# THE PURCHASING OF
# HEALTH CARE BY PRIMARY
# CARE ORGANIZATIONS

# STATE OF HEALTH SERIES

Edited by Chris Ham, Director of Health Services Management Centre, University of Birmingham

# THE PURCHASING OF HEALTH CARE BY PRIMARY CARE ORGANIZATIONS

An Evaluation and Guide
to Future Policy

EDITED BY

# Nicholas Mays, Sally Wyke, Gill Malbon and Nick Goodwin

**Open University Press**
Buckingham · Philadelphia
In association with the King's Fund

Open University Press
Celtic Court
22 Ballmoor
Buckingham
MK18 1XW

e-mail: enquiries@openup.co.uk
world wide web: www.openup.co.uk

and
325 Chestnut Street
Philadelphia, PA 19106, USA

First Published 2001

A catalogue record of this book is available from the British Library

ISBN    0 335 20900 9 (pb)    0 335 20901 7 (hb)

*Library of Congress Cataloging-in-Publication Data is available*

Typeset by Type Study, Scarborough
Printed in Great Britain by St Edmundsbury Press,
Bury St Edmunds, Suffolk

# CONTENTS

# LIST OF FIGURES

# LIST OF TABLES

# LIST OF BOXES

# LIST OF CONTRIBUTORS

*Stephen Abbott* is currently researching how primary care groups are tackling their health improvement role (at the King's Fund), and (at the Health and Community Care Research Unit, University of Liverpool) working on local evaluations of two Personal Medical Services pilots and a national study of the health impact of welfare benefits advice in primary care. His other research interests include health and social care for older people.

*Max Bachmann* is a public health physician and health services researcher who worked in the Department of Social Medicine, University of Bristol while working on the national evaluation of total purchasing pilot projects. His research interests include health care evaluation, epidemiology and economics of health care, dynamics of specialist and generalist services, and chronic disease management. He is now head of the Department of Community Health, University of the Orange Free State, South Africa.

*Kate Baxter* is Lecturer in Health Economics in the Department of Social Medicine, University of Bristol. She was a Research Associate at the time of the National Evaluation, and was responsible for the survey of budgetary management as well as undertaking fieldwork with a number of sites. Her current interests include health economics and policy, primary care organizations, general practitioners as purchasers and commissioners, and evaluations of primary care interventions.

*Gwyn Bevan* is Reader in Policy Analysis in the Department of Operational Research at the London School of Economics and Political Science. He has worked for the United Medical and Dental

Schools of Guy's and St Thomas's Hospitals, the Universities of Warwick and Bristol, for London Economics, HM Treasury and the National Coal Board. His main research interests are developing methods of resource allocation that can be integrated with primary care and ways of reducing inequalities in health.

*Jennifer Dixon* is a health policy analyst at the King's Fund in London, and was previously policy adviser to Sir Alan Langlands in the NHS Executive. She trained in medicine, public health, and health services research and has written widely on health services reforms and policy.

*David Evans* works in primary care and public health research and development. He is Senior Research Fellow in the Faculty of Health and Social Care at the University of the West of England and Public Health Development Manager, Avon Health Authority.

*Linda Gask* is Reader in Psychiatry, University of Manchester, based at the National Primary Care Research and Development Centre and the Royal Preston Hospital. Honorary Consultant Psychiatrist, Guild Community Trust. Research interest is mental health care in primary care settings.

*Nick Goodwin* is Lecturer at the Health Services Management Centre, University of Birmingham. Nick's portfolio of interests includes research into the development of joint commissioning organizations and the mechanisms required to establish integrated care working successfully. Within primary care, Nick has been active in the evaluation of several primary care innovations including GP fundholding, total purchasing, primary care commissioning, and Primary Care Groups.

*Amanda Killoran* has a background in health services management and health promotion. For part of the evaluation she was a Visiting Fellow in policy analysis with the King's Fund Policy Institute on secondment from the then Health Education Authority where she was Head of Development. She is currently Senior Adviser for Planning and Communication with the new Health Development Agency.

*John Lee* worked as a Research Associate at the National Primary Care Research and Development Centre at the University of Manchester while involved with the Total Purchasing Evaluation. He has a PhD which looked at the impact of the 1990 National Health Service (NHS) and Community Care Act on mental health services. John is now a Research Associate at the Sainsbury Centre for Mental Health.

*Brenda Leese* has a background in science and is currently a Senior Research Fellow in the National Primary Care Research and Development Centre at the University of Manchester. Her main research interests are in the areas of general practice structure and organization, and the factors affecting the recruitment and retention of general practitioners.

*Hugh McLeod* is a member of the Health Economics Facility at the Health Services Management Centre, University of Birmingham. Hugh's main research interest is the use of quantitative data in the evaluation of programmes designed to pilot new policy initiatives.

*Gill Malbon* was a health policy analyst at the King's Fund Policy Institute where she worked on the national evaluation of total purchasing pilot projects. She has recently helped to set up the national evaluation of Primary Care Groups/Trusts with the King's Fund Primary Care Programme. Gill has particular interests in the development of commissioning by primary care practitioners and the links between health and social care. She is currently working as a Research Associate at the Audit Commission.

*Nicholas Mays* was Director of Health Services Research at the King's Fund Policy Institute when the national evaluation of total purchasing pilot projects was undertaken. He led the Total Purchasing National Evaluation Team (TP-NET). He is currently Health Adviser in the Social Policy Branch of the New Zealand Treasury based in Wellington as well as holding visiting professorships at the London School of Hygiene and Tropical Medicine and the London School of Economics.

*Michael Place* works for the York Health Economics Consortium at the University of York, where he has been a Research Fellow since completing his MSc in Health Economics at York in 1995. He has worked on a wide variety of projects, ranging from an evaluation of the Powered Wheelchair and Voucher Scheme Initiative (for the NHS and Department of Health) to a study of the roles, functions and costs of Primary Care Trusts (for the NHS Executive).

*John Posnett* is Professor of Health Economics at the University of York. Until recently he was Director of the York Health Economics Consortium and has been Director of the Graduate Programme in Health Economics at York. His main areas of current interest are the methodology of economic evaluation and cost-effectiveness evaluation in wound care.

*James Raftery* has worked as a health economist at District, Regional and Department of Health levels. He currently heads a 10-strong team of health economists based in the Health Services Management Centre in the University of Birmingham, funded by the West Midlands Regional office of the NHS Executive. He is also co-director, along with Professor Andrew Stevens, of the National Horizon Scanning Centre at the University of Birmingham. He has co-edited a series of health care needs assessments and has published widely in academic journals. Educated at Southampton, Dublin and London, his PhD was on the economics of psychiatric hospitals over the period 1845–1985.

*Judith Scott* is a Research Fellow in the Transport Research Institute at Napier University but during the course of the total purchasing pilots evaluation was Research Fellow in the Department of General Practice at the University of Edinburgh. The main emphasis of her research is qualitative with a focus on the patient–client perspective; this has included projects on the management of chronic pain and the mental health needs of young homeless people. Current interests include access, mobility and wayfinding issues from a visual impairment perspective.

*Andrew Street* is a health economist at the Centre for Health Economics, and is funded by the Medical Research Council and Northern and Yorkshire Region. He has previously worked in Australia at the National Centre for Health Program Evaluation, Monash University and the Victorian Department of Health and Community Services. This was followed by a five-year spell with the York Health Economics Consortium. His current research focuses on hospital performance and the development and use of performance indicators.

*Sally Wyke* is Senior Research Fellow in the Primary Care Research Group, University of Edinburgh and Foundation Director of the Scottish School of Primary Care. Her research interests are in the evaluation of primary care policy and organization and in lay management of illness and use of services.

# SERIES EDITOR'S INTRODUCTION

Health services in many developed countries have come under critical scrutiny in recent years. In part this is because of increasing expenditure, much of it funded from public sources, and the pressure this has put on governments seeking to control public spending. Also important has been the perception that resources allocated to health services are not always deployed in an optimal fashion. Thus at a time when the scope for increasing expenditure is extremely limited, there is a need to search for ways of using existing budgets more efficiently. A further concern has been the desire to ensure access to health care of various groups on an equitable basis. In some countries this has been linked to a wish to enhance patient choice and to make service providers more responsive to patients as 'consumers'.

Underlying these specific concerns are a number of more fundamental developments which have a significant bearing on the performance of health services. Three are worth highlighting. First, there are demographic changes, including the ageing population and the decline in the proportion of the population of working age. These changes will both increase the demand for health care and at the same time limit the ability of health services to respond to this demand.

Second, advances in medical science will also give rise to new demands within the health services. These advances cover a range of possibilities, including innovations in surgery, drug therapy, screening and diagnosis. The pace of innovation quickened as the end of the century approached, with significant implications for the funding and provision of services.

Third, public expectations of health services are rising as those who use services demand higher standards of care. In part, this is stimulated by developments within the health service, including the availability of new technology. More fundamentally, it stems from the emergence of a more educated and informed population, in which people are accustomed to being treated as consumers rather than patients.

Against this background, policy-makers in a number of countries are reviewing the future of health services. Those countries which have traditionally relied on a market in health care are making greater use of regulation and planning. Equally, those countries which have traditionally relied on regulation and planning are moving towards a more competitive approach. In no country is there complete satisfaction with existing methods of financing and delivery, and everywhere there is a search for new policy instruments.

The aim of this series is to contribute to debate about the future of health services through an analysis of major issues in health policy. These issues have been chosen because they are both of current interest and of enduring importance. The series is intended to be accessible to students and informed lay readers as well as to specialists working in this field. The aim is to go beyond a textbook approach to health policy analysis and to encourage authors to move debate about their issue forward. In this sense, each book presents a summary of current research and thinking, and an exploration of future policy directions.

Professor Chris Ham
Director of Health Services Management Centre
University of Birmingham

# PREFACE AND ACKNOWLEDGEMENTS

This book marks the culmination of the national evaluation of the general practitioner total purchasing experiment in the UK. The programme of closely interrelated studies which constituted the project was funded over three years of fieldwork by the Department of Health and the Scottish Office Health Department. Additional resources were provided for preparing a range of reports and policy commentaries derived from the findings. In all, it has taken five years to complete all the elements in the work and to integrate them in book form. Despite the inevitable passage of time, we believe that the study remains highly relevant today as primary care-based commissioning and service development takes shape throughout the English National Health Service (NHS).

The scale and complexity of the evaluation called for a large, multidisciplinary team from a number of universities and the King's Fund. The Total Purchasing National Evaluation Team, or TP-NET as it dubbed itself, met frequently in the course of the project to coordinate the many strands of the study. Meetings were often detailed and lengthy, but rarely, if ever, dull. It is fair to say that all, or most, of us learned a great deal from one another, particularly through the exchange of ideas and insights between disciplines. It was a great experience.

This is an opportunity to thank the contributors to the programme of research who are not authors of chapters in this book, but who deserve mention for their enthusiastic input, particularly in the formative stages of the project. We would like to thank Julian Le Grand, Jo-Ann Mulligan, Colin Sanderson, Martin Roland, John Howie, Jennie Popay, Susan Myles, Helen Stoddart and Howard Glennerster for a range of help and support.

Ray Robinson played a particularly important role in the evaluation which is not reflected in the authorship of the chapters which follow. In addition to leading the empirical work on total purchasing pilots' approaches to service contracting, he was active within TP-NET in helping the rest of the team make sense of the emerging findings and draw out their policy implications. He was encouraging and challenging by turns and always good to work with.

TP-NET worked closely with the Department of Health, which commissioned the evaluation as part of its policy research programme. Our liaison officer in the Department of Health in London was Alan Glanz. Carrying out the fieldwork in a potentially sensitive political environment and trying to feed emerging findings into the various policy-making processes in the Department, NHS Executive Total Purchasing Steering Group (chaired by David Hewlett) and elsewhere was made so much easier with Alan's help. It was a positive pleasure (a rare sentiment to report in researcher–government relations!) to work with such a thoughtful, research-literate liaison officer.

Last, but by no means least, we would like to thank Kim Stirling and Ken Judge above other colleagues at the King's Fund who offered encouragement to the study. The phrase 'secretarial support' does not do justice to the wide-ranging role which Kim played in acting as the administrative glue which held together a disparate bunch of researchers who liked to think of themselves grandly as a team, but who, without Kim, would have been closer to a rabble. Ken Judge made an essential strategic contribution without being directly involved in the study. He recognized the importance of the study and gave it his strong support, which allowed Nicholas Mays to devote a considerable amount of his time to leading TP-NET.

Nicholas Mays
Sally Wyke
Gill Malbon
Nick Goodwin

# HEALTH SERVICE DEVELOPMENT: WHAT CAN BE LEARNED FROM THE UK TOTAL PURCHASING EXPERIMENT?

Nicholas Mays,
Nick Goodwin,
Gill Malbon and Sally Wyke

## PROBLEMS OF WESTERN HEALTH SYSTEMS

It is easy to identify the weaknesses of the health systems of Western countries. It is far more difficult to find ways of rectifying these weaknesses which either do not lead to further problems or which are unacceptable to health care professionals, patients and the wider public.

It is also easy to identify aspects of health systems in all Western countries that could be made more appropriate, efficient and equitable. Unexplained variations in patterns and levels of prescribing in primary care and of referrals for specialist services are common. Rising, but poorly understood, demand for unplanned admission to hospitals is widely experienced. Despite increasing rates of elective treatment, there are lengthening waiting lists in systems that do not ration services by price. There are inconsistent decisions on the reimbursement of specific new drugs and treatments and unwillingness on the part of clinicians to ration resources on behalf of the state or insurers.

The main responses to this challenge in the last decade have been to encourage contractual relationships between organizations charged with procuring or purchasing health care services and those charged with providing these services; to attempt to break down barriers between funding streams and budgets within the health sector; to encourage providers to work to clear budgetary limits; and to encourage contestability, if not outright competition, between providers for the contracts of public and private purchasers (Saltman *et al.* 1998). One specific means to encourage cost consciousness and efficiency, and to improve the use of resources across primary and secondary care, has been to allocate all or part of the health care budget on a capitation basis to organizations which are then responsible for securing the delivery of all or most of the health care for their enrolled populations. In health care systems which have lacked strong primary care, this generally involves requiring patients, often for the first time, to use the general practitioner (GP) for their first contact care and then to require general practitioners to act as 'gatekeepers' to more costly and specialized services. Such organizational and budgetary developments are generally referred to as *managed care*.

Managed care has developed most fully in the USA, where there is a huge variety of types of managed care arrangements. Managed care can mean many different things to different people. Managed care organizations typically involve the sharing of financial risk between the 'insurer' (usually a specialist firm, which works on behalf of an employer, or the government in the form of the Medicare or Medicaid programmes) and 'providers' (these can be institutions like hospitals or groups of physicians). Managed care organizations also normally place some restrictions on the clinical decision-making autonomy of providers and their staff or sub-contracted clinicians, as well as some restrictions on patients' choice of physician. Finally, they usually encourage more vertically integrated forms of service delivery, such as offering all services to patients with a particular chronic condition (e.g. diabetes, asthma or mental health services) through a single delivery organization rather than through separate primary, secondary and tertiary service providers as is common in other health systems (Robinson and Steiner 1998).

Managed care organizations vary in the degree to which the insurer/purchaser and the service provider functions are integrated and the extent to which providers deal exclusively with a single insurer/purchaser. In the USA, integration of purchasers and providers generally occurs when both work for the same organization. By contrast, in the best-known UK version of managed care – GP

fundholding – the GPs led the purchasing function and also provided general medical and some ambulatory services for their
patients. Any controls over utilization put in place were initiated
and implemented by the doctors themselves.

## *WORKING FOR PATIENTS* AND THE
## INTRODUCTION OF GP FUNDHOLDING

GP fundholding was part of the quasi-market changes introduced
into the UK National Health Service (NHS) in 1991/92 and was the
forerunner of total purchasing and, eventually, of primary care
groups (PCGs). The NHS White Paper *Working for Patients*
(Secretaries of State, 1989) proposed the creation of an internal or
quasi-market within the tax-funded NHS. Before that date, health
authorities (boards in Scotland) had been responsible for planning
and delivering health services to the populations within their
boundaries and to other patients who came into their areas to use
the services which they directly managed. *Working for Patients*
separated responsibility for purchasing services from responsibility for providing services. NHS acute hospitals, and other
provider organizations responsible for community health services
and mental health services, were to become NHS trusts, separate
from the health authorities. The main purchasing function was
assigned to health authorities, which were to concentrate on
assessing the needs of, and purchasing services for, their resident
populations. They ceased to have any direct responsibility for provision. Health authorities were funded through a needs-weighted
capitation formula.

In addition to the health authority as purchaser, the White Paper
introduced the parallel innovation of GP fundholding – a peculiarly
British kind of managed care organization. Larger general practices
were encouraged to take responsibility for managing budgets
that covered a range of elective hospital and community health
services (HCHS), non-medical practice staff costs and the costs of
their GP prescribing. The fundholders were permitted to vire
money between the various elements in these budgets, allowing
partial budgetary integration. The HCHS part of the budget was
top-sliced from the budget of the local health authority, initially
on a historic basis but increasingly on the basis of some form of
capitation formula. The health authority continued to have
responsibility for purchasing emergency services for the patients

of fundholding and non-fundholding practices alike. Fundholders were responsible to the regional tier of the NHS for the exercise of their purchasing responsibilities and not to the local health authority.

The idea behind fundholding was that the GP, unlike the health authority bureaucrat, had direct and close knowledge of individual patients' needs and of the quality and appropriateness of the elective health care which patients received at the hands of local providers through their traditional role as a referral agent. This knowledge could be used by the GPs with budgets to secure better services within available resources either from the existing providers or by shifting activity from hospitals to more convenient locations. It would be more difficult for a hospital consultant or manager to convince a local GP than a health authority purchaser about the impracticality of making a service more convenient for patients! With their share of the budget that had up until then been tied to the hospital, the fundholding practices might choose to enhance facilities at practice level, thereby obviating the need for more costly hospital referrals. In addition, the allocation of a budget to the practice would encourage the GPs to place downward pressure on their prescribing costs and on unnecessary or discretionary tests or referrals to the hospital outpatient department.

Both the health authority purchasers and the GP fundholders, on a smaller scale, and over a narrower scope, had the potential to manage clinical care in the UK in ways that were becoming familiar in the US under managed care (Robinson and Steiner 1998). However, GP fundholding gave the purchaser a direct incentive to manage the use of resources in order to produce savings that could be ploughed back into either facilities at practice level or more and better patient care for patients of the practice. It was closer than health authority purchasing to the thinking behind US managed care, since it brought resource management closer to the point of clinical decision making.

Thus the NHS quasi-market included two contrasting forms of purchaser organization. One was based on the former planning responsibilities of the health authority and for a population typically between 250,000 and 350,000 patients. The other was based on the long-established role of the GP as the patient's advocate and informed referral agent and was available to practices with populations of 11,000 or more (subsequently progressively reduced to 5000). Smaller practices were permitted to enter the scheme by grouping together in multifunds with a shared management infrastructure. Under fundholding, general practices had to take financial responsibility for the consequences of their practitioners' prescribing and referral decisions for the first time (except for patients who incurred expenditure of more than £6000 per year). In return for this partial budgetary responsibility, fundholders were allowed to make and keep a negotiated share of any savings that they were able to accrue out of their allocations through more resource-conscious decision making. Although savings could not be converted directly into the take-home pay of GPs, they could be used to invest in practice infrastructure such as buildings and equipment. Legally, this investment became part of the equity of the GP partnership and could be realized when a partner retired or left the practice, providing a personal financial incentive towards effective budgetary management. Health authorities were not permitted to keep savings in the same way and there were no direct financial incentives affecting the behaviour of their salaried staff.

Particularly in the first few years of the quasi-market in the UK, GP fundholders – by virtue of their smaller size of population, control over a minority of the HCHS budget (approximately 20 per cent of their patients' resource use) and stronger political support – were permitted far greater freedom than the health authorities to commit resources as they saw fit and to shift work between providers. Their activities were less likely to 'destabilize' local hospital providers (a major political concern). Fundholding practices also received a relatively generous management allowance to compensate them for the additional accounting, clerical and information technology costs of the scheme.

## THE CONSEQUENCES OF GP FUNDHOLDING

By 1996/97 approximately half the practices in the NHS in England and Wales had become fundholders (Mays and Dixon 1996). Yet, the GP fundholding scheme itself, and the evidence about its costs and benefits, proved controversial. There was consensus that it represented a genuine innovation with the potential to alter the balance of previous power relationships (for example between hospital specialists and primary care generalists). But there was agreement on little else.

Critics of the scheme disliked the fact that it was implemented in such a way that two 'tiers' of practices and patients were created in the NHS, depending on whether GPs were fundholders or not. This was felt to have led systematically to the disadvantage of non-fundholding practices' patients. In addition, fundholding GPs were felt to have received generous support for practice management and computerization that was not available to non-fundholders. Ironically, the 'two-tier' criticism implied that GP purchasing was more effective (albeit at a cost in management allowances), at least compared with the purchasing activities of the health authorities. However, the health authorities had a far wider purchasing responsibility than the fundholders, were given far less freedom to innovate and shift resources between providers, and had little new investment in management. Proponents argued that 'two-tierism' was not intrinsic to the scheme, but a feature of its voluntary, staged introduction; that fundholding was increasingly available to a wider range of practices; and that many of the benefits secured by fundholders, such as prompter discharge information, became available to non-fundholders' patients as providers altered their operating procedures.

The second main criticism of GP fundholding was that it fragmented NHS planning, thereby undermining national priorities and targets, and led to a large number of small-volume contracts which, in turn, increased the NHS's administrative and managerial costs to no noticeable benefit in terms of patient care. It is generally accepted that the quasi-market, as a whole, increased transaction costs in the NHS. Fundholding contributed to this. Supporters – among whom were many fundholding GPs – argued that small-scale, decentralized purchasing, despite its costs, had resulted in improvements in the process of care through more timely information to GPs about their hospitalized patients, shorter waiting times for elective surgery and outpatient appointments and more responsiveness to patients' needs. The research evidence on fundholding tends to support such claims, but there is far less evidence concerning the effects of fundholding on quality of care, efficiency and equity of access to services (Goodwin 1998).

The third main criticism of fundholding was that it would, inevitably, lead to discrimination against costly patients. They would either be under-served or removed from fundholding practices' lists. This seems to have remained a theoretical rather than an endemic problem under fundholding for two reasons. First, a 'stop-loss' arrangement was built into the scheme in which GP fundholders were financially responsible up to a per-patient cost limit, at which point financial responsibility reverted to the health authority.

Second, fundholders' budgets were based mainly on historic expenditure patterns rather than exclusively on weighted capitation. Furthermore, unlike managed care organizations in the USA, fundholding GPs' personal remuneration from the NHS's general medical services (GMS) budget was not directly affected by over- or underspending on the fundholding budget. The only sanction that could be imposed on a practice was its removal from the scheme. This reduced GPs' personal incentives to deter or under-serve potentially costly patients.

In sum, the extensive, if far from ideal, body of research on GP fundholding suggests that the scheme probably produced at least some of its intended consequences, for example by curbing the rate of increase in GP prescribing costs, at least for several years, and by generating more practice-level services, which were assumed to be more relevant to patients' wishes. Fundholders were able to make savings and were far more likely to be under budget than health authorities, though whether this was due to better purchasing, not having responsibility for emergency care, more generous funding, lower prices or healthier patients, is not clear.

It seems that providers were more responsive to the demands of GP fundholders than to those of health authority purchasers. This appears to have been because fundholders were marginal buyers of services with a budget for mainly elective work that was protected from the pressures of emergency care, rather than because they had superior purchasing skills. Fundholders also tended to be able to negotiate cost per case contracts. Thus fundholders represented a source of additional income for providers facing tight budget constraints set by health authority purchasers via block contracts (Mays *et al.* 2000).

However, the claim that fundholding led to an inequitable service, at least in terms of differential waiting times for in-patient treatment, and higher administrative costs appears to have been borne out.

## TRENDS IN NHS PURCHASING ORGANIZATION AFTER THE INTRODUCTION OF FUNDHOLDING

Despite mixed views of the scheme, GP fundholding continued to enjoy the full support of the Conservative government in the UK in the mid-1990s. It was seen as the only way forward and health authority chief executives were under some pressure to encourage take-up of the scheme. The government was convinced that fund-holding, with the opportunity to make and keep 'savings', sharpened incentives to generate more efficient services.

The original GP fundholding scheme was based on large practices, each holding a budget independently. Over time, the population threshold was reduced, allowing smaller and smaller practices to enter. From April 1996, practices with lists of 5000 or more patients were eligible and a new form of 'community' fundholding (contrasted with 'standard' fundholding) was introduced for practices between 3000 and 5000 patients to hold a budget for all the non-hospital services in the fundholding envelope (NHS Executive 1994a). As smaller practices entered the scheme, so they increasingly banded together into either fundholding consortia (loose alliances of fundholding practices) or multifunds (groups of fundholding practices which pooled their management allowances to establish a common management infrastructure and coordinate their purchasing, while retaining responsibility for practice-level budgets). An increasing proportion of new fundholders became part of these collectives of practices. Most multifunds had populations between 50,000 and 80,000 patients, but some were as large as 300,000. They were seen as a way of increasing the purchasing power of small practices and decreasing the amount of time that their GPs needed to spend on fundholding administration.

However, the 'two-tier' criticism of GP fundholding remained strong and some GPs remained reluctant to manage budgets on behalf of government. Some health authorities and GPs, who were ideologically opposed to fundholding, developed a range of alternative schemes through which GPs were able to influence the purchasing of their local health authority by holding 'shadow' or 'indicative' budgets for a range of services. Unlike fundholding, these schemes grew up without the early support of government. This trend was referred to variously as *locality commissioning, GP-sensitive purchasing* or *GP commissioning*. The schemes took a wide variety of forms depending on the size of population covered, the degree of decision-making autonomy and budgetary delegation from the health authority, the extent to which they were organized around geographic communities or amalgams of practices and the way in which the local GPs were involved in decision making (Mays and Dixon 1996). By the latter half of the 1990s, the vast majority of health authorities in England were purchasing HCHS with input from either sub-district advisory bodies based on GPs or more autonomous organizations which had some form of budgetary control, however weak.

Since locality commissioning and GP commissioning groups did not hold budgets in their own right or negotiate separate contracts, their proponents argued that their administrative costs were a fraction of those of fundholding, while still enabling GPs to make beneficial changes to local services (Black *et al.* 1994; Graffy and Williams 1994). It was also argued that these approaches facilitated collective decisions and avoided the fragmentation of decisions and services generated by fundholding with practice-level budgets. The patchy evidence suggests that such schemes could operate with lower administrative costs than their fundholding equivalents and could bring about desired service changes, particularly in community health services rather than acute hospital services (Mulligan 1998). However, the only study which incorporated a crude comparison of the performance of locality and GP commissioning groups versus fundholding concluded that the more the groups resembled fundholders (e.g. in terms of having extensive budgetary freedom), the more they were able to bring about the local service changes which they desired (Glennerster *et al.* 1998). Generally, those schemes where budgetary delegation was more formal tended to be associated with improvements in quality, choice and responsiveness of services, at least in the short term (Le Grand *et al.* 1997).

While collective alternatives to fundholding were becoming more prevalent, the range of services included in the standard fundholding package also widened. For example, from April 1996, fundholders were able to purchase specialist nursing care (e.g. diabetic nursing).

Despite the widening of the scope of fundholding, it was still conceived of as a mechanism for GPs to influence patterns of resource consumption in relation to services (e.g. outpatient referrals and community nursing) and activities (e.g. prescribing for their patients), which were directly amenable to GP influence through their day-to-day work. However, a number of prominent fundholding GPs were frustrated by what they saw as the artificial and unhelpful budgetary separation between fundholding and non-fundholding goods and services. For example, GP purchasers were confined to looking for savings and opportunities to substitute primary care for hospital services in service areas, such as elective surgery, where lengths of stay were relatively brief. They could see that there were opportunities in other service areas to make better use of resources by altering the pattern of care, but were unable to do anything about it except by attempting to influence the purchasing activities of the local health authorities.

## THE EMERGENCE OF TOTAL PURCHASING

In response to this bottom-up pressure from some fundholders, four informal, pioneer total purchasing pilot projects began in April 1994, with the support of Regional Offices of the NHS Executive. Three of these projects were made up of small groups of individual, experienced, fundholding practices. The fourth included non-fundholding as well as fundholding practices in a defined geographical area. These pioneer total purchasers began to work together to take on additional purchasing responsibilities delegated to them by their local health authorities.

Very soon after this, the NHS Executive decided to launch a larger scale, three-year, national initiative along the same lines as part of the development of a so-called primary care-led NHS (Department of Health 1994a). In one strand of the initiative, selected, volunteer standard fundholding practices were recruited to purchase a single, additional service (e.g. mental health services, maternity, palliative care and certain complementary therapies) as if it were part of their normal fund. These projects were known as extended fundholding pilots. In the other strand, volunteer standard fundholding practices were recruited either singly or in groups to purchase potentially all HCHS for their patients, also on a pilot basis over three years. These were known as total purchasing pilots (TPPs). For the first time, GPs could purchase services such as accident and emergency (A&E), maternity, in-patient mental health and in-patient general medical and geriatric medicine. Figure 1.1 locates the TPPs and extended fundholding pilots within the plurality of local purchasing organizations that had grown up in the NHS by the mid-1990s.

Both sets of pilots were to be the subject of a national evaluation, unlike the original fundholding scheme (Mays *et al.* on behalf of TP-NET, 1997a). The NHS Executive indicated that the eventual role of the health authority would be to concentrate on developing a broad health and health care strategy for the area, while monitoring and holding to account groups of GP practices that would be responsible for purchasing services.

Although the remit, aims and objectives of the TPPs were not

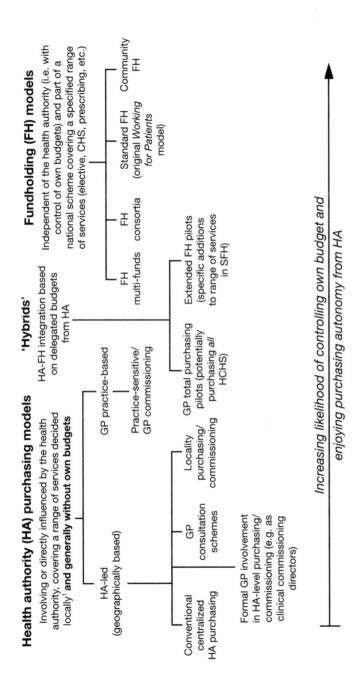

**Figure 1.1**  A typology of purchasing organizations in the NHS, 1996/97

*Note:* [1] Some FH practice involvement in some schemes, but generally involving non-FH practices

*Source:* Mays *et al.* (1998)

spelled out by the NHS Executive, and it was not at all clear at the outset how the pilots would organize themselves, after a few months of monitoring their evolution, the evaluation team was able to produce the following definition of total purchasing:

> Where either one general practitioner practice, or a consortium of practices, is delegated money by the relevant health authority/board to purchase potentially all of the community, secondary and tertiary health care not included in standard fundholding for patients on their lists.
>
> (Mays *et al.* on behalf of TP-NET 1997b: 5)

Since legislation would have been required to allow fundholders to hold extended budgets as of right, the additional budgets held by both TPPs and extended fundholders remained the legal responsibility of the local health authority. The TPPs were also required to ensure that the fundholding budget and the total purchasing budget were kept separate. These administrative details affected the development of the pilots since the informal status of the TPP budget meant that, de facto, the pilots could only function with at least some cooperation between the practices and the local health authority. The TPPs became subcommittees of their local health authority, albeit with varying levels of day-to-day autonomy.

The necessary cooperation between TPPs and local health authorities meant that, although total purchasing was viewed by government as the logical widening of the scope of standard fundholding, the TPPs also had a considerable amount in common with the range of locality and GP commissioning schemes. In particular, each depended on building collaboration between general practices and the staff of the health authority. TPPs had to negotiate a management budget and/or staffing with the local health authority. Over time, it became apparent that fundholding and non-fundholding approaches to GP involvement in purchasing were converging in practice. In addition, much of the ideological heat was ebbing away from the debate about fundholding, to be replaced by a broad acceptance of the potential benefits of involving primary care providers in the purchasing of HCHS by devolving budgetary responsibility to organizations below health authority level (Mays and Dixon 1996).

Although the pilots were labelled total purchasers by the NHS Executive, it became apparent in the early stages of their preparation for live purchasing (1995/96) that the TPPs would not be compelled to take responsibility for all the HCHS used by their patients. Instead, the TPPs emerged as *selective* purchasers, choosing which service areas and which purchasing issues they wished to engage with. This enabled them to concentrate their efforts on solving problems in local service provision secure in the knowledge that the health authority would continue to purchase and monitor the other services on which their patients depended. In a crude, practical way, this approach to purchasing has some similarities with the economic technique of marginal analysis. Under this approach to purchasing, it is only necessary to focus on altering the deployment of resources at the *margin*, rather than assessing the total needs of the population and reviewing all the services that relate to those needs. Instead, the focus is on investment and disinvestment decisions at the margin where substitution of one set of inputs for another can be demonstrated to improve cost-effectiveness.

## LABOUR'S POLICY ON FUNDHOLDING AND GP INVOLVEMENT IN PURCHASING

While the Conservative government's TPPs were organizing themselves and defining their purchasing objectives in 1995/96, the Labour Party in opposition was developing its broad policy towards the fundholding scheme and the alternative. Labour was determined to abolish single-practice fundholding on the grounds that it was excessively costly to administer budgets at practice level and that the scheme was inequitable in its current 'two-tier' form (Labour Party 1995). Beyond this, Labour's stance was one of pragmatic adjustment. The purchaser–provider separation would be maintained along with the continuation of GP involvement in the purchasing process. In place of fundholding, a system of *GP commissioning* would be developed in consultation with GPs, in which groups of practices in an area would work in partnership with their local health authority to purchase HCHS. The term *commissioning*, rather than *purchasing*, was used to indicate that the practices would be involved as much in developing new forms of provision as purchasing from a preset menu of existing services. All practices would be able to participate, unlike under fundholding. Bureaucracy would be minimized by abolishing the costly billing process associated with individual practices holding their own budgets and purchasing separately. As a result of these adaptations to previous policy, all patients would have equal access to treatment rather than privileges going to the patients of fundholders. Labour's position was premised on the assumption that the savings in administrative costs generated by a more collective approach would offset the effects of diluting the incentives to efficient budgetary management that existed under fundholding at individual practice level.

## MAKING SOME VERSIONS OF FUNDHOLDING UNIVERSAL: THE LABOUR GOVERNMENT'S POLICY ON COMMISSIONING HCHS

The main elements of Labour's policy in relation to fundholding remained unchanged through the general election campaign and can be seen clearly in the Labour government's NHS White Papers of 1997 and early 1998 (Secretary of State for Health 1997; Secretary of State for Scotland 1997; Secretary of State for Wales 1998). Organizations based in primary care, structured around quite large groups of general practices and led, for the most part, by GPs, now take the main responsibility for improving the health and health care of their patients working within the framework of a local health improvement programme (HImP). The local health authority/board, which remains in place, but with a more strategic function, has ultimate responsibility for successfully negotiating the HImP with all the local NHS agencies and local government.

In England and Wales, the merits of primary care-driven commissioning, linking clinical and resource management decisions at the same point in the system (i.e. at GP level), are clearly articulated in the White Papers. Thus, in England PCGs and primary care trusts (PCTs), and in Wales local health groups (LHGs) took responsibility for commissioning HCHS as well as providing primary care from April 1999. In Scotland, by contrast, health boards continue to commission all hospital care, while PCTs and local health care co-operatives (LHCCs) plan and develop the provision of primary and community health services. LHCCs have responsibility only for control of their cash-limited prescribing budget. Although they are not commissioners of care, they are able to influence the strategic configuration of local services (e.g. a shift from hospital to community-based services) through access to a joint investment fund controlled by the PCTs. The Scottish model casts the primary care-based organizations as developers of better primary care rather than as commissioners of services from others and so marks a shift away from fundholding, locality commissioning and total purchasing. It strengthens opportunities for integration between

community and primary care services while weakening opportunities for vertical integration (or 'virtual' integration) through
commissioning. As a result, the PCGs/PCTs in England and LHGs
in Wales have more in common with the former TPPs than the PCTs
and LHCCs in Scotland.

The main responsibilities of PCGs/PCTs are as follows:

- to contribute to the development of the local HImP;
- to commission HCHS from local providers, excluding specialized
  mental health services and services for people with learning dis-
  abilities;
- to develop primary care services through the practices in the
  PCG and to integrate primary care and community health
  services (and, in the case of PCTs, to *deliver* community health
  services);
- to monitor the quality of local services;
- to promote the health of the population.

The government envisages that it will take a decade for the arrangements introduced in 1999 to mature fully. The approach is explicitly
evolutionary. Thus PCGs in England and LHGs in Wales were free
to start operating at a number of different levels in April 1999 with
the clear expectation that they would progress from less to more
autonomous roles and from an advisory to a budget-holding capacity (see Box 1.1).

All PCGs are allocated a budget, which covers HCHS, GP
prescribing and the practice infrastructure part of GMS. As PCGs
move between 'levels', it is envisaged that their budgets will
become increasingly integrated. It is possible that the HCHS
budget of the PCG may be merged, over time, with the entire
resources for GMS available to the constituent general practices in
order to produce a fully integrated budget for PCTs. Such a
development would be sure to require the abandonment of the
national GP contract through which, at present, the vast majority of
NHS GPs are remunerated. At this highest level, PCTs are accountable to the local health authority not only for commissioning all
HCHS, but also for the delivery of community health services to
their populations, thereby integrating purchaser and provider functions for community health services in a single organization. PCTs
therefore bear some similarities to US managed care organizations
charged with meeting the entire health care needs of a registered
population. The key difference is that PCTs are not currently in
competition with one another for patients. At lower levels of PCGs,

---

**Box 1.1   Options for primary care groups**

PCGs will:

Level 1: at a minimum, support the health authority in commissioning care for its population, acting in an advisory capacity.

Level 2: take devolved responsibility for managing a delegated budget for health care in the area, formally, as a subcommittee of the health authority.

Level 3: become established as free-standing bodies accountable to the health authority for commissioning care.

Level 4: become established as free-standing bodies accountable to the health authority for commissioning care and with added responsibility for the provision of community health services for their population.

*Source*: Mays *et al*. 1998a.

---

the separation between purchase and provision of HCHS and GMS remains more apparent, since PCGs do not provide all the community health services for their patients, but rather purchase some community health services from the local NHS community trust. At each level, the HCHS resource entitlement of the PCG/PCT is determined through a needs-weighted capitation formula similar to that used to set the budgets of health authorities/boards.

## SIMILARITIES AND DIFFERENCES BETWEEN TOTAL PURCHASING PILOTS AND PRIMARY CARE GROUPS/TRUSTS

It seems almost inevitable that the research-based evaluation of innovations can scarcely ever keep pace with changes in public policy. Although early and interim reports were made on the current evaluation before the election of a new government, the study of the TPPs still had almost a year to run in May 1997 when Labour came to power. The Labour government's plans for fundholding and GP involvement in purchasing were published three to four months before the scheduled end of the TPPs in April 1998. As a result, the TPPs themselves had to adapt to a changing policy environment. In some cases, it became apparent to the participants in the pilots that they had lost the support of the local health authority, which was anticipating the abolition of all forms of fundholding. The research too had to be undertaken with an eye to its future relevance as well as its significance as a record of a major attempt to pilot a new way of purchasing HCHS.

The continuing policy relevance of the national evaluation of the TPPs to readers in the UK depends, in part, on the degree of similarity between the pilots and PCGs/PCTs and other agencies that were put in place in April 1999. This can be seen from Table 1.1, which compares TPPs, PCGs/PCTs, LHGs and Scottish PCTs and LHCCs (Killoran *et al.* on behalf of TP-NET, 1999a).

Perhaps the most fundamental difference between TPPs and the arrangements that have replaced the Conservatives' version of the NHS quasi-market is that TPPs were time-limited experiments whereas PCGs/PCTs, LHGs and the like are the basic building blocks of the organization of the NHS in their respective countries of the UK. They are regarded as central to the development of the local health system in each area, whereas the TPPs, although they had strong government support, were often minor players with pilot status. It can be seen from Table 1.1 that most TPPs were considerably smaller than the agencies which have replaced them and the range of locality and GP commissioning groups which had grown up below district level in the NHS in the 1990s. On the other hand, the PCGs/PCTs and other GP groups (apart from LHCCs) comprise all the practices in an area, which have varying levels of service commissioning experience, different ideas about health system development and different standards of primary care delivery. The TPPs comprised volunteer standard fundholding practices which tended to have reached similar levels of practice development and which had chosen to work together on a pilot basis.

Table 1.1 further indicates that PCGs/PCTs and LHGs, in particular, have a wider range of specified responsibilities than the TPPs. Whereas total purchasing was introduced with an emphasis on the purchasing role of the GPs, PCGs were introduced with an emphasis on the development of the primary medical and nursing care offered by the practices within the group, as well as on commissioning secondary care services. Thus there is a dual emphasis on developing the GMS and related community health services provided by and at the practices themselves, and on the expertise of

**Table 1.1** Comparison of total purchasing pilots, primary care groups, local health groups and local health care cooperatives

| TPPs | PCGs (England) and LHGs (Wales) | PCTs and LHCCs (Scotland) |
|---|---|---|
| • Small (approximately 30,000 population; range 8000–80,000 population) | • Large (approximately 100,000 population; range 50,000–250,000 population) | • Large (but small LHCCs possible; range 25,000–150,000 population) |
| • Responsible for commissioning potentially all HCHS | • Responsible for commissioning potentially all HCHS | • PCTs responsible for planning and providing primary and community health services through LHCCs. Not responsible for commissioning hospital services |
| • GP led | • GP and nurse led | • Primary care team led |
| • Volunteer and highly selective practices, and time-limited (three years) | • Compulsory – all practices and not time-limited | • Practices can 'opt out' of participation in LHCCs, but all will be accountable to the PCT |
| • Rural and suburban | • All parts of England and Wales | • All parts of Scotland |
| • Many simple/informal projects | • More complex formal organizations | • More complex organizations |
| • Ring-fenced total purchasing budget and standard fundholding budget (GMS not included) | • Moving towards integrated budgets, including standard fundholding, total purchasing and GMS | • Moving towards integrated community health services, prescribing and GMS budgets |

- Some pilots still with indicative budgets and some with fully delegated budgets after two years

- Intended to be a purchasing organization rather than concerned with the provider role of practices (although in practice did influence provider roles)

- No structure of 'clinical governance' between the GPs in different practices

---

- Moving towards delegated and independent budgets (i.e. legally the responsibility of PCGs and LHGs)

- Responsibilities for commissioning services plus health improvement and primary care development

- Arrangements for clinical governance aimed at improving quality and consistency of primary care delivery

---

- Moving towards delegated and independent budgets for primary and community health services at PCT level and for prescribing at LHCC level

- Responsibilities for health improvement and primary and community care development. Responsibility for development of overall service through HImP and joint investment plan

- Arrangements for clinical governance aimed at improving quality and consistency of primary care delivery

GPs as commissioners of services which will be delivered by other agencies such as acute hospitals. TPPs, by contrast, tended to avoid the pursuit of goals that directly affected the internal management of any of their constituent practices. In addition, a wider range of professionals than TPPs manages PCGs/PCTs. Their boards comprise community nurses and members of the professions allied to medicine, as well as local GPs. Given their fundholding origins, the clinician members of TPPs' governing bodies were all GPs rather than other members of the primary health care team.

Despite the differences between TPPs and the range of new primary care organizations put in place in the NHS by the Labour government in 1999, there are sufficient similarities for the findings of the evaluation of the TPPs to provide useful lessons for current NHS policy and practice (Killoran *et al.* on behalf of the TP-NET, 1999b). Despite originating in a different context, total purchasing involved groups of general practices working together as a subcommittee of the local health authority to change and develop hospital and community health through the use of a shared, delegated budget as do the PCGs. Level 2 PCGs operate in a very similar manner to the TPPs as subcommittees of the health authority with a budget delegated to them by the local health authority. The experience of building TPPs as organizations and their effectiveness in securing change and improvements in services are both highly relevant for the development of primary care-based organizations in the NHS.

## RELEVANCE OF THE EXPERIENCE OF THE TOTAL PURCHASING PILOTS BEYOND THE NHS

Since the early 1990s, a number of countries other than the UK have experimented with new ways of managing more efficiently the financial risks associated with rising demand for health services. Usually, the broad approach has been to integrate the finance and delivery of care by breaking down conventional budgetary and organizational distinctions, for example between primary care physicians and specialist providers, to avoid cost shifting and service fragmentation, and to align incentives appropriately throughout the health system. Innovations have included developing new ways of organizing and reimbursing primary care physicians and allied workers (usually involving strategies such as grouping physicians together, paying doctors by capitation to avoid over-service and introducing patient enrolment with a specific primary care provider). Other linked developments have consisted of extending budgetary delegation to primary care physicians to enable them to purchase a wider range of health services for their patients, including incentives for them to substitute less costly primary care for secondary care services. Thus experiments with GP budget holding have taken place in countries as diverse as Russia (Saltman *et al.* 1998) and New Zealand (Malcolm and Powell 1996).

Developments in New Zealand are especially interesting not only because of the similarities between the tax-funded New Zealand and UK health systems, but also because two different forms of so-called 'managed care' involving GPs have emerged. One is based, as in the UK TPPs and locality commissioning schemes, on groups of general practices or practitioners, known as independent practitioner associations (IPAs). The other is based on integrated care organizations (ICOs) separate from the GPs.

The separation between hospital services and GMS has been as marked if not more so in New Zealand as in the UK. GPs are self-employed practitioners, are paid on a fee-for-service basis and receive only a minority of their incomes from the public purse. By contrast, acute hospitals are publicly owned and financed, have been funded largely through output-based and block contracts and employ salaried staff. Neither part of the system has had any incentive to consider the impact of its actions on the other. Although the GPs, as in the UK, act as gatekeepers to specialist care, this amounts to a very weak form of integration. The only practical link, traditionally, between the hospitals and the GPs has been the exchange of information about patients referred across the primary–secondary divide (Ashton 1998).

GP budget holding in New Zealand developed initially under the auspices of IPAs rather than as a direct result of government policy. IPAs are large groupings of single-handed and group practices which came into being spontaneously in the early 1990s in response to a perceived threat from government and the then regional health authorities (RHAs) to the GPs' contracts and reimbursement arrangements for GMS. By banding together, mainly into limited liability companies, the GPs believed that they would be better able to negotiate with the payers.

Approximately 70 per cent of New Zealand's 3100 GPs are now members of IPAs, which vary widely in size (Malcolm *et al.* 1999) – some are very large organizations. For example, the Pegasus IPA in Christchurch has 330 GPs. Over half the IPAs have budgets for services other than GMS (which remains a series of fee-for-service subsidies to individual practitioners). However, unlike fundholding in the UK, the budgets do not currently include hospital outpatient or in-patient services, being restricted to GP pharmaceuticals, laboratory tests and, in some cases, a limited range of community health services. An exception is the Pegasus IPA which developed a contract with the national purchasing agency (which then was the Health Funding Authority) designed to allow investment in primary care in order to reduce hospital admissions. The budgets, which are mostly historical, are held by the IPA and not at practice or practitioner level. In practice, it appears that the budgets have been more indicative than genuine, in that money changes hands only if the IPA is in surplus at the end of the financial year. Any surpluses are shared between the purchaser and the association, but up to now overspends have largely been absorbed by the purchaser. Despite this, some of the IPAs have evaluated their budget holding and have reported impressive savings, particularly on laboratory test expenditure, suggesting considerable slack in historic budgets (Kerr *et al.* 1996). The incentives generated by having a budgetary constraint are further weakened in the IPA setting by the fact that patients, except those on low incomes, have to make a co-payment for each GP consultation, thereby allowing GPs to increase the available resources from private sources.

Despite the continuing separation of hospital and GP services, the IPA budget-holding schemes have not been extended to hospital services for two main reasons: a widespread perception that the costs of GP fundholding in the UK have exceeded the benefits, based on an interpretation of the Audit Commission's study of fundholding focused on the extent of savings made by fundholders compared to the costs of running the scheme (Audit Commission 1996); and a concern in some quarters that GPs who operate as self-employed business people, and are perceived as such, should not control major flows of resources to public hospitals. As a result, government has been interested in other ways of bringing about service integration and improving incentives to efficiency. In the late 1990s, a number of pilot ICOs were developed by the health funding authority to organize the integration of service delivery and eventually to subcontract with providers, including hospitals and IPAs (Ashton 1998).

Two forms of ICOs emerged in 1998 in response to a health

funding authority request for proposals to develop and test new ways of delivering integrated health services:

- collaborations between different types and levels of provider organizations to form an ICO delivering services in new ways (collaborative provider model of integration);
- independent management organizations, which planned to manage funds from the Health Funding Authority to purchase and coordinate services from a range of providers for a defined population (devolved sub-purchaser model of integration).

A number of ICO pilots based on improving inter-provider relations are currently underway. However, proposals for the second, risk-bearing, form of ICO, which involve private insurers, were deferred by the Health Funding Authority and have now been abandoned with the election of a new government in November 1999. The reasons for this decision have not been made public, but there are well-known risks with managed care arrangements based on fixed budgets, such as the possibility that the organization might under-serve needy patients in order to contain costs; 'cream skim' (selectively enrol low-cost patients and discourage potentially high-cost patients); cost shift to other budgets; and increase administrative costs in excess of any efficiency gains (Robinson and Steiner 1998; Cumming 2000). It is likely that there were also concerns at passing responsibility for financial risk to new bodies outside the public sector that would have been local monopoly purchasers.

The evaluation of the ICO pilots is under way, but no results have yet been published. In the meantime, the experience of the TPPs may provide some insights into the development of both IPA-based budget holding and risk-bearing ICOs, despite the differences between the schemes. Budget holding by IPAs appears to have more in common with British GP fundholding and total purchasing than the proposals for ICOs. Whereas the proposals clearly intended the purchasing ICOs to be fully risk-bearing, independent organizations, TPPs managed risk in the context of the health authority's purchasing. Whereas the risk-bearing ICOs proposed taking the entire health care budget for their patients, the TPPs excluded the GMS funds paid to the GPs for their own services. Nonetheless, the activities and consequences of the TPPs indicate the potential of GP-led purchasing in the NHS and the organizational challenges facing any purchasing organization based on individual GP practices.

## CONCLUSIONS

Governments in a number of Western countries are attempting to improve the efficiency, appropriateness and equity of their health systems. One of the main mechanisms is to devolve purchasing responsibility from national and regional to more local agencies, which are allocated budgets that span both primary and secondary services. This book draws on an extensive government-funded evaluation of the UK total purchasing experiment to shed light on a number of important general questions raised by these policies:

- The key tasks of devolved purchasing include: assessing population needs and views; developing a purchasing plan and setting priorities; building relations with providers; specifying, negotiating and monitoring contracts; managing clinical risk; and managing expenditure within budget. How long does it take for GP-led collectives to develop sufficient organizational maturity and robustness to enable them to undertake these tasks? What do they need to do to develop these functions?
- Which service areas do GPs demonstrate the strongest motivation to purchase effectively? In which service areas do GPs have the appropriate expertise to manage relationships with specialist providers?
- Can GP-led organizations successfully use their purchasing power to alter the pattern of use of more costly secondary care in ways that could potentially improve the allocative efficiency of the health system?
- What other activities do GP-led organizations engage in in relation to service development?
- What are the ingredients of more and less successful GP-led purchasing in the context of the NHS?
- What effect does the splitting of the purchasing function between health authorities and primary care have on the overall costs of organizing and managing the health system? Are these costs justified by any gains brought about by more local purchasing?
- As the scale of GP-led purchasing organizations holding a purchasing or providing budget grows from single-practice fundholders through larger TPPs to PCGs/PCTs in England, how is this likely to affect the incentives facing practices and individual GPs to make more efficient use of health care resources? Is there still a place for individual practices to hold budgets and, if so, for which services?

- How can budgets be allocated to GP-led organizations that are sensitive to the needs of their different populations?
- On balance, is there merit in persisting with the development of models of devolved purchasing based either on GP practices, or primary care more widely; or do other forms of managed care organizations offer greater potential to improve the quality and efficiency of publicly funded health services?
- What lessons can be drawn from the experience of such a large and complex evaluation?

# 2

# DESIGNING THE EVALUATION OF THE TOTAL PURCHASING EXPERIMENT: PROBLEMS AND SOLUTIONS

Nicholas Mays and
Sally Wyke

The national total purchasing initiative was one of the first major quasi-market policy developments in the NHS to be evaluated independently from the outset. Previous policy changes, such as the introduction of standard fundholding, had been introduced without parallel evaluation. The main focus of contemporary health services research was on the evaluation of specific clinical interventions rather than changes to organization and economic incentives. There were no straightforward models of research design from which to borrow; no off-the-shelf packages.

While there was a commitment from the UK government to some form of evaluation of total purchasing, this did not mean that ministers of the time were open-minded about the merits of this form of general practitioner-led purchasing. There was strong support in the government for extending GPs' control over purchasing budgets. As a result, the pilots were not introduced in such a way as to facilitate evaluation. For example, there was no opportunity to compare TPPs that had been admitted to the scheme with similarly eligible practices that had not been included in the scheme, for experimental purposes. Similarly, although it was made apparent to participants in the pilots that there would be an evaluation, there was no requirement for the projects to collect any data themselves to assist the evaluators. There was a feeling among the evaluators that politicians accepted evaluation as a necessary evil.

The evaluation was to interfere as little as possible with the implementation of the projects.

Total purchasing had been introduced officially in the autumn of 1994, following the publication of the NHS Executive's Executive Letter EL (94) 79 (NHS Executive 1994a). After a brief approval process, in which few applications were turned down, 53 pilots were sanctioned to start a year of preparation in April 1995 before becoming 'live' purchasers 12 months later. There were hints that a second wave of pilots was likely to follow a year behind the others. Box 2.1 summarizes what was known about total purchasing as it was introduced.

---

**Box 2.1    The introduction of total purchasing into the NHS: what was not known and what was known about the scheme**

*What was not known*

- aims and objectives of the scheme and how it would operate;
- the particular weakness of the prevailing purchasing arrangements to which total purchasing was a response;
- what total purchasers were expected to achieve.

*What was known*

- total purchasing was to function within existing legislation;
- total purchasing practices could not hold budgets for services beyond the scope of standard fundholding;
- resources to be deployed by the total purchasers would remain ultimately the responsibility of the health authority;
- there would be no set management allowance from government: this would need to be negotiated locally;
- total purchasers would rely heavily on the cooperation of their local health authorities;
- total purchasers would comprise groups of volunteer fundholding practices: they were originally envisaged as quite large groups, but in the event some single-handed practices were allowed to enter the scheme;
- it was to be a time-limited scheme over three years (two cycles of live purchasing).

In summary, there was a general belief prevalent in government at the time that there was merit in giving GPs more influence over NHS purchasing by means of delegated budgets. This belief led to the introduction of total purchasing, but with no clear statement of aims, objectives or processes to be used in setting it up. Total purchasing would be codified gradually through the process of local implementation in 53 parts of the NHS. This approach to designing self-inventing institutions was typical of many of the quasi-market changes in the UK welfare state in the late 1980s and early 1990s (Klein 1995). Governments seemed to have lost confidence in expert planning and in the design of social institutions. Instead, policy makers preferred to allow institutions to develop adaptively through the play of events. While this strategy might have suited the government, it was not open to the evaluators who were required to specify their evaluation in sufficient detail to win the tendering process.

## THE DEPARTMENT OF HEALTH RESEARCH BRIEF

An evaluation brief was prepared by the Department of Health to tender for proposals for the evaluation. In the absence of detailed policy documents on total purchasing, or information on prototype TPPs, this brief was of crucial importance in offering an indirect idea of the potential objectives of the scheme.

The brief was clear that total purchasing was to be seen as 'the extension of GP fundholding', indicating that, in general terms, the Department and the NHS Executive might be expecting similar consequences to those associated with fundholding. The aim of the evaluation was 'to assess the costs and benefits attributable to the *extension* of GP fundholding to total purchasing'. The more specific objectives were to collect evidence on:

- the factors associated with successful set-up and operation of total purchasing;
- the costs and effectiveness of total purchasing;
- the benefits to patients through total purchasing.

This evidence was collected in order to indicate the 'best models for further development of fundholder-based purchasing in a primary care-led NHS' (Department of Health, Research and Development Division 1995: 1–2). Data were to be collected from all the 53 TPPs, though sampling was permitted for specific parts of the study. The study was to follow the TPPs for three years – one year for the pilots to prepare for active contracting, followed by two purchasing cycles for the first-wave TPPs. The assumption was that the evaluators would adopt a conventional stance, independent and separate from the policy and implementation process.

Thus the evaluation brief required some form of marginal analysis of the costs and benefits of total purchasing over the status quo (which then consisted of health authority purchasing with volunteer fundholding practices purchasing elective services for their patients). However, it also required a description of how the individual projects were established and run with a view to identifying the features of more and less 'successful' pilots. The former implied that the most important question was whether total purchasing was in some sense better than the status quo. The latter implied that total purchasing was either a good thing or, at least, agreed government policy for some time, such that the most important question was which *form* of TPP was the most 'successful' and should be replicated. Both implied a comparative design, but of very different types. Taken together, they suggested that the evaluation would need to employ a range of different methods of data collection and analysis.

Under the *costs* of total purchasing, the Department of Health research brief indicated that the study was to include a focus on the operating costs of the scheme (i.e. the costs of negotiating, specifying and monitoring contracts and managing spending between purchasers and providers) and policies to minimize these costs. This suggested a concern that the TPPs might increase the overall management and transaction costs in the NHS internal market by increasing the number of purchasing organizations. The research was also to look at budgetary management, overspends and underspends and the use made of any savings from TPPs' budgets. This suggested that there might be straightforward budgetary incentives in total purchasing similar to those present in fundholding, linked to the ability of projects to make and spend their own savings. It was not clear how this could be reconciled with the fact that the resources of the TPPs were to remain the responsibility of the local health authority, but no doubt this would become clearer over time.

The brief divided the *effects* of total purchasing into two parts – 'effectiveness' and 'benefits to patients'. Under 'effectiveness', a range of aspects of health services were listed in which TPPs might be expected to bring about change, such as referral and investigation patterns, quality standards in contracts, prescribing patterns, the balance between primary and secondary care and provider configuration. There was also an interest in detecting any divergence between TPP, health authority and national purchasing priorities and strategies. 'Benefits to patients' suggested that the Department believed it possible that the TPPs might be able to improve service responsiveness to patients' wishes, lower waiting times, improve access to primary and secondary care, raise levels of patient satisfaction and improve health outcomes. Researchers were asked to give some thought as to how these effects might be assessed with one-year pre-total purchasing and two-year post-total purchasing to work with.

Finally, the research brief highlighted a number of specific services for special attention as part of the evaluation. The list included all the services that had not previously been included in the fundholding scheme, such as accident and emergency (A&E) services, emergency medical in-patient care, in-patient services for people with serious mental health problems, maternity care, and community and continuing care of older people. There was a concern to assess the extent to which the TPPs opted to use different providers, altered the content of services, differed from the local health authority in their strategies and met the requirements of national policies, where relevant, in these new service areas.

It was clear that GPs could directly influence the pattern of non-urgent services used by their patients through their referral behaviour. Glennerster *et al.* (1994) had shown that fundholding practices had been able to use the fact that they were 'closer to the pains and preferences of patients' to make micro-efficiency gains in relation to non-emergency services. However, it appeared less immediately plausible that GPs would be able to influence the unplanned areas of health services such as attendance at A&E departments, even if they were given budgetary incentives to do so. In addition, there was no clear evidence that fundholders had the knowledge or motivation to pursue quality and cost improvements in services such as in-patient mental health services. On the other hand, being able to demonstrate that TPPs had some ability to influence these new services would be crucial in assessing whether total purchasing had potential as an alternative way of organizing HCHS purchasing.

## FEATURES OF TOTAL PURCHASING WHICH SHAPED THE EVALUATION DESIGN

The process of designing the national evaluation of the TPPs in England and Scotland exemplifies many of the issues and dilemmas familiar to evaluators of other complex social programmes. While the research brief presented an ambitious and somewhat idealized view of what an evaluation could cover, the reality was likely to be equally influenced by the way in which the total purchasing initiative was being developed. Box 2.2 summarizes the main features of the total purchasing initiative that had some bearing on the evaluation design.

The fact that total purchasing was new and had deliberately not been specified in detail meant that the researchers were hampered by a lack of *a priori* descriptive knowledge of what they were to evaluate. Beyond the likelihood that TPPs would be engaged in

---

**Box 2.2    Features of the total purchasing initiative relevant to the evaluation design**

- no detailed statement of aims, objectives or processes of implementation – TPPs largely defined through local implementation;
- innovation with potential to influence a wide range of aspects of the local health system;
- organizational as well as economic dimension required in the evaluation;
- pilot scheme was not implemented to facilitate an experimental/quasi-experimental research design;
- pilots knew that they would be evaluated through a national study, but were not required to collect data for the evaluation;
- pilots required to collaborate with the local health authority because they lacked legislative identity in their own right to hold extended budgets;
- large number of pilots spread across England and Scotland operating in different contexts, but all to be evaluated;
- other forms of GP involvement in purchasing HCHS with similarities to total purchasing were present widely in the NHS.

some form of budgetary delegation from the health authority, it was not clear whether they would be risk-bearing or even whether they would have their own distinct contracts for services. It was likely that the projects would be diverse. Because of the degree of uncertainty, it was decided that the early stages of the evaluation should be exploratory and descriptive. Face-to-face interviews using mostly open questions were suited to identifying the most relevant of a wide range of potential issues for subsequent study (Barbour 1999). Research on the effects of TPPs on specific service areas would not be finalized until the team had a better grasp of how total purchasing was being implemented in practice.

The large number of pilots permitted to enter the scheme in the first wave in October 1995 and the commitment by the Secretary of State that *all* the projects should be included in the national evaluation had two important implications for the evaluation. First, a quasi-experimental design which compared the first wave of TPPs with groups of similar practices eligible for the scheme, but which had not been entered, was not possible. Second, the evaluation resources had to be spread relatively thinly.

## OTHER ISSUES TO BE RESOLVED IN DESIGNING THE EVALUATION

Box 2.3 summarizes the wide range of issues that the Department of Health research brief left relatively open.

### Policy questions and appropriate comparisons

The identification of the most important, durable policy questions, and therefore the most relevant comparisons to shape the design, continued to exercise the attention of the TP-NET for a considerable time both before and after the evaluation had formally begun. As mostly academic researchers, independent of government, most members of the evaluation team were mainly interested in answering the question of whether total purchasing was 'better', in some sense, than prevailing arrangements. To do this, they wanted to compare the TPPs with suitable non-TPPs. This desire was partly a response from the academic community to the earlier decision of government not to sponsor such research when fundholding had been introduced in 1991. There was some discomfort among the TP-NET members with the requirement to research the 'best'

---

**Box 2.3  Issues to be resolved in the design of the evaluation**

- identification of the most important, durable policy questions and feasible comparisons to guide the design (e.g. TPP versus fundholding and health authority purchasing; marginal costs and benefits of total purchasing over fundholding and health authority purchasing; TPP versus alternative forms of extended general practice-based purchasing such as locality commissioning; and comparisons between the TPPs themselves;
- identification of potential effects (costs and benefits) to be measured in the absence of good information on the objectives and nature of the intervention and the degree to which the study should test prior research questions or be undertaken inductively;
- stance of the evaluation and nature of feedback – conventional objective research stance, action-research or more interactive style of relationship with policy makers and participants in pilots;
- relative emphasis on study of structure, inputs and processes as against outputs and health outcomes (e.g. likelihood of changes in outcomes in timescale of pilots);
- participants', policy makers' and evaluators' definitions of progress and success of pilots and the relative weight to give to each;
- defining the boundary of a case (i.e. TPP alone or TPP plus its local health service context);
- range of qualitative and quantitative data to collect and how to reconcile different types and sources of data;
- balance between data collection from 100 per cent sample and from subsamples of TPPs.

---

models of TPP for further development of a primary care-led NHS, since this objective seemed to be politically slanted and unduly restrictive in assuming that total purchasing would work.

The major practical difficulty faced in comparing the effect of the TPPs with the status quo ante was the fact that the best TPP comparator should have been the activities of its local health authority together with local fundholding practices. These purchasers were likely to have been using many of the same providers as the TPPs, thereby enhancing comparisons. However, since the health authority was also involved in the TPP, this would have meant comparing the health authority with itself – a tricky task. Comparing areas with TPPs with socio-economically similar areas without TPPs risked confounding due to different patterns of provision available in each area. Careful matching of population characteristics and provider characteristics could still have been undermined by the possible existence of schemes for GP involvement in purchasing similar to total purchasing in comparator districts, such as certain forms of locality commissioning.

On a more conceptual level, it was not self-evident whether TPPs should be viewed as *alternatives* to either the health authority as purchaser (or, indeed, other devolved approaches to local purchasing), or a *complement* to the health authority, acting to develop good practice which could then be adopted more generally. Subsequently, the NHS in England seems to have adopted the latter approach since PCGs now operate within the framework of the health authority's health improvement programme (Secretary of State for Health 1997). Yet another way of considering the TPPs was as precursors to a new form of *collaboration* between health authority purchasers and general practice-based purchasers after a period when fundholding practices and health authorities had operated largely in parallel and separately. Each interpretation of the current or likely future role of total purchasing required that priority be given to answering a different research question.

It became apparent from an early stage that some form of GP-led purchasing, whether 'total' or an extension beyond fundholding, was supported by all the main political parties (Mays and Dixon 1996). As a result, the comparison of the effects of TPPs with the status quo ante became decreasingly important for policy. The question of how something like total purchasing could most effectively be introduced, managed and sustained became far more salient and was likely to have the most lasting appeal to policy makers. Such a question also had the additional strength of recognizing, implicitly, that total purchasing was likely to be implemented very differently in different places and with differing consequences. The early stages of fieldwork began to demonstrate that total purchasing was not a 'magic bullet' or, indeed, a single entity, which could be compared easily to something else, but rather a new part of the local NHS. Its effects were unlikely to be attributable, in any straightforward way, to the presence or absence of budgetary incentives since TPPs were also new forms of NHS organization. The quality of the leadership and management of the TPPs was likely to be as important, if not more so, for their effective operation, as the earlier Audit Commission evaluation of fundholding had shown (Audit Commission 1996).

In the event, different components of the evaluation were designed to look at different policy questions. This increased the likelihood that at least some of the evaluation's findings would still be relevant by the time they became available. Thus one part of the study involved collecting detailed information on the context, structure, organization, management costs, purchasing objectives and reported service changes of all the TPPs to identify which types of TPP appeared to be more successful than others and in which contexts. This component was able to begin to answer the questions of how and why some TPPs appeared to make greater progress than others in bringing about potentially desirable service changes. Case studies of a subsample of projects were then undertaken in order to explain the relationship between the context of the TPP and the mechanisms which it used to bring about service change to understand outcomes and rate of progress.

Another component focused on the nature of specific services purchased, their costs, and patients' views of those services. This compared a subsample of TPPs interested in the specific service, a subsample without a special interest, a matched sample of non-TPP practices with a special interest and a matched subsample of fundholders without a special interest. This part of the evaluation was intended to shed some light on whether TPPs were, in any sense, superior purchasers when compared with non-TPP purchasers.

**Stance of the evaluation**

Following the Department of Health's research brief, the evaluation team adopted a relatively conventional stance in relation to the pilots. It was made clear that the research process was to be entirely separate from the process of implementing the pilots and the performance management activities undertaken by the health authorities and the NHS Executive Regional Offices of the NHS Executive. A commitment was made by the evaluation team to provide regular summaries of aggregated, anonymized findings to participants in the TPPs as well as to regional and national managers and policy makers from the earliest opportunity. There was considerable pressure from the NHS Executive for early feedback from the evaluators on the progress of the pilots. The research team was also aware that the support of the participants in the pilots for the evaluation could be dented if they heard little or nothing from the evaluators for some time. In addition, members of the TP-NET made numerous presentations on the work in progress at TPP, district, regional and national levels, as well as organizing meetings, workshops and seminars on particular aspects of the evaluation and of total purchasing (for example, risk management strategies).

### Process versus outcome evaluation

The relative emphasis in the data collection on the structure of TPPs, inputs, processes, outputs (e.g. service changes), patients' views and health outcomes was determined by what was practicable and by a judgement as to which could legitimately be attributed with reasonable confidence to the actions of the TPPs.

One of the commonest criticisms of the eventual design (see Figure 2.1) – particularly from audiences unfamiliar with the realities of programme evaluation but influenced by the doctrine of evidence-based policy making and the centrality of health outcomes to health services policy – was the lack of attention to measuring changes in population health status associated with total purchasing. This criticism implied that the principal test of total purchasing as a policy lay in improved health outcomes. However, the three-year timescale of the pilots made it extremely unlikely that clear-cut changes in population health could be identified and attributed unequivocally to the presence or absence of total purchasers. Instead, it appeared more feasible to discover, first of all, how the participants in the pilots defined their objectives and their perceptions of how their projects were progressing. This could be followed by seeing if total purchasers could bring about the service changes they were aiming for and then to quantify the effects of those changes in service delivery. This could be accompanied by an investigation of patients' experiences of specific services purchased by the TPPs. It would also be of considerable value to policy makers to know whether TPPs were capable of purchasing exactly the same services at lower cost than their comparators, irrespective of whether health outcomes were improved or not. Indeed, given that health outcomes are determined by a wide range of factors, most outside the direct control of purchasers, it would have been inappropriate to base a judgement about the worth of total purchasing on outcomes (Cumming and Scott 1998).

A final drawback with an evaluation design which gave predominant weight to health outcome assessment was the fact that there would have been little to report until after the end of the three-year pilot period. This would have guaranteed that the findings of the evaluation would have been too late to influence decisions about what to do when the initiative came to an end, even assuming that such decisions had not already been taken. By contrast, early descriptions of the similarities and differences between the ways in which the pilots chose to organize themselves, or of their purchasing objectives, would enable policy makers at the Department of Health to obtain a rapid understanding of where their *laissez faire* policy *vis-à-vis* the TPPs was leading. It might then be possible to adjust the terms of reference of the projects if problems were emerging.

**Internal versus external assessment of pilots' progress**

Apart from the specific issue of the relative focus on processes, outputs and outcomes in the evaluation, it became apparent that there was merit in being able to report on the relative progress or even 'success' of projects over time. In the absence of a clear policy statement, and without first-hand knowledge of how TPPs would operate, it would have been rash for the evaluation team to develop its own means of assessing TPPs' progress from the outset. It was recognized that there was a place in the evaluation for participants' own interpretations of the extent to which their projects were on track and questions on this were included in interviews from the beginning of the study. In addition, it was recognized that external to the pilots themselves, policy makers at different levels and the evaluators had their own expectations and views on what would constitute more and less 'successful' total purchasing. After the projects had been in existence for about 18 months (i.e. they were in their first live purchasing year), it was possible for the evaluation team to devise its own assessment of the progress of each pilot. This was derived from the views put forward by participants in the TPPs as to the progress of their projects, analysis of the strategic challenges facing GP-led purchasing if it were to remain a feature of the NHS, and a judgement about which indicators would be available in the first live year (Mays *et al.* 1998a). One early assessment, designed to capture the extent to which each pilot was in a position to operate as a fully fledged purchaser, was based on the following questions:

- Have the practices in the original pilot stayed together?
- Has the TPP purchased any services directly?
- Has the TPP brought about any service changes?
- Has the TPP brought about a shift in the location of care?
- Has the TPP made effective external links?
- Has the TPP stayed within budget?

(Mays *et al.* 1998a)

Other criteria used later in the life of the evaluation were the TPPs' self-reported successes in achieving their own objectives, and TPPs' reported success in achieving objectives in specifically total purchasing-related areas, including their management of unplanned use of acute hospital services.

## MAIN COMPONENTS OF THE EVALUATION

The evaluation design that resulted from consideration of the issues discussed earlier in this chapter was observational rather than experimental. The design employed a range of qualitative and quantitative methods of data collection, reflecting the complex and multifaceted nature of the total purchasing initiative, which both altered budgetary incentives and led to the creation of new forms of organization in the local NHS. Some parts of the evaluation focused on understanding the development of the TPPs; other parts compared TPPs with one another in order to try to identify the determinants of more and less successful pilots. Other components compared the TPPs with parts of the NHS where there were no TPPs. Some of the comparisons concerned the patients of different types of purchaser organization (TPPs and non-TPPs), while others concerned the processes undertaken in the purchaser organizations themselves.

Fifty-three first-wave TPPs were studied over a three-year period which began with their preparatory year (1995/96), before continuing for two live purchasing cycles in 1996/97 and 1997/98. Thirty-five second wave TPPs began their preparatory year in 1996/97 and were followed during that period and for a further 12 months of live purchasing in 1997/98. The design of the evaluation of the first and second waves differed.

## EVALUATION OF FIRST-WAVE TOTAL PURCHASING PILOTS, 1995–98

The evaluation of the first-wave projects comprised a large number of interrelated elements, some of which were carried out at all pilots and some of which were carried out only at subsamples of TPPs. This 'thick and thin' design was chosen to make the best use of the research resources available. Figure 2.1 summarizes the evaluation programme.

## SET-UP AND OPERATION OF THE TOTAL PURCHASING PILOTS

This part of the evaluation was undertaken at all first-wave projects and began in the second half of their preparatory year between September and December 1995. The first round of data collection was focused on how total purchasing was being implemented (see Chapter 3). It was undertaken through a mixture of face-to-face interviews, diary cards administered to samples of participants at projects, postal questionnaires, telephone interviews, analysis of routine data and the analysis of documents. Approximately 300 face-to-face interviews were undertaken with lead GPs, TPP project managers, senior managers from the local health authority (health board in Scotland), representatives of the local NHS trusts (provider organizations), and staff from local authority social services departments (social work departments in Scotland). In addition, a series of telephone interview and postal questionnaire surveys was run in parallel with the TPP site visits. These covered the contracting process, risk management arrangements, financial management, and how TPPs' budgets were set (see Chapters 9 and 10). A second round of interviews and related data collection using the same methods was undertaken in February and March 1997. This concentrated on the pilots' experience of total purchasing in the first live year (1996/97), their perceptions of how successful their projects had been, their specific achievements against their main objectives and the enabling factors and obstacles which they had encountered (see Chapters 4 and 5). Data were also collected at interview on the amount of time and money spent on managing the pilots (Chapter 8), whether the project had stayed within budget (Chapter 10), the project's plans for 1997/98, and accountability arrangements (Chapter 11).

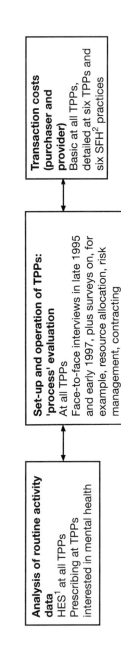

**Figure 2.1**  Main components of the national evaluation of first-wave total purchasing pilots

*Notes:* [1] HES = hospital episode statistics
[2] SFH = standard fundholding
[3] EAs = emergency admissions
[4] EFH = extended fundholding pilot

Further data on progress against achievements, management costs and the involvement of the TPPs in the development of the PCGs which succeeded them throughout the NHS in England were collected by a mixture of telephone interviews and postal question-naires from participants at all first-wave TPPs at the end of the second live year, 1997/98 (see Chapter 4). The aim of this, the third year of the evaluation, was also to identify different types of TPPs and their impact (benefits and costs), taking account of their local contexts, in order to be able to identify the ingredients of success-ful devolved purchasing based in primary care. By then, it was apparent that 'success' was likely to be related to the context of the pilot, the content of its purchasing objectives, its managerial resources and the processes through which it attempted to imple-ment its objectives.

To study this, in addition to monitoring progress at all the first-wave TPPs, a subsample of 12 TPPs was selected for more detailed case study investigation. Single-practice TPPs were excluded from this since it had become apparent after the change of government in May 1997 that budget holding at individual practice level was likely to be abolished, irrespective of its particular attractions. Multi-practice TPPs were selected as case studies in order to enable investigation of the emerging types of TPPs, their organizational features and the financial and managerial tools and levers which they used to bring about service changes (see Chapter 5). The case studies were also used to look at the extent to which the TPPs con-tributed to and complemented existing and future local commis-sioning arrangements (for example, the new PCGs, which began to be planned alongside the TPPs in the second half of 1997/98), the management investment required to support total purchasing, the ability of the TPPs to bring about change, and the implications for maintaining such investment in the longer term. By identifying examples of 'best practice', the findings provided an empirical basis for practical guidance to inform the development of local commis-sioning arrangements such as the PCGs developed from *The New NHS* White Paper in England (Secretary of State for Health 1997) (see Chapter 14 and see also Goodwin *et al.* 2000).

**Transaction costs**

Since the advent of the TPPs added to the number of purchasing entities at local level in the NHS and, potentially, increased the number of transactions between purchasers and providers, it was important to be able to look at the full cost implications wherever these costs fell. The direct managerial costs of the TPPs were estimated at all first- and second-wave TPPs. The wider transaction costs associated with total purchasing compared to previous health authority purchasing in the presence of fundholding practices were analysed in detail at a subsample of six TPPs (see Chapter 8).

**Analysis of changes in hospital activity**

One element in the rationale for extending fundholding into total purchasing was to give practices, for the first time, an incentive to manage their patients' use of unplanned acute hospital services. Any savings that they made by reducing the use of acute services could be reinvested in additional patient care for their patients, thereby making their practices increasingly attractive to potential patients. If TPPs were able to manage demand for acute services better than the health authority, it was important to be able to document it. As a result, the changes in hospital activity (i.e. in patient episodes and lengths of stay) before and after the advent of total purchasing were compared between TPP and non-TPP populations using routine NHS hospital episode statistics. The pattern of TPP patients' use of hospital services was compared both with the pattern in a subgroup of local non-TPP practices using the same hospitals and with the whole of the remainder of the health authority population (see Chapter 7).

**The development of specific services purchased by general practitioners for the first time through total purchasing**

Substudies were undertaken to examine patterns of care purchased, service costs, and patients' responses to four services purchased by TPPs in comparison with the same services purchased by the health authority. The services were chosen because NHS GPs had not purchased them previously and because each represented a test of the capacity of GPs to manage the purchasing process effectively. The four service areas were emergency admissions (see Chapter 7), community and continuing care for people with complex needs (mainly older people), services for people with serious mental health problems, and maternity care (see Chapter 6). In the case of the latter two services, the evaluation of the TPPs was linked to an evaluation of a series of pilot extensions to fundholding in which volunteer fundholding practices took purchasing responsibility for one additional service beyond the scope of fundholding. In each of the four service areas, the focus was on a small subsample of TPPs that had made the particular service area a priority in their purchasing strategy.

### Assessing the accountability of TPPs

Chapter 11 describes in more detail how three elements of accountability – managerial, financial and public – were assessed to see how far first-wave TPPs were held to account in their first live year (1996/97). The information was collected via the semi-structured interviews conducted with all first-wave TPPs in England and Scotland as described above. These interviews included questions on the extent to which formal structures existed locally to demonstrate the accountability of the TPP. Questions were not asked about professional accountability for clinical care since the main focus of the study was on the GPs as purchasers of services. Questions were also asked about how accountability systems were operating in practice. Semi-structured interviews conducted with a manager responsible for total purchasing at each of the eight NHS Executive Regional Offices in England, and a representative from the Scottish NHS Management Executive, also asked questions of accountability.

## EVALUATION OF SECOND-WAVE TOTAL PURCHASING PILOTS, 1996–98

A second wave of TPPs was admitted to the national pilot scheme a year after the first wave. Data modelled on the study of the establishment and operation of the first wave were collected from all second-wave projects, but in less detail. Telephone interviews and postal questionnaires, rather than face-to-face interviews, were carried out with lead GPs and TPP project managers at the second-wave pilots during their preparatory year between October 1996 and March 1997. Similar supplementary sources of information such as purchasing plans and other documents were also collected and used to supplement the interviews and questionnaires.

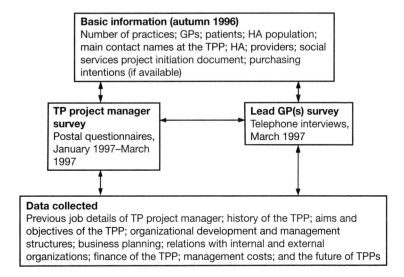

**Figure 2.2**   Data collection on the national evaluation of second-wave total purchasing pilot projects

Figure 2.2 shows the main topics covered in the postal questionnaires and telephone interviews in the second-wave preparatory year (1996/97) and at the end of a year of active purchasing in the Spring of 1998 when the focus was on evidence of their initial purchasing achievements. The majority of the questions used with the second wave were structured and precoded based on an analysis of data collected from the first-wave pilots. Investigation was thus informed by what had been learned about total purchasing from the earlier wave.

## CONCLUSIONS

Many of the issues which the TP-NET grappled with in designing, modifying and undertaking the national evaluation of TPPs have been discussed and illuminated far more elegantly by Ray Pawson and Nick Tilley in their 1997 book, *Realistic Evaluation*. The book powerfully advances the case for an approach to programme evaluation which avoids both the inflexibility and lack of explanatory power of the traditional experiment or quasi-experiment, and the relativism of so-called 'fourth generation evaluation'. The book is particularly helpful for the policy-relevant evaluation of complex programmes but, unfortunately, appeared at a relatively late stage in the evolution of the TPP evaluation. Nonetheless, insights from the book have helped to explain some of the difficulties encountered in beginning the design of the evaluation from the perspective of a modified version of the conventional, 'black box' experimental approach. Pawson and Tilley's approach, by contrast, focuses on the relations between the mechanisms of an intervention and the context in bringing about particular outcomes. They argue that 'outcomes are explained by the action of particular mechanisms in particular contexts' (Pawson and Tilley, 1997: 59). Rather than prompting the evaluator to focus exclusively on the question of whether one programme is on average better than another in producing some outcome, Pawson and Tilley prompt the evaluator to try to answer the question of why a programme works, for whom and in what circumstances, given that social programmes, by their nature, tend to produce a wide range of outcomes. They also stress the role of prior theory in building explanations, and making evaluations accumulate until social programmes, and the mechanisms through which they work or do not work, are understood. Such insights contributed to the design and analysis of the case studies in 1997/98 (see Chapter 5). Chapter 12 reflects further on what the current evaluation has taught us in the light of Pawson and Tilley's insights.

# 3

# DEVELOPING PRIMARY CARE ORGANIZATIONS

## Nick Goodwin, Brenda Leese, Kate Baxter, Stephen Abbott, Gill Malbon and Amanda Killoran

Until recently, primary care in the UK has been based on a small business model, with general practitioners working as independent contractors to the NHS, usually within a partnership. Over time, the size of partnerships has increased with an associated rise in the employment of practice-based staff including practice managers, nurses and other practice-attached community health service staff as part of a primary health care team. However, the basic organizational form of 'the practice' has not significantly altered. The structure even survived the advent of the multifund of fundholding practices, an arrangement in which fundholding practices agreed to pool their management allowances to provide combined administrative services such as finance and personnel management. In this arrangement, any savings achieved against practice budgets were specific to practices themselves and were not shared with others in the multifund. Consequently, practices were able to maintain their integrity and financial independence.

Within both the total purchasing experiment, and the subsequent NHS primary care reforms which began in 1998/99, groups of general practices functioning collaboratively have been seen as fundamental to planning and delivering local health services. This implies collective responsibility for managing budgets as well as for service development. The experience of larger TPPs was that before any goals could be achieved, attention had to be paid to the development of the pilot as a health care organization. So while most smaller TPPs were able to achieve their chosen objectives with relatively little investment in organizational development, the largest TPPs required substantial time and investment before progress could be made. After three years, including one preparatory year, some TPPs were still at a relatively early stage in becoming effective commissioning organizations (Mays *et al.* 1998a; Killoran *et al.* 1999b). By the second live year, however, many larger pilots had caught up in terms of their ability to achieve objectives (Malbon *et al.* 1999). This related not only to the time it took for larger TPPs to develop their organizations, but also to the context in which they were working. Of particular importance were relationships with their local health authorities and providers (see Chapter 5 for a more detailed discussion of the importance of context in the organizational development of TPPs).

This chapter draws on data collected in face-to-face interviews conducted in all 53 first-wave TPPs, and on the case studies of 12 larger TPPs carried out in the second live year as described in Chapter 2. The chapter first examines the profile of the first-wave TPPs before considering the organizational characteristics of the pilots in more detail. The chapter concludes with an examination of the lessons that can be learned from TPPs for the development of primary care organizations as effective multi-practice groups and, in particular, the motivation and ability of GPs to act collectively.

## PROFILE OF FIRST-WAVE TOTAL PURCHASING PILOTS IN 1996/97 AND 1997/98

Table 3.1 gives the basic features of the first wave of national TPPs in England and Scotland, which were studied between 1995 and 1998. Fifty-three first-wave TPPs were examined in the first year and 41 out of 53 TPPs in the second year. Of the TPPs that were not included in the analysis of the second year, four had ceased to operate as TPPs from April 1998 while the others had failed to respond to telephone or postal interviews. The characteristics of the non-responders were as varied as those of responders. Given that total purchasing was to end officially in March 1998 (unless given approval to continue until March 1999 by the local health authority), and that the agenda for the development of the larger PCGs had already been set, the lack of participation in the second year of the evaluation by some TPPs also may have reflected a perception that the final stages of the national evaluation of TPPs was already irrelevant to future policy development.

**Table 3.1** Basic characteristics of first-wave total purchasing pilots, 1996/97 and 1997/98

| Characteristics | 1996/97 | 1997/98 |
|---|---|---|
| *Basic features* | | |
| Number of TPPs | 53 | 41[1] |
| % of single-practice TPPs | 36 | 44 |
| % of multi-practice TPPs | 64 | 56 |
| *Size* | | |
| Mean number of practices per TPP | 3 | 3 |
| Median number of practices per TPP | 3 | 3 |
| Mean number of GPs per TPP | 17 | 17 |
| Median number of GPs per TPP | 16 | 14 |
| *TPP patient population* | | |
| Range in patient population | 8100–84,700 | 6653–81,000 |
| Mean TPP patient population | 31,300 | 29,384 |
| Median TPP patient population | 28,200 | 24,500 |
| *Health authority patient population* | | |
| Mean percentage of health authority population served by TPPs | 6 | 6 |
| Median percentage of health authority population served by TPPs | 6 | 5 |
| Mid-range (25%–75%) of health authority population served by TPPs | 3–8 | 3–7 |
| *Organizational features[2]* | | |
| % of TPPs with a dedicated TP manager | 66 | – |
| % of TPPs with a 'complex' organizational structure | 38 | – |
| % of TPPs with a 'simple' organizational structure | 30 | – |
| *Management costs at 1997/98 prices, £* | | |
| Mean per capita cost | 2.96 | 3.10 |
| Median per capita cost | 2.82 | 3.08 |
| Range of per capita cost | 0.02–7.08 | 0.05–7.07 |

*Notes*:

[1] Four TPPs dropped out of the evaluation by June 1998. Two four-practice projects had divided into eight single-practice TPPs (53 + 6 = 59 and 59 − 4 = 55) and 14 practices did not respond (55 − 14 = 41).

[2] These data were not collected for TPPs in 1997/98.

As Table 3.1 shows, TPPs varied widely in size, from large multi-practice pilots with a population coverage of more than 80,000 to small, single-practice TPPs covering a population of less than 7000. Indeed, approximately one-third of first-wave TPPs contained just a single practice. The diversity in the size of the TPPs was matched by differences along many other dimensions including the level of management costs per capita and the complexity of organization. In addition, by their final year, this diversity continued and there was little sense of organizational convergence between TPPs. This is reflected in the management costs which showed no sign of decreasing despite the fact that set-up costs incurred in years 1 and 2 ought to have come to an end. The pilots were on average slightly smaller in the second live year than the first. However, this can be directly attributed to the fact that two multi-practice projects broke up into eight separate projects.

## DECISION-MAKING STRUCTURES

The development of PCGs in England provided detailed guidance on how to structure their organization (NHS Executive 1998d). However, by contrast, TPPs were free to decide how to develop their organizations, albeit within the confines of being a health authority subcommittee. Consequently, total purchasers developed a wide variety of organizational forms from simple to complex structures dependent on a range of characteristics including the number of practices within the pilots; the scope of their commissioning activities; and the degree of collaboration with, or independent from, their host health authority (Mays *et al.* 1997a).

Despite variations between pilots, TPPs typically had decision-making structures as outlined in Figure 3.1. Organizational analyses of the TPPs (particularly those researched in depth through case studies in 1997/98) highlight the importance within this structure of the executive, or decision-making board within multi-practice pilots (Goodwin *et al.* 2000). The executive board most often comprised lead GPs from the practices within the TPP acting as pilot directors (usually one from each practice), with a project manager in attendance as a secretary or as a fellow director. The executive board's function was to determine the focus of the TPP, and to make and oversee the implementation of commissioning and service development plans (i.e. a management role).

Within the overall structure of TPPs, executive groups were

**Role and membership**

| | |
|---|---|
| **HEALTH AUTHORITY BOARD** | The health authority board comprised staff from the health authority only. This board discussed health authority policy towards the TPP and gave strategic direction to health authority members on the TPP project board. Typically, the board consisted of the chief executive, senior managers and the directors of public health, finance and contracting. |

**Governance role**

| | |
|---|---|
| **TPP PROJECT BOARD** | The TPP project board acted as the steering group to the pilot and was usually designated as a subcommittee of the health authority. This board gave strategic guidance to the executive board and often held full delegated power over the TPP. The board typically comprised a pilot manager, lead GPs and directors from the health authority and was sometimes extended to local providers and region. |

**Management role**

| | |
|---|---|
| **TPP EXECUTIVE BOARD** | The TPP executive board was the decision-making group of the project dealing with day-to-day administration. This board was likely to comprise the pilot manager, lead and other GPs, fundholding and practice managers. Lower level health authority managers were sometimes represented on the executive board for such issues as finance, purchasing and public health matters. |

**Support role**

| | |
|---|---|
| **TPP SUB GROUPS** | Comprising informal groups with no specific task (e.g. a lead practitioner or pilot manager group) and formal groups assigned to various tasks (e.g. finance, information, purchasing and contracting) often led or supported by the health authority and local providers. The TPP subgroups and *ad hoc* groups feed information and proposals to the executive board for discussion and ratification. |

**Figure 3.1**   Organizational structure of a hypothetical total purchasing pilot

*Note*: In some TPPs, particularly smaller ones, the TPP project board and TPP executive board is combined into a single decision-making body.

usually distinct from the TPP project board (except for some small pilots where one board fulfilled both tasks). Project boards typically included senior officers from the host health authority with a key role to steer the development of the pilot from a strategic, governance point of view. Since the legislation required for delegating NHS money outside the scope of fundholding to organizations other than health authorities was not in place during the life of the TPPs, the TPP project board represented the interests of the health authority as the legal 'owner' of the pilot. And in all TPPs, the health authority retained the ultimate right of veto over any total purchasing activity since it controlled and was responsible for NHS funds for total purchasing.

As subcommittees of the health authority, TPPs did not have formal constitutions, which meant that the willingness of all the GPs within TPPs to invest the executive board with the authority to shape strategic direction varied. The extent of support and investment in decision making emerged as the TPPs' programmes were implemented. Generally, where willingness to divest power to an executive group by GPs was most in evidence, progress was faster. The willingness to delegate power to an executive group was often associated with a consensus commitment to working on a specific local health care issue (for example, protecting a local hospital or improving mental health care), but it was also important that all GPs had sufficient trust in the leadership of the TPP for this to occur.

In many respects, PCG boards in the NHS now carry out the managerial functions of TPP executive groups and also some of the governance duties of the TPP board. Unlike TPPs, PCGs are distinct bodies formally accountable to health authorities (not simply subcommittees) and their boards include representatives from health authorities, social services departments, nurses from the local community health services provider, the public, and local GPs. Since TPP executives typically involved GPs only, the arrangements for PCGs are both more formal and wider ranging than those for TPPs. Questions of accountability and representation are complex: unlike GPs (the majority of whom will continue as at present to be self-employed contractors), many non-GP members on PCG boards are employed by other organizations, such as NHS community health services trusts, local authority social services, and other professional bodies. Developing custom and practice in dealing with these issues, and managing the possible conflicts of interests inherent in such arrangements, is taking time to be resolved (Smith *et al.* 2000b). TPPs rarely included such representatives in their organizational structure, but when they did so such representatives were generally not invited to share executive responsibility for decisions with the GPs.

A noticeable feature of most TPPs, as volunteer schemes, was their reliance on a few highly motivated individuals whose vision and leadership drove the TPP forward. In the early stages, TPPs tended to be dominated by a single innovative practitioner or occasionally a project manager, or perhaps both (Leese and Mahon 1999a). Many, but not all, lead GPs were able to give time to total purchasing only by employing locums, by 'stealing' time from their clinical workloads, or by fitting TPP activities into spare time such as lunchtimes and evenings. Indeed, this appears to have been a common element in the development of alternative forms of primary care organization such as GP commissioning groups (Earwicker 1998; Regen *et al.* 1999). As a result, the majority of GPs in TPPs remained marginal to, and often ambivalent about, TPP activity. Given the overall low level of input from the GP community as a whole, the sustainability of TPPs was questionable, particularly since there was evidence from some pilots to show that the loss or removal of a key player could be devastating to the future progress of projects (Mays *et al.* 1998a). Nevertheless, TPPs needed the energy, determination and vision of such leaders in order to become established and to pursue their objectives successfully in a relatively short time. PCGs and other primary care organizations are unlikely to succeed without this.

Despite the importance of leadership, analysis of data from the 11 case studies of TPPs in their second live year suggested that successful TPPs also created a sense of collective ownership of the pilot among the practices (Goodwin *et al.* 2000). In particular, greater participation by non-lead GPs led to a reduction in the workloads of the leads. The development of collective commitment came partly from interpractice communication, which was achieved in a number of ways. In many cases, TPPs created a number of subgroups in order to enable the participation of the non-lead practitioners, and sometimes of other stakeholders. The subgroups either concentrated on clinical areas (such as breast cancer) or on managerial aspects (such as the management of extra-contractual referrals). An extreme example was a TPP with 25 subgroups across 12 practices involving 30 GPs!

Subgroup structures within TPPs also helped to ensure the participation of GPs in some aspect of total purchasing work outside the boundaries of their own practice. At best, subgroup working was beneficial to the creation of the TPP organization in three ways: first, it helped reduce work pressures on the lead GPs; second, it enabled a more collective sense of responsibility for the TPP as a whole to develop; and third, greater collective responsibility led to more support for the executive board to lead the project on behalf of constituent practices. Some level of interpractice working became the norm for most GPs in the more successful TPPs and, generally, the subgroup structure seems to have been successful in increasing organizational cohesion, although not all TPPs used it, and not all subgroups adopted a truly corporate perspective. It is reasonable to predict that many primary care organizations will use subgroups as a means of managing workload and encouraging participation and the development of specialist expertise, particularly as not all practices will be represented on their full boards. In turn, where GPs in TPPs did see themselves as part of a single clinical group (which was more likely in smaller TPPs), the TPPs tended to be better at managing their budgets than in TPPs which were less corporate (Bevan *et al.* 1998).

As a short-lived pilot scheme of voluntary collaborators, total purchasing offered few incentives to encourage reluctant members to participate fully. If the TPP did not proceed satisfactorily, one or more of the practices could leave the collaboration at any time, with no significant loss to themselves. Within the 'new NHS', membership of primary care commissioning organizations is compulsory and they function as geographical monopolies, making it virtually impossible for GPs to leave the group. A breakdown in relationships, or failure to achieve ambitions, impact on all practices within the group, and their patients. Therefore, on the one hand, it could be argued that PCGs might provide an incentive to participate since success for individual practices is more likely when all members become actively involved in group activities. On the other hand, as Street and Place (1998) show, PCGs, like TPPs, will theoretically suffer from 'free rider' problems – that is, when a GP accepts the benefits of total purchasing such as additional services, but not the restraints on his or her clinical freedom to commit resources.

A small number of TPPs attempted to develop democratic structures that avoided executive groups, believing these to be too hierarchical given the independent practices and practitioners in the TPP. In other words, these TPPs were essentially organizations that attempted to coordinate the work of independent purchasing practices in which all practices were involved in all or most decisions. The Department of Health's guidance on PCG boards (NHS Executive 1998d), however, rules out this form of coordination. But it is useful to observe that in two case study pilots, where such a 'flattening' of structure was attempted, quite strong informal leadership arrangements developed. In another two pilots, care had been taken to appoint a project manager who could not be identified with any one practice, so as to avoid suspicions that any one practice was dominant or accusations of divided loyalties. However, neither TPP was notably successful in establishing itself as an effective organization. It may be that collective organizations such as PCGs would be well advised to confront potential problems of hierarchy, conflict and mistrust between practices rather than to seek to avoid them. Certainly, the multi-agency composition of PCG boards requires even greater corporate ability to manage debate and dissent creatively. There are interprofessional as well as interpractice issues at stake in PCGs which did not exist in TPPs.

**MANAGEMENT SKILLS**

A common aspect of the largest and most successful projects was the employment of a competent project manager working full-time on total purchasing, with sufficient skills to be able to cover a wide range of sophisticated tasks including financial risk management, the facilitation of group decision making on purchasing priorities and the linking of clinical and budget management, as well as the more obvious tasks such as contracting, information gathering, the development of information technology systems and human resources management.

In some cases, project managers had a small team of support staff and developed leadership roles. Some became one of the executive directors of the TPP (in two of the 11 TPPs studied in depth they were titled 'chief executives' of the TPP). When this happened, non-lead GPs were more willing to delegate responsibility for their practice's interests to the project manager as an active member of the executive board, but one who was not affiliated with any particular practice. This could be regarded as a major organizational development in primary care in England.

Lack of project management capacity inhibited some TPPs. A few were forced to withdraw because they lacked a project manager, which led to excessive calls on GP time and poor communication within the TPP. In one case study pilot, a TPP project manager was employed with no experience of contracting, resulting in unrealistic and unreasonable contracting demands being made of both local NHS trusts and the health authority. As a result, the perceived ability of the TPP to run its affairs professionally was undermined, leading to lack of support from external agencies for the TPP's objectives. The experiences of TPPs with good and bad project managers indicate the importance of non-clinical management support in developing primary care organizations.

## INFORMATION MANAGEMENT AND TECHNOLOGY

A key task facing TPPs was the ability to obtain information to allow priorities to be set and purchasing decisions to be made. Information was also required to inform budget setting, to prepare purchasing and business plans, and to carry out contracting and monitoring functions. For all of these tasks, TPPs had to invest considerable time and effort in the negotiation and development of information systems, since most TPPs indicated that such systems – for example, to examine the pattern and nature of services used by TPP populations – were inadequate (Mahon *et al.* 1998; Robinson *et al.* 1998). In particular, the lack of central guidance on information systems and an absence of standard software for total purchasing meant that each pilot developed individualized systems, most often based on modified fundholding software which was usually found to be inadequate (Mays *et al.* 1998a).

The problems TPPs encountered in obtaining and managing information related to its quality, usability and accessibility. For example, while TPPs could often obtain information from several sources, including NHS trusts and the health authority, it was not always in a form that was readily usable by the pilots and often presented an incomplete record of the information needed. A common experience for many TPPs, therefore, was having to put together a jigsaw of information from the different sources available (Mahon *et al.* 1998). In addition, particularly in the preparatory stages, TPPs themselves were not always sure of the information they wanted from NHS trusts and in what format, making it difficult for providers to respond to demands. In addition, TPPs were often suspicious of information provided to them by health authorities and there was a generally limited understanding between projects and their health authorities about the information necessary to support devolved purchasing.

(Mays *et al.* 1998a)

A common problem for TPPs was related to the poor activity and cost data available from NHS trusts, which hampered efforts to monitor and change services through contracting. This was a particular problem for TPPs interested in influencing mental health services and community health services. Many NHS trusts were unable to produce adequate information on the use of services by TPP patients, and their resultant costs to support devolved purchasing, since they had not previously been required to provide information at a practice or individual patient level. While problems with data availability contributed to difficulties in achieving objectives, TPPs appeared to act as catalysts for change by alerting NHS trusts, health authorities and indeed the practices within TPPs themselves to the information requirements of primary care-based purchasers. As a result, TPPs generally reported improvements in the accuracy and timeliness of information during their lifetime as they pressed for better information systems to be put in place (Mahon *et al.* 1998).

The multiplicity of existing information systems in primary care means that both money and time is required to tackle information issues adequately. As the total purchasing experiment drew to its end, staff within TPPs often expressed concern over information technology deficits and incompatibilities between practices that would become future collaborators in PCGs. Consequently, there has been concern that the information technology to support PCGs may be inadequate and that significant investment is likely to be required to improve the activity and cost data available (Street and Place 1998).

Additional evidence from TPPs also indicates that a cultural barrier needs to be overcome in the use and sharing of information systems. In some TPPs, progress was slow because the ability to share information and information systems, both between practices and also between the TPP and NHS trusts, first required an understanding of the different cultures and ways of working of the various groups involved. So while many information technology and information barriers could be described as technical, the real barriers to change were often those of existing traditions and the values of the different stakeholders (Leese and Mahon 1999a).

## ALLIANCES AND COLLABORATIONS

In order to improve their capacity to influence the delivery of health care services, many TPPs recognized the need for the development of alliances with other agencies including their host health authority, NHS trusts and social services departments. Indeed, the character of relationships between the various stake-holders in total purchasing influenced the process of change. More specifically, where relationships between the TPP and other agen-cies were cooperative or collaborative, it was more likely that TPPs would achieve their objectives (Mays *et al.* 1998b).

The most important alliance to be made by TPPs was with their host health authority, since a good relationship with the health authority was significantly related to a TPP's ability to achieve objectives (see Chapter 4). For example, good relations with the health authority manifested themselves in a greater likelihood for health authorities to let go – that is, allow TPPs to take on additional budgetary responsibilities – and meant that TPPs were potentially more likely to be supported and resourced. While both TPPs and health authorities acknowledged a large culture gap between the different organizations, more successful pilots invested in steps to promote shared learning and improve relationships. On the other hand, where TPPs were at odds with their health auth-ority and did not acknowledge their differences, pilots experienced difficulties in making progress (Mahon *et al.* 1998). For PCGs, a key lesson from TPPs is the importance of achieving effective working relationships with their health authorities. However, the increased emphasis in PCGs on formal accountability on the one hand and the devolution of commissioning responsibilities from health authorities on the other means that future relationships are likely to be rather different from those experienced by TPPs. Nevertheless, it will be important for PCGs to develop and sustain good relation-ships with their health authority, at least at levels 1 and 2, and also among the GPs within the individual practices of the groups (Leese and Mahon 1999b).

The ability of TPPs to influence service change was also affected by their relationships with NHS trusts. In general, it was neither suf-ficient nor adequate for TPPs solely to use the contracting mechan-ism as a lever for change without first securing input or feedback from the providers on the implications of contract changes. A collaborative approach to service development was required, manifest in coopting representatives of provider organizations on to subgroups. Typically, this was undertaken to devise ways to enhance particular services, such as maternity, mental health and continuing care of the elderly. Where such collaborations were successful, it was usually the case that the other agencies were equally keen to achieve change. For example, work on maternity services revealed that change was facilitated when working relationships between TPPs, health authority staff, NHS trust managers and midwives were close (Myles *et al.* 1999).

Developing relationships with social services departments was also an important focus for many TPPs with respect to managing emergency admissions, care of the elderly and mental health. Some TPPs achieved a high degree of collaboration and joint working, despite initial scepticism from social services staff. For example, one second-wave TPP covering a whole town (rather similar to a PCG) had created an inclusive multi-agency public health subgroup to address the full range of health issues faced by a deprived urban population. The fact that such interagency collaboration was stressed so forcefully by participants in total purchasing as an enabling factor to service change confirms the need for similar relationships to be developed in future primary care organizations.

Emerging policy in both England and Scotland in the late 1990s (Department of Health 1998d; Scottish Office 1998), and the development of Health Action Zones (HAZs) in England, has emphasized the importance of flexible partnership working in health and social care. The Health Act 1999, in particular, has permitted radically new forms of service delivery between health and social care agencies including lead commissioning, pooled budgets and integrated provision (Department of Health 1999). Local health groups in Wales are also encouraged to work with local authorities, in particular to coordinate HImPs (Secretary of State for Wales 1998). Furthermore, PCGs are required to contribute to the HImPs of their respective health authorities. All of these developments emphasize the importance of closer working relationships for primary care organizations, not only with providers and social services, but also with other local authority departments and voluntary organizations. This can only be achieved by building on the improved relationships evident in some of the TPPs (Leese and Mahon 1999b).

## RESOURCES FOR MANAGEMENT

A further message for primary care organizations in relation to organizational development is that effective organizational management arrangements require adequate financial resources. As Chapter 4 will discuss, there was a significant relationship between higher achieving TPPs and higher direct management costs per capita, particularly in the case of larger pilots in their second year (Malbon *et al.* 1999). This suggested that greater investment in the management infrastructure of the TPP, including information systems, was associated with achieving service objectives. However, as Chapter 8 reveals, the level of management spending varied widely between the pilots, largely because there was no blueprint as to how to go about total purchasing. In addition, costs appeared to bear no relation to the characteristics of the population served.

The level of management resources used by TPPs was closely related to communication, coordination and decision making within organizations rather than commissioning and contracting with external providers. In multi-practice TPPs, for example, the costs of coordination were significant, and increased as the size of the project increased. As discussed above, multi-practice TPPs needed to invest in relationships and develop subgroups within which individual GPs and other organizations could communicate effectively. Therefore the costs of primary care-led purchasing throughout the English NHS might well be higher than for total purchasing. Future primary care organizations will need to be aware that engaging all their GPs and other stakeholder groups is likely to increase their management costs, at least in the first few years. Organizational cohesion is likely to be achieved both by developing communications and decision-making systems to inform and engage all PCG staff and by developing and achieving a harmonized group-wide information technology capability – but at significant cost.

## COLLECTIVE RESPONSIBILITY AND CORPORATE GOVERNANCE

One of the biggest challenges facing emerging primary care organizations is the development of corporacy and corporate governance in order to manage a budget. Under total purchasing, many GPs and practices remained only loosely connected with the TPP and its goals, with a substantial number tolerating their involvement as long as budgets remained indicative and/or did not involve managing resource reductions as some PCGs will have to do. Many were happy to be a part of a TPP only if this meant a limited impact on their 'core business' and practice-based fundholding activities. Indeed, the extent to which all GPs and practices were signed up to total purchasing varied widely. While TPPs were able to improve the level of participation through subgroups, the willingness to invest in executive groups varied. On the whole, TPPs did not engender consistent collective responsibility and as result there tended not to be a corporate approach to the management of finances.

As Street and Place (1998) argue, the development of corporacy is likely to succeed only where there is a perception that working as part of a larger organization delivers greater benefits than can be achieved through isolated practice-based working. Otherwise there is little impetus to participate since there are no financial or professional incentives. Since it takes time to develop, collective trust was not an established feature of TPPs (Leese and Mahon 1999b). Much of the success of PCGs, therefore, will rely on goodwill and the confidence that a significant number of practices are contributing to the collective. A key organizational development issue for PCGs and future primary care organizations will be how to establish collective responsibility across a group of GPs and practices that will be larger in size and likely to represent different interests. Similarly, good relationships are likely to be even more important for the success of the much larger PCGs (Mahon *et al.* 1998). The experience of the TPPs suggests that GP members of PCG boards, at least at the outset, are likely to represent the narrow interests of their specific constituency (practice or group of practices), rather than, as good corporate governance would dictate, act strategically on behalf of the entire group. However, it should be possible to develop such behaviour over time.

## LESSONS ON ORGANIZATIONAL DEVELOPMENT

The organization and subsequent development of TPPs provide a number of key lessons for the successful development of large primary care organizations based on individual general practices. In particular, new primary care organizations need:

- a strong executive management team with an identified leader and with the mandate to take decisions on behalf of the wider group;
- a clear vision and agenda for action;
- a sense of collective responsibility and corporacy (i.e. to involve all GPs in planning and managing the use of resources);
- sophisticated project management capacity;
- appropriate clinical and management information systems;
- adequate funding of organizational and management arrangements;
- time to develop without further policy upheaval.

Organizations are likely to be more effective where all criteria are met, although clearly balances need to be found – for example between executive efficiency on the one hand and inclusivity and partnership on the other. As well as following the example of successful TPPs in these respects, primary care organizations also need to tackle the challenge of involving the public in policy-making decisions, which TPPs had not succeeded in doing (see Chapter 11).

## ACHIEVING NEW PRIMARY CARE ORGANIZATIONS: THE IMPORTANCE OF CONTEXT

The key emerging characteristics of a successful TPP organization described above are appropriate markers for the development of any primary care organization. However, the ability of TPPs to develop some or all of these appropriate characteristics was heavily influenced by the context in which they developed. As Chapter 5 explores, whether an innovation works is very much dependent on the context or circumstances in which it is implemented.

The importance of context in shaping the development of TPP organizations can be demonstrated on a number of levels. In particular, the culture and history of the participant GPs and practices were often instrumental in shaping the organizational design and the resulting system of representation. For example, the participants in some TPPs were keen to establish a system in which no single GP or practice was predominant, instead with an emphasis on collegiate or collective decision making. Such approaches were often characterized by the development of a flat, participative structure in which there was no designated lead GP or executive management group. In other cases, often where there was a recent history of collective project management through a fundholding multifund, a more hierarchical organizational structure with delegated executive powers could develop. This was often characterized by the establishment of an executive, or governance, group to which the TPP's practices were confident to delegate power for important management decisions.

The financial context of TPPs – that is, availability of adequate management resources and flexibility of budgets – also had a significant impact on their ability to develop organizations fit for the task. In particular, it appears that the most successful larger TPPs had developed a dedicated management support structure containing a skilled project manager and other support staff, investment in information technology, and resources for practitioner time spent on management tasks. The next chapter examines the relationship between resources and achievement in more detail, but it comes as no surprise that, generally, the better resourced projects were also those that had the opportunity to develop better organizational support systems (see Chapter 4).

When large primary care organizations are being established, variable local contexts are likely to play an important part in the organizations that emerge. While the establishment of PCGs has been, and will be, far more influenced by directives from the centre than TPPs ever were, a range of organizational variations will inevitably emerge. These variations in PCGs will reflect different combinations of practices with different historical and cultural backgrounds as well as differences in local service configurations. As with total purchasing, flexibility can help to ensure that organizations can be tailored to suit the characteristics of their locality.

## CONCLUSIONS – IMPLICATIONS FOR THE DEVELOPMENT OF PRIMARY CARE ORGANIZATIONS

The total purchasing experiment clearly showed that significant investment in time, money and human resources was required to create the necessary organizational arrangements to enable commissioning to be addressed. This was particularly important in the larger pilots. This suggests that the development of new primary care organizations requires a period of organizational development of at least one year and possibly longer. Indeed, the requirement for such organizational development is reflected in the progress of more recent primary care organizations in the UK. The early focus of primary care groups in England, for example, was dominated by issues relating to the development of administrative and support structures and in the negotiation of management budgets (Smith *et al.* 2000a). Similarly, the first year of primary care commissioning group pilots in Northern Ireland was characterized by the need to establish organizational structures and develop new relationships between professional groups, not least because these commissioning groups were established as cross-agency organizations including representation from providers and social services as well as primary care (McCay *et al.* 2000).

As the next chapter will show, persistent issues of organizational development often restricted what TPPs could achieve. Indeed, after three years, including one preparatory year, some TPPs had yet to establish themselves as effective commissioning organizations (Mays *et al.* 1998b). However, by the second 'live' year of total purchasing, many of the larger pilots had 'caught up' in terms of their ability to achieve objectives, suggesting that previous investment in organizational development had begun to bear fruit (Malbon *et al.* 1999). This time lag between organizational development and addressing service change has also been reflected in the development of primary care groups in England. During the second year of their development there has been a shift in emphasis away from organizational imperatives to issues related to primary care developments, clinical governance, and health improvement, with numerous examples of tangible service changes being reported (Smith *et al.* 2000a). However, despite such progress, commissioning was a core function where primary care groups had made slow, if any, progress. Thus, while there is evidence to argue that investment in new primary care organizations will, given time, result in local service changes, there is less evidence to suggest that they will be equipped to address the commissioning agenda.

# 4

# WHAT DID TOTAL PURCHASING PILOTS ACHIEVE?

## Gill Malbon, Nicholas Mays, Sally Wyke and Hugh McLeod

Chapter 1 outlined the political and policy context in which total purchasing was introduced. Total purchasing was seen by the NHS Executive and ministers as very much an extension of general practitioner fundholding. GP fundholders had focused on purchasing elective surgical services for their patients and the TPPs would extend this to non-elective areas. Total purchasers were expected to use their first-hand knowledge of their patients to purchase potentially all HCHS for their patients. They were seen primarily as purchasing organizations and were expected to use their budgetary leverage and the contracting process to negotiate changes in service delivery that would deliver cost savings, efficiency gains and quality improvements.

However, early in the evaluation it became clear that total purchasing was far from straightforward for many TPPs. Many had goals and motivations which were not directly related to purchasing secondary care. For example, some were centrally concerned to keep open a threatened local community or general hospital; others wanted to use the opportunity of total purchasing for investment (from whichever source) to develop intermediate care or to achieve better coordination of care for their patients. By the end of the first year of live purchasing, it had become clear that TPPs had not interpreted their remit solely as purchasers of secondary care. Less than half (44 per cent) of first-wave TPPs were directly purchasing services in total purchasing-related areas to achieve changes in secondary care as well as in non-hospital and primary care (Mays *et al.* 1998).

So, if they were not all purchasing secondary care as expected, what were TPPs doing? How could their endeavours be evaluated? What did total purchasers achieve? This chapter examines the achievements of total purchasers in different ways and give examples of some of the services they were attempting to influence and to deliver. The next chapter examines the factors associated with their successes and the mechanisms they used to achieve their goals, and investigates the relationship between the context in which TPPs were operating, the mechanisms they used to achieve their goals, and the outcomes of their endeavours.

## MEASURING THE SUCCESS OF TOTAL
## PURCHASING PILOTS

Judging the success or otherwise of any developing NHS primary care organization depends very much on national goals and local priorities. As it became clear that total purchasers were operating as selective purchasers, and some were not attempting to achieve service change in any of the service areas new to GP purchasing via total purchasing, a two-fold judgement of progress was used. Based on their stated purchasing objectives and corroborated by reports of their progress and achievements, each TPP was placed into one of five hierarchical performance groups. First, the achievements of the TPPs were assessed in terms of their own objectives. Projects' own objectives varied greatly in scope and ambition and many could have been undertaken by standard fundholding practices. Second, the TPPs' achievements were assessed in relation to their ability to make change in total purchasing-related areas – for example, service areas new to GP-led purchasing: maternity care; services for the seriously mentally ill; care of the frail elderly in the community; A&E services; emergency admissions; in-patient length of stay; and alternatives to acute hospital in-patient services. Pilots making changes in total purchasing-related service areas were thought to be more likely than others to be influencing local health services in a major way, given the scale of such services. Such TPPs were also judged to be more likely to be *developing* the potential of primary care-based purchasing, rather than simply consolidating the technique acquired via standard fundholding in relation to elective care.

In order to maximize the reliability of the ratings, three researchers independently placed each TPP into one of the five performance categories. Discrepancies in placement were discussed until consensus was reached. Broadly, TPPs in Group 5 (the highest achieving band) attained (and could provide corroborating evidence of) all their planned objectives, together with other developments. Those in Group 1 (the lowest achievement band) had achieved none of their planned goals.

Figure 4.1 shows the distribution of TPPs according to their reported achievement of their own objectives. The wide range of achievements reported by the 50 TPPs responding in 1996/97 was continued by the 40 responding in 1997/98. Most TPPs overestimated what they could do in the two years in which they were live purchasers. Simply being conferred with TPP status did not necessarily lead to success in achieving objectives. For some TPPs, the context in which they developed was more conducive to success. Others had some difficulty organizing themselves (see Chapters 3 and 8). These issues will be discussed further in Chapter 5.

Figure 4.2 shows that a similar range of success was seen when TPPs' achievements were assessed in total purchasing-related service areas, although there was an overall increase in the reported achievements of TPPs in these areas between 1996/97 and 1997/98. More TPPs achieved more of their objectives in total purchasing-related areas in the second live year. However, it must be noted that a fifth fewer of the TPPs responded to the relevant questionnaires in the second year. Some of the non-respondents left the total

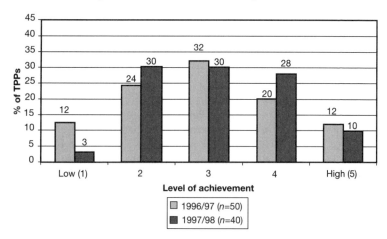

**Figure 4.1**   Total purchasing pilots by level of achievement in their own terms, 1996/97 and 1997/98

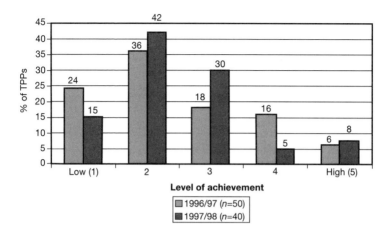

**Figure 4.2**  Total purchasing pilots by level of achievement in total purchasing-related areas, 1996/97 and 1997/98

purchasing programme in 1997/98, and they may have been among the least successful pilots in 1996/97.

## SERVICE AREAS TARGETED BY TPPS

The variation in level of achievement of TPPs, whether they were judged by achievement of their own objectives or by specific achievements in total purchasing-related areas, begs the question of what the TPPs were trying to achieve and why. Which service areas did GPs in the total purchasing organizations decide to focus on, what were they attempting to do early on, and how successful were they in achieving these specific objectives?

Table 4.1 shows the main service areas selected by the TPPs in the two purchasing cycles studied and the proportion of objectives reported as achieved in each year.

Objectives in relation to early discharge, development of the primary health care team, and needs assessment/information management were most likely to be achieved, at least in the first year. However, TPPs clearly learned from their experience over the life of the total purchasing experiment. If objectives were not easy to achieve – such as managing demand for emergency services or altering local mental health services – they dropped them. The

**Table 4.1**   Achievements and non-achievements of first-wave total purchasing pilots by service area, 1996/97 and 1997/98

| Service area of four main purchasing objectives | Main objectives | % reported achieved | Main objectives | % reported achieved |
|---|---|---|---|---|
| | **1996/97** | | **1997/98** | |
| Early discharge (e.g. discharge coordinator) | 22 | 64 | 18 | 72 |
| Community and continuing care (e.g. integrated nursing; home beds) | 19 | 53 | 36 | 67 |
| Maternity services (particularly community midwifery) | 27 | 52 | 10 | 70 |
| Managing emergency services (e.g. intermediate care and primary care projects) | 32 | 44 | 16 | 75 |
| Mental health services (primarily community based) | 28 | 39 | 20 | 75 |
| Develop primary health care team | 15 | 87 | 10 | 70 |
| Information/needs assessment | 12 | 83 | 22 | 64 |
| Other[1] | 35 | 59 | 40 | 72 |
| | **190** | **54** | **172** | **70** |

*Note*:
[1] Wide variety including oncology, cardiology, school health, palliative care, etc.

number of English TPPs included in the study of pilots with objectives in reducing emergency hospital admissions fell from 55 per cent (27 out of 49) in 1996/97 to 33 per cent (16 out of 49) in 1997/98 (McLeod and Raftery 2000) (see Chapter 7 for a detailed analysis of TPPs' actions in this field). There were also fewer objectives in the area of mental health services, which had been a difficult area in the previous year (although those TPPs that did focus on these areas had success in 1997/98). There were also fewer TPP objectives in maternity services, reflecting either early success in achieving these objectives or the loss of national impetus in the area as national policy for maternity care slipped down the list of NHS priorities (Wyke *et al.* 1999) (see Chapter 6 for more on maternity services).

However, TPPs set themselves more objectives in community and continuing care in 1997/98, possibly because they had had experience of setting up services at a primary and community level and had already found it an easier area in which to focus. The larger number of objectives in information gathering and population needs assessment over time may have reflected a recognition of the enormous need for information. As a result of these shifts in focus between the two live years of purchasing, there was far less variation in achievements between service areas in the second versus the first live year of purchasing. Table 4.1 therefore presents a picture of TPPs learning what kinds of objectives they could manage over time, and focusing their efforts in achievable goals.

More detailed examination of the specific service developments through which TPPs attempted to reach their objectives showed that there were strong similarities between service areas in the approaches adopted to change. Tables 4.2, 4.3 and 4.4 present more detailed information on what TPPs were trying to do in three service areas – emergency services, mental health services and community and continuing care.

The tables show that while some TPPs attempted to influence secondary care providers directly through contracting and related activity (see Chapter 7), most achieved change through primary care-based service developments, and that these primary care-based developments were *similar* whatever the specific service goal. For

**Table 4.2** Achievements and non-achievements in managing emergency services, 1997/98

| Main objectives | Number of achievements | Number of non-achievements |
| --- | --- | --- |
| *Contracting* | | |
| Change in contract currency | 3 | 1 |
| *Intermediate care/vertical integration* | | |
| Intermediate care facility | 3 | 0 |
| Increased primary care to reduce emergency admissions | 3 | 0 |
| Rapid response out-of-hours team to reduce emergency admissions | 1 | 2 |
| Pre-operative assessment scheme | 1 | 1 |
| *Other* | | |
| Research to assess ways of reducing emergency admissions | 1 | 0 |
| **Total** | **12** | **4** |

**Table 4.3**   Achievements and non-achievements in mental health, 1997/98

| Main objectives | Number of achievements | Number of non-achievements |
|---|---|---|
| *Contracting* | | |
| Contracting for emergencies | 1 | 1 |
| Change of contract currency | 0 | 1 |
| Change of provider | 1 | 0 |
| *Intermediate care/vertical integration* | | |
| Common service specification between providers | 1 | 0 |
| Developing district-wide mental health strategy | 3 | 1 |
| *Primary care-based developments/horizontal integration* | | |
| Enhanced community mental health team (including community psychiatric nurses (CPNs), counsellors, psychologists, etc.) | 7 | 2 |
| Practice-based CPNs | 2 | 0 |
| **Total** | **15** | **5** |

example, TPPs that stated that their main objectives were to make better use of the resources they had historically expended on emergency services put in place services such as intermediate care facilities (for example, nursing home beds). Those that stated that their main objective was to develop better community care for the frail elderly also bought access to more nursing home places. Similarly, total purchasers wanting to enhance care for either mentally ill people or for frail older people with complex needs for continuing and community care put in place similar services at primary care level, mainly through enlarging membership of the primary care team to include additional professional specialists.

The service developments and mechanisms used in these service areas are summarized in Table 4.5. From this, it can be seen that the majority of the objectives of the TPPs were pursued through relatively simple primary care extensions, and that these approaches to achieving objectives were likely to be successful. Few if any of the mechanisms used were entirely novel, but the total purchasing

**Table 4.4** Achievements and non-achievements in community and continuing care, 1997/98

| Main objectives | Number of achievements | Number of non-achievements |
|---|---|---|
| *Contracting* | | |
| Redirecting resources from acute to community services | 2 | 0 |
| Changing contract currency | 1 | 1 |
| Changing provider | 1 | 0 |
| *Intermediate care/vertical integration* | | |
| Developing the local community hospital | 1 | 2 |
| Setting up a hospital-at-home scheme/GP out-of-hours service | 1 | 4 |
| Utilizing GP beds | 0 | 1 |
| Purchasing nursing home beds | 6 | 3 |
| *Primary care-based developments/horizontal integration* | | |
| Improving the community team, integrating community and practice nursing | 7 | 1 |
| Developing care packages and shared protocols with social services | 2 | 0 |
| Employing an attached social worker | 2 | 0 |
| Undertaking health and social care needs assessment | 1 | 0 |
| **Total** | **24** | **12** |

initiative was clearly encouraging the practices to look at the local balance and location of the care offered to their patients as intended (Malbon *et al.* 1999). Far fewer TPPs tackled changing patterns of specialist, secondary care through the contracting process, although those that did were mainly successful by the second year. Chapter 7 reports on the 16 English TPPs that aimed to reduce emergency service use at acute hospitals. These TPPs introduced a range of alternative services and were generally successful. Less successful were approaches that involved developing more complex primary care-based services, particularly those including out-of-hours care.

**Table 4.5**   Broad categorization of developments in relation to emergency services, mental health and community and continuing care reported by TPPs in 1997/98

| Mechanism/development | Number of objectives | Reported achieved (%) |
|---|---|---|
| Influencing secondary care (contract currency, change providers) | 14 | 10 (71%) |
| Complex primary care developments (requiring coordination of out-of-hours care, such as hospital-at-home or rapid response team to prevent hospital admission) | 8 | 2 (25%) |
| More straightforward expansion of the primary care team (e.g. integration of practice and community nursing, or practice-attached community psychiatric nurse) | 46 | 35 (76%) |
| Strategic developments (district-wide protocols and strategies) | 5 | 4 (80%) |

## THE POTENTIAL OF TOTAL PURCHASING – DEVELOPING INTEGRATED CARE

Chapter 1 discussed how part of the rationale for giving practices wider budgetary responsibility was to encourage practices to consider the effects of their referral and other clinical actions on resource use either in hospital or in the community. It was hypothesized, following the example of standard fundholding, that giving groups of general practices control over a wider range of resources would encourage them to consider the potential for making better use of a wider range of facilities in secondary care in which previously GPs had had little or no interest. It was expected that total purchasers would have an incentive to make the best use of their allocated budgets wherever their patients received treatment through adapting various forms of vertical and horizontal service integration (i.e. linking hospital and non-hospital forms of care *vertically* and linking various forms of health and social care in the community *horizontally*).

Whatever their original objectives – whether to extend or

improve primary care services, or to reduce emergency hospital admissions for older people – many of the TPPs attempted to develop services in order to bring about greater integration between primary and community care services (for example community psychiatric nursing), between primary, community and social services, or between primary and secondary care services. For example, TPPs attempted to integrate primary and other community health services by developing practice-attached midwifery; practice-based community psychiatric nursing; practice-attached self-managed community nursing teams; new physiotherapy services; practice-attached community pharmacy services for prescribing advice; and specialist nursing for the care of chronic conditions. They attempted to integrate primary, community and social care services by putting in place TPP-attached community care coordinators; and multidisciplinary proactive care teams for care of older people or mentally ill people. Finally, they worked to integrate primary, community and secondary care services by developing community beds as alternatives to acute hospital beds (for example GP beds in community hospitals, nursing home beds, places in hospital-at-home schemes); hospital discharge coordinators to speed discharge; multidisciplinary elderly care teams with access to day care and respite facilities; and testing the provision in primary care of facilities formerly available only in hospital after a consultant referral.

Some of the examples of primary and community care integration did not require TPP status to be achieved, but the total purchasing experiment may have made it easier for the practices to develop the services. For one thing, where the pilot involved more than one practice, the beginnings of inter-practice organization were in place via the TPP to facilitate sharing information on a range of issues. A good example of this is from the TPP illustrated in Box 4.1. This innovation is not entirely novel and has been developed elsewhere in non-TPP practices, but was perceived as a real success by TPP and health authority respondents, with the potential for other practices to learn from their experience.

Very often, where TPPs managed to integrate primary, community and local authority social care services, they had an impact on secondary care services too. The TPP illustrated in Box 4.2 provides such an example.

An example of how a larger TPP commissioned a full range of integrated services which resulted in patients achieving appropriate care in the least costly setting is provided in Box 4.3.

**Box 4.1 Community pharmacy advisory service**

| Context | Service development | Achieving change | Outcome |
|---------|---------------------|------------------|---------|
| Locality-based TPP: 16 practices, 35 GPs | Part-time community pharmacist funded jointly by TPP and health authority to advise on more cost-effective prescribing by GPs and local hospital specialists | Monthly reports by pharmacist adviser to subgroup of GPs with recommendations for change | Some containment of prescribing costs |
| Deprived, urban population 67,000 | | | Greater prescribing of statins and more cost-effective prescribing of wound-healing drugs |
| No budget | Additional aims to enhance the primary care role of community pharmacists | Production of joint hospital/primary care formulary agreed by GPs and consultants | Greater engagement of GPs in TPP strategies |
| | | Review of repeat prescribing | Greater shared understanding of prescribing issues. More consistent prescribing |
| | | Initiated discussions between GPs and community pharmacists | Pharmacists unwilling to extend role without further additional incentives (payments) |

**Box 4.2  Integrated provision for older people**

| Context | Service development | Achieving change | Outcome |
|---|---|---|---|
| Single-practice TPP with two surgeries | Community care coordinator – an experienced social worker acting as bridge between the practice, social services and voluntary sector | Variety of mechanisms to achieve change: | Ability to address less severe problems has potential to prevent health crises |
| Population 16,000 in relatively deprived urban area | | – changed community nursing contract to obtain practice-based self-managed community nursing team | Initial assessments shared between health and social care |
| The TPP had a delegated budget for hospital and community health services and independent contracts | Admission and discharge coordinator | – joint funding of community care coordinator with local social services department | Much speedier referral and assessment |
| | Multidisciplinary elderly care team – coordinated by manager of self-managed nursing team. Health and social care professionals involved and community geriatrician | Direct employment of discharge coordinator | Proactive care for older people with health problems |
| | | Contract with community health services provider for community geriatrician sessions | |

**Box 4.3  Intermediate care**

| Context | Service development | Achieving change | Outcome |
|---|---|---|---|
| Non-geographical locality-based TPP, eight practices (42 GPs) | Range of interrelated services: | Design informed by knowledge of other schemes, needs assessment and literature review | Emergency admissions prevented, hospital discharges speeded up |
| 81,000 urban population | GP referrals to intermediate care team | | Sharing of experience with emerging primary care groups across the district |
| Budget holding, direct purchasing with own contracts | Discharge planning team | Involvement of all key stakeholders | |
| | Intermediate care beds, including: hospital-at-home, spot purchase of nursing home beds | Heavy marketing to A&E consultants, nurses, hospital-at-home nurses and all TPP GPs | |
| | Discharge alert register | Peer pressure on GPs via a league table of referrals scheme | |
| | | Ongoing systematic review and evaluation | |

## MANAGING EMERGENCY HOSPITAL ACTIVITY

One of the toughest tests for TPPs was whether they were able to alter the pattern of use of emergency hospital services (see Chapter 7). Only 16 pilots in England were found to have pursued objectives of reducing acute hospital emergency admissions and/or length of stay during the two live years of the project. Hospital episode statistics were used to compare changes in activity for these TPPs and comparator practices. In order to provide an overall measure of change, relevant activity in the second live year was compared to that in the preparatory year. Eleven of the 16 pilots (69 per cent) experienced a reduction in the total number of occupied bed days in the targeted specialties which was greater than the reduction (or, in some cases, an increase) experienced by the comparator, and in each case the difference was statistically significant.

Nine of the 16 TPPs were multi-practice, and seven of these were successful in terms of the above criteria. Those multi-practice pilots targeting emergency admissions tended to increase their use of community hospitals or hospital-at-home services, while those pilots targeting length of stay tended to introduce discharge liaison nurses or more comprehensive rehabilitation teams.

Fourteen of these TPPs held 'independent' (i.e contracts separate to, and distinct from, those developed by their host health authority) contracts with their main hospital providers. They attempted to fund the alternative services to acute hospital care by reducing their expenditure on their patients' acute hospital use. The independent contracts were usually based on health authorities' provider contracts, in which activity was priced using finished consultant episodes at average specialty cost. The TPPs were generally unable to negotiate contracts using prices based on admissions or length of stay, which would more closely link changes in activity to changes in funding. With few exceptions, the pilots usually funded their initiatives using additional funds, such as winter pressures resources, rather than through changes to contracts.

## TOTAL PURCHASING – DEVELOPING PRIMARY MANAGED CARE?

Many of the techniques and approaches used by TPPs to develop services (including forms of integrated care) would be familiar in managed care settings in other health systems (Robinson and

Steiner 1998). Myles *et al.* (1998) identified a range of managed care techniques at national health policy, systems management and disease management levels in TPPs which related to developing community and continuing care services. For example, TPPs were using utilization review of admissions discharge planning, and performance management of contracts, and were making genuine attempts to share information. They concluded: 'The models of care being developed by the TPPs taking part in this study could represent the progenitor of primary managed care approaches to providing services for older people with complex needs in the UK.' Similar approaches are being adopted by the range of primary care organizations in the 'new NHS' (Secretary of State for Health 1997).

**SUMMARY**

This chapter has shown that TPPs varied widely in their abilities to achieve their objectives, but learned from their experience over time. No matter what their stated intentions, the majority of achievements made by these primary care-based purchasing organizations were made using relatively simple extensions of the primary care team and/or the development of intermediate care services, such as nursing home provision. TPPs may have put the primary care-based services in place to try to reduce their patients' likelihood of emergency admissions or reduce their lengths of hospital stay. Originally, many TPPs were hopeful that the reduced use of services would result in savings to their budget, which could be used to finance further investment in the primary care sector. However, in practice the total purchasing experiment, for most TPPs, was more about changing the delivery of primary and intermediate care services than about achieving efficient and high-quality secondary care services – if for no other reason than the fact that extracting resources from hospital contracts proved so difficult to achieve. Many TPPs successfully managed to develop more integrated services. The following chapter examines the factors associated with their differing levels of success, as well as how and why TPPs were, or were not, successful.

# 5

# HOW WAS CHANGE ACHIEVED?

## Sally Wyke, Gill Malbon, Nicholas Mays and Nick Goodwin

The extent to which a particular TPP was successful in achieving its objectives was dependent on interactions between the context in which the TPP was developing, the content of its objectives (what the pilot was trying to achieve) and the mechanisms developed to achieve them (how the pilot tried to achieve its objectives) (see Mays *et al.* 1998b). Chapter 4 described the content of TPPs' objectives, their relative achievements and the services they put in place. This chapter examines the contexts in which TPPs developed and the mechanisms they used to achieve change. Understanding the complex interactions between content, context and change mechanisms should shed light on how other types of primary care organization can assess the situation in which they operate and develop strategies to achieve their potential in the particular circumstances in which they work.

## CONTEXTS IN WHICH TOTAL PURCHASING PILOTS DEVELOPED

Whether an innovation, such as a social intervention, works, and to what degree, is very much dependent on the context or circumstances in which it is implemented (Pettigrew *et al.* 1992; Pawson and Tilley 1997). This was certainly the case with total purchasing in that some pilots worked well in some places some of the time, while others did not. The receptiveness of the cultural, political, historical, geographical and financial contexts in which TPPs were developing influenced their relative success in achieving their objectives and in demonstrating the potential of the scheme as a whole.

### Bridging the cultural divide

The cultural context refers to deep-rooted assumptions and values that permeate organizations and are associated with individuals' expectations of objectives, styles of working and speed of change. General practice-based organizations such as TPPs had very different cultures from formal bureaucracies like health authorities and social service departments, and bridging the cultural divide between individuals working in these organizations often took time and created tensions (Mays *et al.* 1998a).

The relationship between a total purchaser and its local health authority was particularly influential. For example, it was common for health authority staff to experience culture shock when faced with a TPP in its early stages, particularly since TPPs were trying to challenge established practice. The following reaction from a member of staff at a health authority responsible for a TPP was typical:

[Total purchasing] has posed an obstacle to integrated working [between secondary and primary care] and has led to a cultural climate which is, at the least, ambivalent towards the scheme. This has manifested itself at both the health authority board level and among health authority managers . . . I would say that some managers feel threatened by general practitioner-led purchasing and total purchasing is the extreme of these threats. However, I believe that these are largely cultural problems and much of the early period of the TPP's development process has been devoted to overcoming these problems.

In the early days of the total purchasing experiment, the cultural divide between the pilot project and host health authority was often very wide and both had to take considerable time to understand each other's aspirations and needs. Many health authority managers had had relatively little direct contact with GPs in the past and the process of negotiation between health authority and TPP was often far from easy and relationships tended to be characterized by friction. The response of one lead GP to the process exemplifies this friction; in particular, the common perception that the health authority was not supportive enough of the pilot while at the same time not being willing to give the TPP greater autonomy in its commissioning role:

> Initially, relations were difficult. A recurrent problem was that the health authority felt that the TPP project manager was not up to scratch with the corresponding feeling that the TPP as a whole could not be left to get up to its own devices. The issue of who is answerable to whom remains a problem unresolved. This is a problem with the potential to bust the TPP apart.

While the process of adaptation to total purchasing was characterized by early friction, relationships between key stakeholders undoubtedly improved over time, especially in the more successful pilots. The language, in particular, changed with phrases like 'from culture shock to culture shared', 'added value', 'breaking down barriers', 'mutual learning' and 'change of ethos' appearing in the interviews undertaken in 1997 as against those in 1996. A later interview, undertaken with the same GP who had highlighted substantial friction between the TPP and its host health authority in the preparatory period, emphasized this shift:

> The strengths of our relationship with [the health authority] have come later and have been manifest in greater dialogue, such that we [the GPs] have a greater understanding of health authority problems and priorities. The level of relationship with the health authority – the balance between paternalism and autonomy – remains unresolved [but] there has developed some form of partnership with the health authority.

The ability of TPPs to bridge the cultural differences between the health authority and the practices of TPPs varied, contributing to the wide variation in levels of achievement noted in Chapter 4. The extent to which TPPs felt their health authority was providing 'fair' or 'good' support was associated with their level of achievement. All pilots that were high achievers (achieved their own objectives) felt that their health authority provided either good or fair support in 1996/97, whereas only 69 per cent of those that were low achievers (achieved few if any of their own objectives) felt the same (see Chapter 4 for a description of how achievement was defined). Although this association was not statistically significant, it supports other qualitative data on the reported importance for participants of a supportive relationship between a TPP and its parent health authority.

The point is well illustrated by the contrasting experiences of two TPPs that were attempting to influence use of secondary care services by reducing length of stay and preventing emergency admissions. Both projects had tried to ensure that the necessary packages of support and care were assembled for individual patients, either to promote early discharge or to prevent admission in the first place. To do this, each appointed a care manager or liaison nurse to facilitate effective relationships between ward staff in the hospital, community nurses and social services. However, the health authority refused one pilot control of a delegated budget for fear that its plans to shift resources out of the hospital would potentially destabilize it. In the case of the other TPP, the health authority delegated a budget for the pilot, supported its independent contracts and supported its goal of reducing lengths of stay. As a result, this TPP was able to reduce lengths of stay and shift resources from acute to intermediate care to sustain this.

Another cultural value generally held by TPP GPs, including lead practitioners, was a strong desire to remain primarily family doctors and advocates of individual patients rather than be managers of services. This desire strongly limited their ability to work in a public health role (i.e. with a population focus) or at an interagency level within their TPPs. Recognition of their cultural commitment to what was seen as the core work of general practice and to finding ways to manage or reconcile competing demands enabled many to manage better their combined roles in TPPs of clinician and budget/service manager.

**The influence of political changes**

The national policy changes in the NHS brought about by the election of a Labour government in May 1997 represented the single biggest contextual influence on the ability of TPPs to achieve their objectives and make progress in 1997/98, their second live year. In Scotland, the move away from primary care-based commissioning which began immediately after the election and before the *New NHS* White Paper of December 1997 led to the end of all TPPs in March 1998. In England, the larger, locality-based TPPs most resembled the primary care groups (PCGs) proposed and were at a considerable contextual advantage in their more sustained development. On the whole, these TPPs had supportive health authorities keen to learn from their experience and were clearly going to continue in some form after the official end of the pilot. In this way they were able to retain commitment and enthusiasm from all staff for the continued development of their initiatives. Such TPPs did not lose impetus, and achievements continued apace. On the other hand, smaller and non-locality-based TPPs suffered from continued uncertainty over their fate and many lost momentum. As a result, some projects simply petered out.

Other national policy had an impact on TPPs' developments. For example, one TPP was keen to identify objectives that reflected national priorities and chose cancer services as a priority as a direct result of the 1995 Calman–Hine national report on cancer services, which recommended the partial reorganization and greater specialization of cancer services. Consequently, the TPP helped reorganize the cancer units run by two separate hospitals into a single team working from two sites. It is unlikely that cancer care services would have been addressed by the TPP in this way had it not been for the Calman–Hine report. In addition, the ability of the TPP to convince providers to cooperate with the approach was greatly aided by the presence of the report. Similarly, TPPs developing initiatives in the field of maternity care did so because it was a national concern in England following publication of national policy goals and approaches in 1993. As maternity care fell from the list of national priorities, so did the local impetus to achieve change in service delivery (Wyke *et al.* 1999b). One of the paradoxical effects of the internal market reforms of 1991 was the way in which they increased the responsiveness of the periphery of the NHS to central initiatives while, at the same time, devolving financial management responsibility (Hughes *et al.* 1997).

**The geographical context**

Working with non-NHS agencies, such as the social services departments of local authorities, was important for some TPPs trying to develop more integrated community care for people with complex needs. Whether TPPs were locality-based or non-locality-based was an important determinant of how successful they were able to be in this area. Most borough councils and social services departments organize their services around localities. Coterminosity – or matching boundaries – between TPPs and other agencies allowed both organizations to consider the per capita budget allocation for their area, and facilitated joint working and the development of pooled budgets and services. In contrast, some attempts at integrating care, for example through the addition of a care coordinator or a social worker to the TPP's primary health care team, foundered because of the differences in service areas covered.

### The financial context and the ability to resource innovations

The financial context was a very important factor determining the ability of the TPPs to bring about change. Total purchasers needed to identify resources for investment in the services they wanted to develop. In the early days, many TPPs had plans to release resources by reducing their patients' use of secondary care. For example, some pilots wanted to invest in primary care-based services in order to reduce length of stay and emergency hospital admissions. As Chapter 7 details, this was an intractable issue.

Provider reluctance to release funds was common. Purchasers wishing to transfer activity from acute hospitals should aim to release funds at average cost. However, in the short term (such as the life of a TPP), hospital providers tend to argue that they can only be expected to lose income at marginal cost, unless they used released capacity to generate additional income. Therefore, most TPPs had to obtain additional resources to fund new developments and so joint or external funding with a range of local agencies was often used to achieve service developments. Successful TPPs usually had to be innovative to establish the funds required. Some used health authority development money, some used general medical services growth funds or savings from standard fundholding budgets to co-fund posts with other agencies. Others used investment from pharmaceutical companies to fund developments such as a 'heart health nurse', or assistant GPs to run specialist intermediate care clinics for specific patient groups (such as those with diabetes). In general, achieving shifts in patterns of care was highly dependent on the local availability of additional sources of money rather than freeing up resources from local hospitals.

TPPs operating in districts with a significant financial deficit faced much greater challenges than those in better placed areas. Various strategies were employed to overcome the potential limitation imposed by a poor financial context. For example, one TPP was constrained by its necessary contributions to the health authority's financial recovery plan, made necessary by falling population numbers, reduced capitation payments and historical overspending. In these cases, pilots had to be even more effective in finding other ways to overcome financial hurdles.

**Table 5.1** Association between management costs per capita and achievement of own objectives

| Characteristics | Low achiever in own terns (n = 13) | High achiever in own terms (n = 15) | Significant (t-test 95%) |
|---|---|---|---|
| Mean management costs per capita, 1997/98 | £1.63 | £3.96 | Significant |
| Median management costs per capita, 1996/97 | £1.46 | £4.28 | – |

A major concern of devolved purchasing is that it will lead to an increase in management and transaction costs (see Chapter 8). As shown in Chapter 3, the level of funding for management costs was left to local negotiation between total purchaser and health authority, so that if the health authority was in financial deficit, or had difficulties meeting its management cost target, the level of management support for the project was likely to be lower. Chapter 3 showed the great variation in level of support of direct spending on management between TPPs. However, Table 5.1 shows a clear association between self-reported performance of TPPs and their management costs, with the better-funded projects more likely to achieve their objectives.

Previous research on the costs and functions of health authority and general practice-based purchasers suggests that the smaller general practice-based purchasers generated, on average, 50–90 per cent of the costs of health authority purchasers for half the number of functions (Millar 1997). Many TPPs appeared to be higher spenders on management in relation to their range of functions than many health authorities, although there was a wide range of management costs in both TPPs and health authorities. The association between performance of total purchasers and their management costs means that this increased investment may be necessary to achieve changes in service provision through devolved purchasing. Unfortunately, no equivalent data were available on the achievements of health authority purchasers in relation to their management costs.

**History and relationships**

Another important contextual theme in the development of total purchasing was the extent to which local NHS history played a part in shaping the way in which projects developed. In particular, history played an important part in defining the objectives of TPPs. Frequently, TPPs concentrated on issues that had been of importance locally for many years and/or used total purchasing as a catalyst to promote initiatives or ideas which had been developed previously. The component of the TPP evaluation which considered community care for people with complex needs highlighted the importance of the historical context, showing that most TPP initiatives in community care were not new:

> [The objectives of total purchasers in community care] are rooted in and strongly shaped by past experience of the practices involved in the TPP and the wider agency relationships within which the TPP is operating ... Practically all of the TPPs' developments were based on previous initiatives ... none of the sites, even with their history of involvement in the community and continuing care area, opted to try anything as new or innovative as a TPP.

Furthermore, there is evidence to suggest that the more successful pilots needed an issue with a local history to provide a clear focus for their work. It appears that the genesis of TPPs was important in this regard, since those that developed from the 'bottom-up' (i.e. those that were clearly GP-led) appeared to have more specific goals and objectives than those that had been formed through 'top-down' pressure (for example, those orchestrated by health authorities in a desire to be seen to be responsive to national initiatives). Therefore, pilots with a specific local agenda for change, and generated from the bottom up, tended to progress more quickly. Mahon *et al.* (1998) were able to show that the early service-specific priorities of TPPs stemmed from perceived long-term local problems with which the GPs were already familiar. Evidence to suggest that total purchasers needed such a background for change in order to progress quickly can also be seen from the community care substudy. It concluded:

> The two case study sites which exhibited the least historical experience in community and continuing care initiatives and more difficult inter-agency relations (either poor inter-personal/working relations or reluctance to share budgets) were also the two sites which proved to be least well-developed in terms of integrated purchasing and provision.
>
> (Myles *et al.* 1999)

History has therefore played an important part in shaping the objectives of TPPs and the pace of change was quickest in those projects which based their objectives on some clearly defined, previously identified local issue. In many cases, TPPs were not pursuing new ideas but instead using their new-found status as total purchasers to address unresolved long-term issues.

In addition to influencing the *content* of TPPs, the history of relationships between key individuals and groups locally had an important impact on the pace of change. For example, a history of joint working between GPs and the managers of mental health providers gave certain projects a comparative advantage in developing new contracts and service agreements over TPPs where relationships were underdeveloped (Gask *et al.* 1998). Also, while every total purchaser appeared to find problems associated with generating information and compatibility between information systems, there were significant differences in the pace of progress on mental health issues related to the extent to which communication links and information systems had been developed previously.

### Summary – the contexts in which total purchasing pilots developed

The contexts in which TPPs developed influenced both the pace of change (how quickly a TPP had been able to make progress) and the context of change (what the TPP had been able to achieve). Where receptive contextual factors converged, it was more likely that objectives would be achieved. Box 5.1 summarizes the 'receptive' and 'unreceptive' contexts in which TPPs developed over the lives of the pilots (the notion of 'receptive' and 'unreceptive' contexts was derived from Pettigrew *et al.* 1992).

### MECHANISMS FOR CHANGE

While context is important in determining the pace of change within TPPs, the mechanisms through which total purchasers tried to achieve their goals ultimately determined the ability of pilots to succeed. This is because people, not contexts, brought about change and because, even in the worst of contexts, some scope to make changes still existed.

Throughout the evaluation, two central and recurrent themes

**Box 5.1  Key receptive and non-receptive contextual variables influencing the ability of total purchasing pilots to achieve their objectives**

| Aspect of context | Receptive | Non-receptive |
|---|---|---|
| **Cultural** | Supportive organizational culture | Opposing organizational culture |
| | Innovation – ability to challenge established practice | Inertia – reliance on established values and working practices |
| | Openness and trust between health authority, TPP and secondary care | Secrecy and mistrust |
| | Commonality – shared values between agencies (TPP, health authority, social services departments) | Incoherence – incompatible values between agencies |
| | Positive self-image and sense of achievement | Lack of clear purpose and no sense of achievement |
| **Political** | Concordance with Labour's policies for primary care (i.e. large, locality-based TPPs) | Lack of concordance with Labour's policies for primary care (i.e. small, non-locality-based TPPs) |
| | National policy backing for service changes (e.g. Calman–Hine) | National/local opposition to service changes proposed |
| | Favourable local political agenda | Obstructive local political agenda |

| | | |
|---|---|---|
| **Historical** | History of working together between practices and between agencies | No history of working together |
| | Advanced and integrated IT system with history of information exchange on activity and costs | Under-development and incompatible IT systems with little previous exchange of information on activity and costs |
| | TPP established through practice/GP-led initiative | Health authority-developed TPP without grassroots support |
| | Local historical issues supporting TP innovations | Lack of purpose behind TP innovations – no local issues with a history to act as a basis |
| **Geographical** | TPP patient population entirely within one health authority | TPP population spread across more than one health authority |
| | Provider/social services catchment area congruent with TPP population | TPP population divided between catchment areas |
| | Potential for provider competition | Monopoly provider only |
| **Financial** | Local financial environment favourable – can identify sources of extra funding | National and local financial environment unfavourable – no sources of local funding |
| | Availability of adequate direct management resources | Management resources inadequate to establish effective total purchasing organization |
| | Local acute trust willing to develop new contracting arrangements | Local acute trust unwilling to facilitate change in contracting arrangements |
| | Flexibility/integration of budgets | Inflexible/ring-fenced budgets |

were identified as important mechanisms through which TPPs achieved their objectives:

- key, able individuals leading change;
- budget holding and contracting.

### Key, able leaders

As we have shown, key individuals had a very important role in providing legitimacy for change for TPPs, and in supporting organizational development. Pilots with the following characteristics were more likely to make progress than those without:

- lead GPs willing to put additional time into the pilot and able to demonstrate the advantages (potential and actual) of total purchasing to the other GPs;
- a project manager with a high degree of technical and managerial skill to act internally as coordinator and facilitator to the pilot and externally as its main representative to external agencies;
- health authority leads who were willing to support TPPs;
- providers that were willing to take an active interest in the TPPs' objectives and to contribute to service developments, rather than acting to protect the status quo.

The importance of key individuals leading change meant that TPPs were fragile, unlike bureaucratic organizations. For example, one lead GP spoke of the importance of the project manager to the continued success of the project:

> We owe an awful lot to [our project manager] and would be lost without her since she has been particularly successful in building personal relationships with [the main acute trust] and with the health authority. She has gained a lot of personal knowledge and really is irreplaceable. I fear that if, for example, she was run over by a bus tomorrow, the project would fold pretty quickly.

Some TPPs lost their project manager during 1997/98 since it was uncertain what their future employment prospects would be once the TP pilot had run its course. In one case, the loss of the project manager had a major negative impact on the ability of the pilot to sustain developments as a group since there was no other individual in the TPP with enough dedicated time to take over project responsibilities. However, in another TPP, project management was taken over by a full-time data manager, whose elevation to the chief coordinating role was significantly helped by the previous development of a cohesive team of GPs and a high level of collaboration and information exchange between the TPP's practices.

So while visionary, energetic leaders were clearly still important as TPPs evolved, some pilots became more stable as more participants became involved and took responsibility for some aspects of development. The most productive TPPs had a virtuous combination of strong leadership and the inclusion of a range of other key players and stakeholders willing to play an active role in the organization. The most effective TPPs in the final year of the total purchasing experiment had:

- formal management of the project by lead GPs or a project manager and willingness of non-lead GPs to devolve decision-making responsibility to them;
- willingness of non-lead TPP members to take on collective project responsibilities.

TPPs with such characteristics enabled the development of sustainable organizations with project leaders who were empowered to make decisions on behalf of constituent practices and practitioners.

### Budget holding and contracting

Total purchasing was intended to give the pilots responsibility for purchasing most emergency hospital services used by their patients. The analysis of pilots with an active interest in managing emergency hospital services in the first live year found that 20 pilots had delegated budgets and independent contracts, and that eight pilots did not have delegated budgets (Raftery and McLeod 1999). The remaining pilots either did not have objectives relating to the management of emergency services or were prevented from pursuing objectives in this area. For example, the aims of some pilots were thwarted because they could not agree a budget with their health authority while other pilots had secured a budget but could not negotiate activity-sensitive contract pricing arrangements (thought to be a prerequisite for making change) with their main provider. Chapter 7 discusses the difficulties experienced by most of the TPPs that attempted to negotiate provider contracts that linked changes in activity more closely to changes in expenditure. Nevertheless, pilots with ambitions to influence emergency hospital use regarded delegated budgets and independent contracts as of key importance.

A range of other factors, including political uncertainty, national policy changes and the limitations of pilot status, resulted in some TPPs deciding not to pursue objectives related to hospital services in the second live year. Chapter 7 discusses the experiences of the 16 English TPPs that persisted with objectives to reduce emergency admissions to acute hospitals and/or hospital length of stay. Fourteen of these pilots had delegated budgets and independent contracts.

In most TPPs, therefore, holding a budget, which in turn provided pilots with the *potential* to hold independent contracts, was an important catalyst to joint working with providers since it encouraged service providers to plan with TPPs the kinds of services they all wanted (Robison *et al.* 1999). Service change could, and did, occur without the signing of formal contracts. However, the work on TPPs and maternity care suggested that the sustainability of changes was greater in those general practice-based purchasers that had enshrined informal agreements in contracts (see Chapter 6). Where there was no formal contract, changes were not as likely to be sustained after the life of the pilot. Thus the evaluation showed that GP involvement in planning care can achieve change if it is accompanied by a collaborative approach with trusts and supported by health authorities and supported by written agreements, i.e. contracts.

## THE INTERACTION BETWEEN CONTEXT AND MECHANISM

The fact that different TPPs progressed to varying degrees can be most fully explained by the *interplay* between contexts and mechanisms. In other words, the ability of a project to achieve its objectives should be regarded as the product of a specific mix of variables that either acted as barriers or catalysts to change. The likelihood of a particular TPP being able to progress, therefore, depended on the overall energy for change at the project's inception and the abilities of those involved in the process to overcome contextual barriers or capitalize on potential advantages as the project developed. This means that it was possible for change to be made in an adverse context (such as a local financial crisis) if the abilities of individuals and their interrelationships were sufficiently well developed. Similarly, a helpful context did not necessarily ensure change, if the abilities and relationships between individuals and groups in the process were poor.

In addition, time was an important factor. Despite appearances, TPPs did not begin from the same starting points. For example, the quality of relationships with providers, and the extent to which practices and GPs in the TPPs had worked together previously, varied. In particular, compared to smaller projects, larger TPPs required considerably more time to set up appropriate organizations before they could progress. Therefore, while smaller TPPs appeared to achieve more in the first live year, over time the larger projects caught up (Malbon *et al.* 1999). The short timescale over which TPPs were operational (two years) meant that few had time to mature as organizations and had shown only their potential as primary care purchasers. By implication, it can be anticipated that the development of future primary care organizations in the NHS will be affected by the time needed to develop as organizations. The first year of PCGs in England, for example, has been dominated by organizational developments rather than advances in the commissioning of care (Smith *et al.* 2000a).

Figure 5.1 attempts to show the interplay between contexts and mechanisms schematically. The vertical axis represents the context in which TPPs operated and the horizontal axis the mechanisms or the way in which TPPs went about their business. Where a context is termed 'receptive', this equates to an advantageous situation

| | | Receptive | **UNDER ACHIEVEMENT**<br><br>Individuals and groups running TP unable to make changes despite receptive context for change<br><br>*Mechanism issue* | **OPTIMAL ACHIEVEMENT**<br><br>Receptive context and appropriate mechanisms lead to change |
|---|---|---|---|---|
| **CONTEXT** | | Non-receptive | **LOW/NO ACHIEVEMENT**<br>*Mechanism and context issue* | **STIFLED ACHIEVEMENT**<br>Individuals and groups running TP able but non-receptive context for change hinders potential progress<br><br>*Context issue* |
| | | | **Inappropriate** | **Appropriate** |
| | | | | **MECHANISM** |

**Figure 5.1** Achieving objectives in total purchasing – the interplay between context and mechanism

where the potential to achieve objectives is high (or the barriers are low), while the opposite is true for 'non-receptive' contexts. Where the process is characterized by 'high ability', this has the effect of making achievements more likely, while 'low ability' indicates the opposite.

The cells in Figure 5.1 represent the range of possible outcomes for a TPP. So where the context was receptive and mechanisms characterized by high ability, the more likely it was that achievements would be made. TPPs that moved closest to this optimal scenario were those that achieved more (see Box 5.2). However, the top left cell in Figure 5.1 describes a situation in which the context for change was receptive, but where mechanisms were not effective. For example, Box 5.3 describes a TPP in a receptive context but with limited outcomes. The bottom right cell describes a situation in which the mechanisms were appropriate but where contextual barriers were difficult to overcome. An example of a small TPP attempting to overcome significant contextual barriers is given in Box 5.4. The final cell in Figure 5.1 describes the worst scenario – a non-receptive context and mechanisms that did not work. It was difficult for any achievements to be made by TPPs in this group (see Box 5.5).

## SUMMARY – THE IMPORTANCE OF THE INTERACTION BETWEEN CONTEXT AND MECHANISM

This chapter has shown that there was a complex interplay between what TPPs were trying to achieve, the context in which they were developing and the effectiveness of the mechanisms through which they were attempting to achieve change. The presence of national policy and wider political change was particularly important in the second live year, and many TPPs fell by the wayside in the context of political uncertainty over the potential future of total purchasing as the extension of the Conservatives' fundholding initiative. National debate concerning particular services (mental health, maternity and cancer services) also had an impact on the ways in which TPPs developed. For example, national policy on maternity care was particularly influential in providing TPPs with firm guidelines for local service development. The support of health authorities was also important. Other analyses (Klein 1995b; Hughes *et al.* 1997) have suggested that the NHS,

**Box 5.2 An example of a total purchasing pilot in a receptive context with appropriate mechanisms of change**

| Context | Aims | Mechanisms | Outcome |
|---|---|---|---|
| Large non-locality TPP in an urban area | To switch provider in order to provide a more coherent community and practice nurse service | Tendered for new contract | Switched provider |
| Mixed cultural context characterized by:<br>• cooperation with the health authority<br>• able and experienced TPP project manager<br>• sophisticated organizational structure with involvement of non-lead GPs<br>• clear vision from lead GP<br>• working over a 2–3 year period (strategic approach) | To set up an intermediate care scheme | Prepared a business plan based on literature reviews and conducted an audit of A&E<br><br>TPP had very specific targets | Achieved an intermediate care scheme, operational since 1997. TPP quarterly monitoring report, which assessed performance against targets, supported TPP's achievement. TPP data were backed up by independent analysis (see Chapter 7) |
| Mixed historical and geographical contexts (for example, pockets of deprivation) | To prevent delay in discharge by reducing the number of emergency admissions and facilitating early discharge | Developed a database of vulnerable patients' social and health details<br><br>Employed a hospital discharge coordinator | Managed to divert 10% of acute admissions to nursing home beds and reduced the rate of admission |
| Financial context:<br>• health authority with large financial deficit<br>• TPP received a capitation-weighted budget | | Sophisticated use of capping the acute contract and diverting 4% to fund alternative provision<br><br>TPP used its large size as a lever for change<br><br>Increased the choice of where care could be delivered | Increased number of admissions to intermediate care by almost 100%<br><br>Gradual increase in use of scheme by GPs (86%)<br><br>Scheme was funded from acute hospital contract<br><br>Achieved multidisciplinary working across secondary/community boundary, and was aiming to become a fully integrated, virtual PCG |

**Box 5.3  An example of a reasonably receptive context, but a total purchasing pilot which did not achieve its potential**

| Context | Aims | Mechanisms | Outcome |
|---|---|---|---|
| Small locality TPP in rural area | To promote independent living by providing comprehensive and coordinated rehabilitation for older people in collaboration with general and local community hospital | Improved local relationships. For example, via subgroup comprising GPs, TPP project manager and community trust representative. Acute trust and social services also consulted | The rehabilitation team was widely perceived to be a success |
| Mixed cultural context:<br>• health authority initially supported the TPP, but support waned over time<br>• dedicated TPP project manager<br>• sophisticated organisational structure with involvement of non-lead GPs<br>• trust unwilling to alter contract currency | | Much enthusiasm from the TPP, but acute trust resistant<br><br>Set up a 'fallers clinic'<br><br>TPP held a budget and invested a substantial proportion of its growth money into the project | However, no systematic audit was undertaken and data were not available on the relative lengths of stay of patients who remained in the acute sector. Even if such data were available, it was suggested there would be considerable difficulties accounting for case-mix as the patients transferred were more likely to have had complex needs |
| Good historical and geographical contexts, for example, low levels of deprivation | | | The TPP believed that the independence of patients seen by the rehabilitation team had improved |
| Financial context:<br>• GPs generously remunerated for TPP work<br>• received a budget<br>• TPP was a capitation 'gainer' | | | Progress made in 1997/98 was not substantially different to 1996/97. A number of smaller scale objectives were put aside as the development of PCGs dominated the TPP's agenda |

**Box 5.4  An example of stifled achievement**

| Context | Aims | Mechanisms | Outcome |
|---|---|---|---|
| Small, two-practice, TPP in rural area | To provide accessible, local services in primary care setting and in local community hospital | GP acting as a leader with vision | Initial changes radical: |
| Cultural context poor: | To work with other agencies to provide integrated, primary managed care | Well-qualified project manager | • TPP ran community hospital |
| • health authority did not delegate budget until as late as December 1997 | | Sophisticated system of sub-groups in clinical and management areas | • innovative joint working with voluntary sector |
| • health authority concerned over destabilization of acute monopoly provider | | Interagency cooperation at operational, but not at strategic level | • integrated approach to mental illness services across primary, community, social and secondary care boundaries |
| • prevailing atmosphere of secrecy and mistrust between TPP, health authority and hospital provider | | No budgetary control | • intermediate care for chronic illness |
| Good historical and geographical contexts | | Sophisticated approach to commissioning including preferred provider and referral matrix; financial incentives, and good monitoring but health authority and trust resistant to its implementation in practice | • innovative approach to care for older vulnerable people. |
| Financial context mixed – innovative approaches to funding enabled some change, despite lack of delegated budget | | | However, progress slowed in second year as negotiations on budget halted and became bitter |
| | | | TPP halted prematurely by health authority in February 1998. Independent enquiry blamed lack of clear of aims on part of the health authority |

**Box 5.5   An example of a total purchasing pilot in a non-receptive context with inappropriate mechanisms of change**

| Context | Aims | Mechanisms | Outcome |
|---|---|---|---|
| Small non-locality in a rural area | To implement *Changing Childbirth* | Discussions with the main acute provider. Main acute provider developed own plans for implementing *Changing Childbirth* and was unwilling to involve the TPP | Maternity project was abandoned |
| Mixed cultural context:<br>• poor relations with the health authority<br>• TPP project manager employed by health authority<br>• undeveloped as an organization<br>• good relations with the community health council<br>• strong lead GP | To release funds from the acute trust contract through early discharge | Initial gains were achieved, but due to the setting of a late budget in 1997/98, the TPP was unable to continue | Unable to achieve further savings |
| Mixed historical and geographical contexts:<br>• low levels of deprivation and unemployment<br>• very different population profile between health authority overall and TPP | To improve information systems | Review of systems in the TPP looking for money to fund project but TPP became aware of the 'planning blight' while waiting for national policy and developments such as NHS Net for general practice information systems | Information systems were reviewed but not improved |
| Financial context:<br>• mixed historic and capitation budget allocated<br>• limited freedom to use budget – for example, unless TPP contracted with its three main providers the health authority insisted on block contracts | | Software houses also not keen to develop for small-scale pilot | |

and/or the internal market, became increasingly sensitive and responsive at local level to national shifts in policy. Currently, health authorities and primary care organizations are responding quickly to another set of major policy changes. As a result, primary care organizations should be given time to establish themselves and to develop before any other radical change is considered. The analysis in this chapter also suggests that, in England, national service frameworks (national guidance for the development of particular service areas) could have an important impact on the way in which local services are developed by health authorities and PCGs.

Investment in a robust management infrastructure was a key factor in the success of TPPs. Leaders and managers able to work interactively with all key players made a big difference. However, achieving the robust structure required took time to develop. Future primary care organizations will need a supportive environment, investment in management, and time to develop if they are to be effective. Some TPPs faced an unsupportive health authority and intransigent local providers when they tried to make service changes (see Chapters 7 and 9 for more on this in relation to resource shifts out of hospitals). There was a good deal of uncertainty and mistrust between agencies (for example, between primary care organizations and hospitals and between some TPPs and certain social services departments). Some TPPs realized that this tension had to be faced and sought to develop a less confrontational and more cooperative approach to developments. This often worked. However, the Department of Health and ministers have to face up to the possibility that in future primary care organizations will want to alter substantially the size, shape and scope of their local acute hospitals' workloads. Even PCGs as *providers* will want to extend the scope of primary care and this will impinge on local hospitals and their budgets. If this is not tolerated and supported by national and local policy, there will be little point in having primary care-led commissioning in England and Wales.

# 6

# PURCHASING MATERNITY CARE, MENTAL HEALTH SERVICES AND COMMUNITY CARE FOR OLDER PEOPLE

Sally Wyke, Linda Gask,
John Lee and Judith Scott

This chapter builds on the analysis in Chapters 3, 4 and 5 by drawing on three substudies, carried out as part of the national evaluation, which examined how total purchasers choosing to be responsible for purchasing maternity care, mental health services, and community care for older people approached their responsibilities and with what results. The three service areas were selected for specific investigation because each represented a major area newly introduced to general practitioner-led purchasing through the total purchasing initiative. Two of the service areas were also subject to another closely related experiment in GP-led purchasing – the extended fundholding pilots – in which individual standard fundholding practices added either maternity care or mental health services to the range of services included in the standard fundholding scheme.

The findings of each of the substudies underlines the following messages from the general assessment of the influences shaping total purchasers' achievements discussed in Chapter 5:

- The degree of organizational development and, in particular, the quality of information management greatly influenced total purchasers' relative success or failure in achieving their service-specific goals.
- Most service development took place through relatively simple extensions to the primary care team, or through the development

of intermediate care, rather than through directly altering the nature of secondary care or specialist services.

- Some TPPs were successful in both horizontal and vertical integration of services – their motivation for integration in both cases was to enhance patient care.
- While budgetary muscle (or the potential to use it) was often a catalyst for change, interagency cooperation over seemingly intractable local problems was equally important. However, the sustainability of change was enhanced when informal agreements were enshrined in more formal NHS contracts.
- The context in which developments took place helped shape the extent to which total purchasers were able to achieve their aims. In particular, the presence or absence of a national policy framework and the political context of a change of government in 1997 were important in shaping the extent to which GPs were able to achieve their goals successfully.

Uniquely in the design of the national evaluation, the maternity care substudy included a comparison of users' views, experiences and resource use between women registered with TPPs purchasing maternity care, extended fundholding practices purchasing maternity care and those registered in practices where the local health authority retained responsibility for purchasing care (see Chapter 2). This chapter therefore considers the question of whether GPs with responsibility for purchasing maternity care made a difference to women's experiences or resource use.

## INFORMATION MANAGEMENT FOR PURCHASING

### Information management for maternity care

Improving the availability and quality of information on maternity care activity in order to develop better costing models and more sensitive contracting were explicit aims of most of the general practice-based purchasers studied. Most pilots had multiple aims in this broad area, but TPPs found it easier to gather information and to develop independent contracts than extended fundholders. TPPs achieved seven of the eight aims they had in this area, whereas extended fundholders achieved only two of their ten aims. Gathering information takes a long time and requires cooperation from other NHS providers. Because of political changes during the life of the pilots (see below) the single-practice extended fundholders had little leverage with large acute NHS trusts, and many simply gave up the battle. One extended fundholding practice did develop a sophisticated costing model for maternity care based on gathering detailed data on activity from both hospital and community health services staff. Setting up this system and ensuring it worked took much longer than expected. However, it was complete by the end of the pilot (two years later) and the practice was hoping to use the model to influence future health authority and PCG service agreements with the local hospital.

**Information management for mental health services**

Obtaining adequate information on activity and costs was a significant problem for GP-led purchasers of mental health services. There were few examples of success in this area. As was the case with maternity care, most pilots overcame this problem only by persistence and the gentle persuasion of provider staff over a long period of time.

One pilot undertook a three-week survey of workload of all professionals involved in providing mental health care (including the primary care team, community mental health team and local specialist services). Staff were asked systemically to count and identify the number and range of people with mental health problems they were currently caring for. This enabled the pilot to clarify exactly how services were being utilized locally.

Several pilots set up their own mental illness registers and one of them went even further, developing its own practice-based information system. However, this did cause some problems. Some community psychiatric nurses found themselves providing two sets of activity information, one for the NHS hospital and one for the practice. Of the two, they felt the information for the practice was more useful as the assessment data could be used as a tool for monitoring individual users' well-being or progress. The hospital information on the other hand was more concerned with levels of activity for contracting purposes. The latter placed an extra administrative burden on the nurses which they perceived as having little direct benefit for patient care.

**Information management for community care**

Information management is one of the most intractable problems for the development of integrated services between health and social care agencies involved in caring for older people in the community. The TPPs in the substudy of community care recognized this problem and had gone at least some way to finding solutions. At two of the TPPs, for example, patient-held record cards were used by all agencies. In three of the TPPs, activity information was shared between the TPP and the local social care agency to help cost joint packages of care. In another TPP, referral and assessments were shared between health and social care staff. However, this took a long time to develop, and no working model of information sharing either for coordination or for costing purposes had been adequately developed by the end of the experiment. Shared information technology systems being developed at three of the TPPs were taking even longer and some projects had to be abandoned before completion.

## EXTENDING PRIMARY CARE TEAMS

All pilots, in all three of the service-specific studies, were involved in the development of some form of extended primary care team.

### Practice-based maternity care

Practices worked hard both to maintain and to put in place practice-based maternity care. Most of the GPs appreciated having maternity care based in their practices. They felt it gave them an opportunity to discuss the progress of their pregnant patients directly with midwives and also to maintain a practical role in the delivery of maternity care.

For example, before the introduction of extended fundholding, an experimental pilot of practice-based team midwifery had been introduced in one of the study practices. Under this model, a small team of midwives, employed by the hospital, was attached to the practice to deliver all care to women (accompanying women to hospital to deliver as often as possible). When the invitation to apply for extended fundholding status was received, this model of care had been under threat as the hospital had judged that it could no longer afford to run it. The practice in question applied for extended fundholding status explicitly to be able to apply pressure on the hospital to maintain the service. Other aims were to make some changes to the way in which the service was delivered to women; 'to make it more primary care-based'; and to develop a better system to cost and contract for maternity care in order to reward and resource community-based care properly. The practice was successful in maintaining practice-based team midwifery, and in persuading the health authority and hospital to roll out the model, albeit in reduced form, after the end of the pilot. This was despite the fact that the pilot was not successful in developing its planned more sophisticated costing model for maternity care.

In another example, one of the TPPs successfully managed to change its pattern of midwifery care from a geographical focus (with midwives undertaking antenatal and postnatal care in women's homes and delivering them in hospital) to a practice-based service (with midwives delivering antenatal care from the practice, women being seen occasionally by GPs and delivering in hospital). The GPs in the TPP had not been happy with the team midwifery service set up by the hospital, feeling that they had been excluded from the provision of maternity care without consultation. In order to develop its own contracts, the TPP was in receipt of maternity activity data from the hospital. The GPs had noticed that they had a high ratio of consultant episodes per delivery, caused by a higher than usual rate of antenatal admissions. They argued strongly that this was due to a lack of GP involvement in antenatal care under the team midwifery model, with care being delivered by midwives in patients' homes. The obstetricians supported this interpretation of the data, and the pattern of care was changed to suit the view of the TPP's GPs. The pilot ended before it was possible to ascertain whether GPs had been correct in their assessment of the causes of the high ratio of consultant episodes per delivery.

There were some exceptions to the general observation that GPs preferred to have maternity care delivered in their practice premises. Where existing premises were too small, for example, or where the practice was associated with a small GP maternity unit in a local hospital, then GP-led purchasing was aimed at *maintaining* the hospital unit. In these circumstances, GPs were happy to support the development or maintenance of separate premises for the delivery of care as long as they continued to exercise a high level of control over care.

### Practice-based mental health services – primary mental health service teams

Developing services that were closely linked with primary care was a significant theme in many of the pilots concerned with mental health services. The main example of this was the simple attachment of community psychiatric nurses to primary care teams, but some pilots went further than this by establishing primary mental health teams, consisting of a range of health and social care staff.

In one of the pilot areas, a rural area that included a number of villages with relatively low levels of deprivation but a high number of elderly residents, a primary mental health team was set up. This consisted of a team leader (a community psychiatric nurse), four full whole time equivalent community psychiatric nurses, and one-and-a-half whole time equivalent social workers. Two counsellors, both of whom were already employed by three of the practices under standard fundholding, were employed for an additional 15 hours of counselling within the mental health pilot and both were also seen as an integral part of the primary mental health team. The team was felt to have developed close liaison with those in primary care. It focused particularly on training primary care staff in mental health issues such as sexual abuse, anxiety, depression, mental 'health' versus 'illness', and appropriate prescribing in depression.

### Practice-based community care for older people

The same desire to locate care at practice level was observed in the study of community and continuing care for frail older people. It was common for a TPP to be dissatisfied with its local provider of community health services. A large part of this dissatisfaction was due to providers refusing to organize their staff as self-managed teams based in practices (insisting, instead, on a geographical focus to allow flexibility of nursing cover). The usual TPP response to this dissatisfaction was to change provider, and to write a specific organizational requirement for self-managed practice nursing teams into any new contract. Total purchasers believed that a practice-based, self-managed nursing team enabled better communication and liaison between all staff, as well as a more strategic, integrated approach to care.

## INTEGRATION OF CARE

### Integration of maternity care

Team midwifery, in which a team of midwives delivers all care to women regardless of location, is a form of 'vertically' integrated maternity care since midwives work in both community and hospital settings. Many providers have grappled with the delivery of this type of care since the publication of the *Changing Childbirth* report in England (Department of Health 1993a). However, support for this type of integration from GPs in the maternity study was dependent on some of the care being delivered from their own premises, and on their own terms. Most GPs wanted contact with women and with midwives, and wanted to feel in control of care. If this happened, GPs were happy to support women-centred, vertically integrated pathways of care. If it did not, they did what they could to undermine the service. So unless GPs were actively involved in the planning or delivery of vertical integrated care, there was less support for it than in the areas of mental health and community care for older people.

**Integration of mental health services**

Integration of services between primary care and local social services ('horizontal' integration) was uncommon in the mental health pilots studied. However, when it did occur, it was primarily through the attachment of social work staff to pilot practices. For example, at one pilot, the total purchaser and the local social services department jointly funded a social worker to become part of the primary mental health team. The social worker took referrals from both the community psychiatric nurses in the team and social workers in the social services department. Most of those on her caseload were women under 25 with children. The social worker arranged child-minding for women to attend courses, counselling, or to prepare for a job and, in addition, set up a playgroup for the families of people with mental health problems. Such joint working was very successful when it occurred, and seemed to reflect the GPs' wishes to recreate links with social work that had been present in the past, but had disappeared under the recent pressure on social services departments to reallocate their staff according to different priorities. Such improved relationships tended to occur when there was a practical basis to the relationship, such as joint commissioning of services or joint funding of posts, rather than when the relationship simply consisted of attendance at liaison meetings.

The setting up of a primary mental health team was the commonest form of horizontal integration between primary and community care services which, for example, included the attachment of community psychiatric nurses to practices. An example of both vertical and horizontal integration between primary and secondary care in mental health occurred in one of the pilots. In this example, the practice-attached community psychiatric nurses from the local NHS mental health trust continuing care team were able to increase links and coordination between primary and secondary care for people with severe and enduring mental illness on the practices' lists.

### Integration of community care

All five of the TPPs studied in detail in relation to their efforts to develop community and continuing care for older people were attempting some form of horizontal or vertical integration of care (Myles *et al.* 1999). As so often, they were doing this primarily through practice-based extensions to the primary care team. However, they were also developing intermediate care. Box 6.1 details the extent of integration at one of the TPPs.

## BUDGETS, CONTRACTING AND COLLABORATION

### Contracts, collaboration and achieving sustainable change in maternity care

None of the extended fundholding practices was delegated a budget to purchase maternity care. Despite this, all of the general practice-based purchasers believed that holding a budget (or having the potential to hold it, or in the case of the extended fundholding practices be seen as a purchaser) was important in their potential ability to make changes. They felt that it facilitated and legitimated their involvement in planning maternity care. This point is illustrated by a consideration of who was seen to be important in the planning of maternity care in each of the areas in which the pilots operated. Table 6.1 shows that general practice staff were seen as important stakeholders in the planning of care by all 11 of the general practice-based purchasers, but in only one of the local 'special interest' or standard fundholding practices not involved in purchasing maternity care. Therefore, holding the budget, or being seen to do so by NHS providers, facilitated GP involvement in planning care.

The initiative for involvement in purchasing maternity care often came from the local provider of maternity service; in particular, from the director of midwifery or from community midwives rather than from the GPs. In the case of maternity care,

---

**Box 6.1   Integrated provision of care for older people**

*Horizontal – health and social care, community care co-ordinator*

An experienced social worker whose role was to liaise with the local social services department and to act as a bridge between the practice, social services care managers, and private and voluntary sector providers. Her post was described as being without strict boundaries, to cover 'the grey areas where everything needed negotiation'.

*Horizontal and vertical – multidisciplinary elderly care team*

A team approach aimed at keeping people in their own homes and independent for as long as possible. Health and social care professionals involved were all based in the TPP. The TPP contracted for a community geriatrician for two sessions a month, who attended team meetings and gave access to a day unit and secondary care beds, where appropriate. The team was co-ordinated by the community nursing team manager, who took referrals from any member of the team and decided which professional should carry out an initial, comprehensive assessment of the patient. All elderly people were eligible for referral to the team, including those with relatively simple needs, which meant that patients with less severe problems got care which may have prevented subsequent deterioration. Initial assessments were discussed at team meetings and the person best qualified to tackle each problem was identified.

*Vertical – admission and discharge coordinator*

The TPP-employed nurse identified TPP patients admitted to hospital as an emergency with a view to facilitating early discharge and reducing length of stay (through accessing the services of the multidisciplinary team). The nurse also undertook pre-admission assessments for elective admissions in which patients were assessed for their suitability for early discharge with and without packages of community care.

---

**Table 6.1** Key players in planning maternity care

|  | Purchasing practices (11) | Non-purchasing practices (10) |
|---|---|---|
| *Provider staff* | | |
| Director of midwifery | 3 | 10 |
| Community midwives | 8 | 2 |
| Obstetricians | 2 | 7 |
| *General practice staff* | | |
| GP | 8 | 1 |
| Fund manager | 3 | 0 |
| *Health authority staff* | 5 | 0 |

GP-based purchasing was seen as a means to an end for service change or service reconfiguration that had already been considered desirable by providers. So the provider's staff identified the opportunities which GP-led purchasing offered; gained the support of the general practices or TPPs; initiated further negotiations with other departments in the hospital; and achieved service change (often with increased resources contributed by the hospital itself or by the local health authority). However, analysis of data from the wider study of TPP contracting (Robison *et al.* 1999), and from face-to-face interviews, suggests that change was not sustainable unless two other criteria were met. First, practice staff needed to be actively engaged in the project (rather than just hosting it) and, second, service changes needed to be reflected in formal NHS contracts if services were to be sustainable in more difficult circumstances (such as the hospital being faced with a budget cut, a shortage of midwives or switch of policy focus).

Two examples illustrate this point. In the first example the NHS hospital, led by the director of maternal and child health services, encouraged a local general practice to apply to become an extended fundholding practice. The director had a long-held ambition to set up a team midwifery project in a rural area covering five general practices. The team would provide total midwifery care to all women registered by the five practices. She wanted to use the status that the general practice would have as a Department of Health national pilot to encourage the local health authority to fund the hospital to set up her team. The TPP lead GP and his fund manager supported the project at the beginning, but had little subsequent role in planning the service. They felt excluded and lost interest in the project. The midwifery team was set up but the practice did not push the hospital for activity data on which to base a contract, did not actively pursue developing a contract, and did not pursue the health authority for control over the resources it was investing in the project. The team ran for a while, but was beset by complaints from local GPs about their lack of involvement in the provision of maternity care. The team was disbanded at the end of the pilot.

In the second example, a TPP successfully secured the future of a local GP-led maternity unit, first through negotiation with NHS hospital staff, and second by reflecting these agreements in a contract with the hospital. The GP-led maternity unit, in a small market town, was run by one of two large NHS trusts in a neighbouring city. It was run by midwives, but was under threat mainly because of a lack of GPs to provide obstetric cover. One GP from the TPP led negotiations with the NHS trust to persuade it to sub-contract the TPP to provide obstetric cover. This guaranteed income and enabled the TPP practice to appoint an additional partner with an obstetric interest to provide cover. In return, the TPP contracted all its maternity care from the NHS trust concerned, unless women specifically requested attendance at the second NHS trust in the city. The agreement between the hospital and the TPP included a requirement for GPs to update themselves on obstetric practice. In this example, holding the budget and the ability to contract led to negotiations and agreements between clinical staff which were then enshrined in contracts. The arrangements were also likely to continue after the TPP was replaced by a local PCG.

### Mental health – budgets and collaboration

In common with most of the GP-led purchasing pilots, those focusing on mental health found that while they may have rarely used contracts as a direct lever to achieve change, holding a budget and the potential to alter contracts were important for being taken seriously by other local stakeholders. While most felt that the principal means of achieving change had been through collaboration and joint working with other local agencies, their ability to engage and cooperate with these agencies was strongly related to their status as budget holders and purchasers.

An example of a pilot that did attempt more extensive use of contracting was one that had changed its purchasing arrangements for day care provision. It was felt that existing local day care provision for both elderly people and adults (16–65 years) with mental health problems was not suitable for most users and that the local day centre provided by a secondary care provider did not have the flexibility to cater for individual needs. For elderly people with mental health problems, the pilot moved the contract to an independent provider that ran 17 homes and contracted with it to provide a day care facility in one of these homes. In terms of adult day care, the pilot developed links with a local adult guidance service provided by the local authority. This service was able to offer individuals from the practice help with accessing college courses or finding voluntary work. This pilot also had a 'spot' purchasing budget of £15,000 a year that was used to provide practical support. For example, overalls and wellington boots were bought so that one patient could take up a training placement at a zoo. Money was also given to a patient with depression to enable her to travel and visit her family.

### Community care – changing contracts and collaborative working

Community health services had long been on the list of services purchased by standard fundholding practices. As a result pilots tackling community care services for older people with complex needs felt that they knew where to start – with their contracts for community health services. Four out of the five TPPs in the sub-study on community care used their contracts with community health service providers to shape services in ways that suited their plans. Three changed providers in order to have self-managed teams of community nurses working in their practices. One changed the contract currency for community geriatric services from the number of patients seen to the number of sessions of geriatrician time. This enabled the community geriatrician to give specialist input into a community-based, multidisciplinary, elderly care team. However, while all total purchasers involved in developing community care services felt that holding the budget and the contracting process were important in achieving sustainable change, some felt that joint working and local agreements were important in getting the process moving. One of the lead GPs for community care said that contracts were 'an expression of agreement. They're not used to force a change in services – that's always a last resort.'

## THE IMPORTANCE OF CONTEXT

### Maternity care: the influence of national policy and political change

The *Changing Childbirth* report (Department of Health 1993a) set out a detailed blueprint for the development of maternity care services in England which focused on women as central to their own care and on providing them with choice, information and control over their care. It encouraged the enhancement of continuity of care as a means to achieve these ends and had great influence on developments in maternity care in the mid-1990s. Accordingly, the NHS Management Executive included maternity services in its planning and priorities guidance for 1994/95. This required health authorities to review the maternity services they purchased in the light of the *Changing Childbirth* recommendations, and to develop a strategy to implement any necessary changes. It was expected that this local strategy would be reflected in health authority contracts for 1995/96. In addition, in July 1994 a *Changing Childbirth* implementation team was set up with Department of Health funding. The team worked for three years with a remit to raise awareness about *Changing Childbirth* among professionals and the public, and to act as a resource for purchasers, providers and users' groups involved in the implementation of the recommendations. The extended fundholding pilot practices were hand-picked by Department of Health staff according to their predicted ability to purchase care in line with the recommendations of *Changing Childbirth*. There was some concern that TPPs, by contrast, would ignore these guidelines, and would purchase less expensive services in order to reinvest savings elsewhere in the health care sector. It was also feared that TPPs would seek to employ midwives themselves, therefore cutting them off from peer support and the ability to further maintain or extend their skills beyond the more mundane aspects of antenatal care. In the event, these fears were unfounded since the vast majority of TPPs interested in maternity care stated that their aim was to implement *Changing Childbirth* (or a related aim). There was widespread support for the policy in the TPPs, and the clear guidance provided by *Changing Childbirth* was felt to have aided TPPs' local negotiations with providers in the first year of total purchasing (1995/96).

However, in subsequent years, *Changing Childbirth* slipped down the national policy agenda. It was reported that this caused difficulties, especially for some extended fundholding practices and their midwifery allies, toiling to maintain new forms of service. In addition, the pilots were operating in an uncertain party political climate. Soon after the extended fundholding pilots officially began in April 1996, health authority, provider and practice staff began to recognize the possibility of a Labour general election victory, and to alter their plans subtly. Labour health policy (Labour Party 1995) had made it clear that single-practice fundholding would come to an end if there was a change of government. This meant that hospitals began to feel less urgency in meeting the purchasing demands of GPs. In turn, health authorities did not feel the need to allocate budgets to the TPPs, or to support them in making demands on providers, and practice staff lost the impetus to press providers for service changes or for activity data on which to base formal contracts (see Chapters 7 and 9). One extended fundholder explained that he had abandoned plans to develop a costing model for purchasing maternity care when it became clear that it 'would be thrown out of the window' if Labour won the 1997 election. The fundholder explained: 'We backed off, there was no point, and we have to work with these guys for the next ten years.' Yet the changing political climate did not harm the TPPs so badly. This may have been because their organizational structure was more robust, or because some form of collective GP-based purchasing, in larger rather than in smaller groups, was felt likely to continue beyond the change of government.

**Mental health services**

At the beginning of the study period, the national priority in mental health policy was to focus provision on people with severe and enduring mental illness. The main providers of mental health services developed this policy focus. Most of the GP-based purchasing pilots were primarily around improving care for common (or less severe) disorders, which initially appeared to pose a problem for relationships between providers and the GP purchasers. It certainly seemed that the groundswell of purchasing opinion in primary care, and its new-found power, were going to come into direct conflict with top-down, national policy.

However, this conflict did not materialize. The fact that providers and purchasers had to enter into dialogue actually appeared to help them resolve some of these difficulties and begin to work together on shared aims. These included caring for people with enduring and severe mental health problems as well as more common problems.

Nevertheless, with the move to PCGs, there may well be difficulties extending the services developed in TPPs to wider areas, given that many of the pilots were perceived to be well-staffed and not based in areas of high need and deprivation. It remains to be seen whether quality can be maintained in the face of the current drive towards equity; that is, with all GPs and areas involved in primary care-based purchasing.

### The national context in relation to developments in community care

National priorities also influenced developments in the area of community care for older people. There had been concern for some years at the rise in unplanned admissions to hospital, particularly of older people, in the winter months. The concern stemmed from hospitals' and health authorities' inability to meet the demand, and the resulting lengthening of elective waiting lists. Elective waiting lists are a major indicator of NHS performance according to the government and are also a barometer to the public of how well the government is supporting the NHS. In the winter of 1997/98 extra money was made available to health authorities to invest in ways of reducing or minimizing unplanned use of acute services, so that waiting lists would not be so severely affected as in past winters. These resources were called 'winter pressures' money.

The winter pressures money was invested in ways that supported the development of TPP-initiated schemes in several TPPs. For example, one TPP had plans to manage admissions and discharge problems for older people that were caused by organizational rather than clinical difficulties by developing 'patient-orientated pathways'. It developed the idea for a medical assessment unit, using winter pressures money, which was discussed at a meeting between the local hospital and practice staff concerned with the avoidance of bed blocking. Older patients in crisis were referred to the medical assessment unit either by GPs or by the A&E department. They stayed a maximum of 48 hours while their clinical and other needs were assessed and a care package put in place. Therefore, whereas the TPP had previously struggled to implement its innovative ideas to manage unplanned use of services, the national context of wider concern and the investment of extra resource rapidly enabled an unfulfilled plan to become a reality. The extra funding meant that the TPP no longer had to try to finance its new approach by removing money from the hospital's contracts (see Chapters 7 and 9).

## GENERAL PRACTITIONERS PURCHASING MATERNITY CARE – DID IT MAKE A DIFFERENCE?

As Chapter 2 discussed, it is easy to criticize the design of the national evaluation of total purchasing by pointing out that it did not consider the impact on users of changes in responsibility for purchasing. This criticism was not considered justifiable for most of the services purchased by total purchasers, as changes in service organization or delivery could not be expected to change people's health status, at least in measurable ways, over the life of the study. However, in the area of maternity care – in which the national policy framework, *Changing Childbirth*, emphasized the importance of women's own experiences of care – comparison of women's experiences of information, choice, control and resource use between GP-based purchasing and non-GP-based purchasing practices was judged to be both feasible and important.

*Changing Childbirth* had encouraged both purchasers and providers to consider how vertical integration of care (through team midwifery projects in which midwives delivered all care for women) could be used to deliver women better information, choice and control over care. GP-based purchasers might have been expected to be more effective in shifting services towards a model that delivered quality of care defined from women's perspectives. As budget holders, they might also have been expected to reconsider resource use, and to encourage services that provided more effective use of resources. Figure 6.1 illustrates the way in which type of practice, model of service organization and women's experiences may be related.

**Figure 6.1**   The hypothetical relationship between type of commissioning organization, model of service organization, and women's experiences and resource use

**Table 6.2** Experiences of women receiving maternity care in commissioning and non-commissioning practices

Number (per cent) of women in each type of practice giving specified binary responses to questions about experience of information, choice, control and resource use, together with odds ratios (95 per cent confidence limits) in commissioning as compared to non-commissioning practices, estimated from multi-level models adjusted for case mix. Also shown are the estimated odds ratios per unit increase in category[1] for the case-mix variables in the multi-level models.

| Question | Response | Commissioning | Non-commissioning | OR (95% CI) adjusted for case-mix | Age | Language | Education | Parity |
|---|---|---|---|---|---|---|---|---|
| **Information** | | | | | | | | |
| 1 Did you have enough information about types of antenatal care? | Had enough information | 953 (79) | 507 (79) | 0.98 (0.92–1.03) | 1.02 | 1.10 | 0.96** | 1.03 |
| 2 During antenatal care were you given different advice? | No | 838 (69) | 451 (71) | 0.98 (0.923–1.03) | 1.02 | 1.13 | 0.97** | 1.01 |
| 3 Were there times when you would have liked to have had more information without having to ask? | No or not really | 672 (56) | 348 (55) | 0.99 (0.92–1.07) | 1.02 | 0.95 | 0.98 | 1.06** |
| 4 In labour, did they tell you enough about why things were necessary? | Always | 876 (76) | 482 (78) | 1.00 (0.98–1.03) | 1.02*** | 0.99 | 1.00 | 1.00 |
| 5 Did doctors or midwives tell you enough about what was happening in labour? | Always | 854 (73) | 4474 (76) | 1.00 (0.98–1.03) | 1.01* | 1.02 | 1.00 | 1.00 |
| **Choice** | | | | | | | | |
| 6 Were you given a choice of who to have antenatal care with? | Yes | 654 (53) | 331 (52) | 0.99 (0.84–1.17) | 1.04*** | 1.18 | 0.99 | 1.03* |
| 7 Were you offered the choice of having your child at home? | Yes | 558 (46) | 269 (42) | 1.02 (0.92–1.12) | 1.01 | 0.90 | 1.01 | 0.97* |
| 8 Was the number of antenatal visits discussed with you? | Yes | 413 (34) | 199 (32) | 0.97 (0.84–1.13) | 1.02 | 1.09 | 1.02 | 1.02 |
| 9 Did the midwife discuss the number of postnatal visits? | Yes | 1058 (89) | 537 (87) | 1.03 (0.99–1.07) | 1.01 | 0.91 | 0.99 | 0.99 |

**Control**

| | | | | | | | | |
|---|---|---|---|---|---|---|---|---|
| 10 How involved were you in decisions about your pregnancy? | Fully involved in all decisions | 592 (49) | 330 (52) | 0.97 (0.90–1.04) | 0.99 | 1.12 | 1.01 | 1.07*** |
| 11 Were you fully involved in decisions about where to have your baby? | Yes | 841 (70) | 429 (69) | 0.99 (0.92–1.05) | 1.04** | 0.94 | 1.01 | 1.01 |
| 12 How involved were you in decisions during labour and birth? | Fully involved in all decisions | 653 (54) | 345 (54) | 0.98 (0.90–1.06) | 1.03* | 1.01 | 0.99 | 0.98 |
| 13 Did doctors or midwives take enough notice of your views during labour and birth? | Always | 869 (75) | 480 (78) | 0.97 (0.90–1.04) | 1.01 | 1.08 | 0.99 | 1.02 |
| 14 Were you involved in the decision about when to leave hospital? | Yes | 1032 (91) | 534 (89) | 1.01 (0.97–1.05) | 1.02 | 1.08 | 0.97*** | 1.00 |
| 15 Were you involved in decisions about postnatal care and the care of the baby? | Fully involved in all decisions | 911 (76) | 474 (76) | 1.00 (0.95–1.05) | 1.00 | 0.84* | 0.97* | 1.00 |
| 16 Would you like to have been more or less involved in your care or were you happy with your involvement? | Happy with involvement | 999 (83) | 523 (82) | 1.00 (0.94–1.06) | 1.02 | 0.90 | 0.98 | 1.00 |

**Resource use**

| | | | | | | | | |
|---|---|---|---|---|---|---|---|---|
| 17 Number of antenatal check-ups | More than 10 check-ups | 540 (44) | 316 (49) | 0.97 (0.84–1.13) | 0.99 | 0.91 | 0.99 | 0.98 |
| 18 Number of antenatal admissions | Any antenatal admission | 1062 (87) | 560 (88) | 0.98 (0.94–1.03) | 1.02* | 0.95 | 1.02* | 1.00 |
| 19 Time spent in hospital after birth | Stay more than two days | 542 (47) | 263 (44) | 1.04 (0.94–1.17) | 1.03** | 0.99 | 1.00 | 0.83*** |
| 20 Midwife postnatal home visits | Most days or more often | 856 (73) | 516 (84) | 0.92 (0.82–1.03) | 1.01 | 1.01 | 1.00 | 0.98 |
| 21 GP postnatal home visits | At least twice | 81 (7) | 190 (31) | 0.82 (0.66–1.03) | 0.99 | 1.07 | 1.01 | 1.01 |

*Notes:*

[1] Categories for case-mix variables as follow: Age – 5-year bands between 15 and 35+; Language – Is English first language? Yes/No; Education – None, GCSE, CSE or O-level, A-level or equivalent, degree or equivalent; Parity – each additional child.
Significance shown as * = P < 0.05; ** P < 0.01 or *** P < 0.001.

Chapter 2 outlined how comparison practices were identified, and women's views elicited. In summary, the resulting sample consisted of 21 practices: five extended fundholding practices, together with five practices with a history of interest in maternity care, five standard fundholding practices with no particular interest in maternity care, and six TPPs. For comparisons, the extended fundholding and total purchasing practices were grouped together as general practice-based purchasers, while the special interest and standard fundholding practices were grouped together as non-purchasers. Women's experiences of information, choice and control and resource use were elicited using a structured postal questionnaire sent to all women registered with the 21 study practices who had babies between October 1996 and December 1997.

Three comparisons were made. First, women's experiences and resource use were compared between types of purchaser. Second, differences in models of service organization between types of purchaser were compared. Finally, women's experiences and resource use between models of service organization were compared. For the first and third comparisons, multi-level modelling was used to take account of differences between practices in case mix and in the number of women responding to the questionnaire and because the data were hierarchical in that numbers of women were clustered within practices.

Table 6.2 shows the results of the comparison of women's experiences and resource use between types of purchaser. None of the responses showed a significant difference between purchasing and non-purchasing practices. These findings suggest that giving GPs responsibility for purchasing maternity care did not appear to have a measurable effect sufficient to improve women's experience, or alter their use of resources.

One possible explanation for this finding might be that the presence of strong national policy guidance, in the form of *Changing Childbirth*, reduced the scope for differences in policy between purchasing and non-purchasing practices. Certainly, the objectives of all purchasing practices were strongly influenced by *Changing Childbirth*. Another possible explanation for this finding is that the timescale of the pilot (two years) was too short and that it could reasonably have been expected to take much longer for changes in responsibility for commissioning to result in changes in service organization, clinician behaviour and women's experiences. However, in the current study, most models of service organization were already in operation in the 21 practices at the beginning of the pilot, and little change in organization of care was observed between 1996 and 1998.

Table 6.3 compares models of service organization between types of purchaser. Four models of service organization of care were apparent. Although testing for statistical significance was not appropriate, it can be seen that general practice-based purchasers were more likely to be associated with less traditional, more

**Table 6.3** Association between type of practice and model of service organization including extent of integration between community and hospital care

| | Commissioning general practices | Non-commissioning general practices |
|---|---|---|
| *Caseload team midwifery* – one or two midwives take on a caseload of women and attempt to provide all care to women registered with them. Integration between community and hospital. | 3 | 1 |
| *Non-caseload team midwifery* – a larger team of midwives provides all care to women registered with the team. Team members attempt to meet each woman prior to delivery. Integration between community and hospital. | 2 | 2 |
| *'Traditional' care* – one or more community midwives provide ante-natal care in the practice and post-natal care at home. Delivery by hospital-based midwives. Less integration between community and hospital. | 5 | 6 |
| *GP units* – staffed by midwives, who provide all care from the unit itself. However, women often deliver in the general hospital and return to the unit for postnatal care. Some integration between community and hospital. | 1 | 1 |

**Table 6.4** Comparison of experiences and resource use of women receiving four models of service organization

Odds ratios (95 per cent confidence limits) compare the four models adjusted for case-mix.[1] Statistical testing compares all four models of service organization (i.e. tests the null hypothesis that they are all the same).

| Question | Response | OR (95% CI) for each care model relative to 'traditional' | | | |
| --- | --- | --- | --- | --- | --- |
| | | Caseload team midwifery | Non-caseload team midwifery | GP units | |
| **Information** | | | | | |
| 1 Did you have enough information about types of antenatal care? | Had enough information | 1.03 (0.97–1.09) | 1.02 (0.96–1.07) | 1.08 (1.01–1.15) | |
| 2 During antenatal care were you given different advice? | No | 1.00 (0.93–1.07) | 1.03 (0.97–1.10) | 1.04 (0.97–1.12) | |
| 3 Were there times when you would have liked to have hade more information without having to ask? | No or not really | 1.01 (0.91–1.11) | 1.02 (0.94–1.12) | 1.11 (0.99–1.24) | |
| 4 In labour, did they tell you enough about why things were necessary? | Always | 1.10 (1.01–1.19) | 0.98 (0.91–1.06) | 1.07 (0.98–1.18) | |
| 5 Did doctors or midwives tell you enough about what was happening in labour? | Always | 1.08 (0.98–1.18) | 0.96 (0.98–1.05) | 1.08 (0.97–1.20) | |
| **Choice** | | | | | |
| 6 Were you given a choice of who to have antenatal care with? | Yes | 1.17 (0.94–1.46) | 1.10 (0.89–1.35) | 1.14 (0.87–1.49) | |
| 7 Were you offered the choice of having your child at home? | Yes | 1.13 (1.01–1.27) | 1.14 (1.02–1.27) | 1.10 (0.96–1.26) | |
| 8 Was the number of antenatal visits discussed with you? | Yes | 1.22 (1.01–1.47) | 1.03 (0.86–1.23) | 0.97 (0.77–1.22) | |
| 9 Did the midwife discuss the number of postnatal visits? | Yes | 0.98 (0.94–1.03) | 1.04 (1.00–1.09) | 1.00 (0.95–1.06) | |

**Control**

| | | | | |
|---|---|---|---|---|
| 10 How involved were you in decisions about your pregnancy? | Fully involved in all decisions | 1.10 (1.00–1.20) | 1.02 (0.94–1.10) | 1.09 (0.98–1.21) |
| 11 Were you fully involved in decisions about where to have your baby? | Yes | 1.19 (1.02–1.40) | 1.14 (0.98–1.33) | 1.28 (1.05–1.56)* |
| 12 How involved were you in decisions during labour and birth? | Fully involved in all decisions | 1.14 (1.04–1.25) | 1.08 (1.00–1.18) | 1.12 (1.01–1.24)* |
| 13 Did doctors or midwives take enough notice of your views during labour and birth? | Always | 1.04 (0.94–1.15) | 0.99 (0.91–1.09) | 1.07 (0.95–1.20) |
| 14 Were you involved in the decision about when to leave hospital? | Yes | 1.01 (0.96–1.07) | 1.02 (0.97–1.07) | 1.07 (1.01–1.13) |
| 15 Were you involved in decisions about postnatal care and the care of your baby? | Fully involved in all decisions | 1.04 (0.98–1.10) | 1.00 (0.94–1.06) | 1.05 (0.99–1.13) |
| 16 Would you like to have been more or less involved in your care or were you happy with your involvement? | Happy with involvement | 1.05 (0.97–1.13) | 1.03 (0.96–1.10) | 1.12 (1.02–1.22) |

**Resource use**

| | | | | |
|---|---|---|---|---|
| 17 Number of antenatal check-ups | More than 10 check-ups | 0.94 (0.78–1.13) | 0.83 (0.70–0.99) | 0.89 (0.71–1.12) |
| 18 Number of antenatal admissions | Any antenatal admission | 1.00 (0.94–1.07) | 1.02 (0.97–1.09) | 1.02 (0.95–1.09) |
| 19 Time spent in hospital after birth | Stay more than two days | 0.85 (0.79–0.90) | 0.90 (0.85–0.96) | 1.25 (1.16–1.34)** |
| 20 Midwife postnatal home visits | Most days or more often | 1.08 (0.94–1.25) | 0.96 (0.84–1.10) | 0.88 (0.74–1.04) |
| 21 GP postnatal home visits | At least twice | 1.12 (0.83–1.51) | 1.14 (0.85–1.51) | 1.03 (0.71–1.50) |

*Notes:*

[1] The estimates for the four case-mix variables are similar to those in Table 6.1 and are not shown here.

Significance shown as * = P < 0.05, ** = P < 0.01 or *** = P < 0.001.

vertically integrated approaches to care than the comparison practices. The probable explanation for this lies in the alliances forged between midwifery managers, community midwives and some of the general practice-based purchasers in order either to maintain or develop models of team midwifery, as described above.

Finally, Table 6.4 compares women's experiences and resource use between models of service organization. It shows that only three of the 21 questions varied significantly between models of service organization. Women who were cared for under the more integrated, less traditional models of care were more likely to report feelings of involvement in decisions about where to have their baby, and in decisions during labour and birth, than women who were cared for under the traditional model (in which most had their babies delivered in a district general hospital by midwives they had not necessarily met before). In addition, postnatal lengths of stay were shorter under both models of team midwifery (probably because midwives accompanied women home) and longer under a general practice unit (probably because some women cared for under this model of care would have delivered in a district general hospital and specifically returned to the general practice unit for postnatal care).

## CONCLUSIONS

This chapter has expanded on issues raised in Chapters 3 to 5 and prefaces others discussed in more depth in Chapters 7 and 9. It has shown that access to good information on both hospital and community-based activity is crucial to general practice-based purchasers. Without it, they could not cost care adequately, and lacked a reliable basis on which to contract with providers. Hospital intransigence and lack of political will due to uncertainty concerning the outcome of the general election further hampered the best efforts of pilots in the substudies. Other experiments in GP-based purchasing or commissioning (including PCGs) will need to recognize these barriers to contracting and seek cooperation from all agencies to overcome them.

This chapter has also demonstrated the importance of holding a budget, or the potential to hold a budget. Without one, general practice-based purchasers had difficulty in being taken seriously by health authorities and providers, and were not included in discussions about service planning. The budget acted as a catalyst to encourage joint working and joint solutions to some of the intractable problems of service delivery that have beset health services in developed countries. These include integration between health and social care agencies and between primary and secondary care services for people with complex problems. However, unless informal service agreements and changes to models of organization were formalized in contracts, they were unlikely to be sustainable through more difficult times. For example, good will was not enough to maintain innovative services through a resource crisis. However, if arrangements for innovative services had been enshrined in formal NHS contracts, they were much more likely to be sustained.

Finally, although general practice-based purchasers seemed to be more likely to be associated with more integrated, less traditional models of maternity care, these did not appear to produce a measurable effect sufficient to improve women's experience of care, or alter their use of resources. These findings have a number of implications. First, any straightforward expectation that giving primary care organizations responsibility for commissioning care will improve quality of patient experiences of care, or the pattern of their resource use, should be treated with caution. The presence of strong national policy (such as *Changing Childbirth* or the new NHS national service frameworks) may be equally or more important in a still largely hierarchical system such as the NHS. Second, it is important to be aware that a variety of models of service organization, and approaches to the integration of care, may be appropriate in different circumstances and local contexts and may deliver high-quality care from patients' perspectives. Service organization, or attempts at vertical integration of care, are not proxies for quality of care. It cannot be assumed that any one type of care will suit all patients. The most powerful forces shaping the experience of care may be professionals themselves and their ability to translate national policy aspirations into local services relevant to patients.

# MANAGING EMERGENCY HOSPITAL ACTIVITY

## Hugh McLeod and James Raftery

General practitioner fundholding was focused on the management of GP prescribing and elective care budgets. One of the potential attractions of total purchasing to ambitious fundholding GPs was the opportunity it presented to improve the management of their patients' demand for emergency hospital services. This could be achieved in part by the introduction of alternative care settings for some acute hospital patients, which might be not only clinically more appropriate, but also less resource intensive.

As well as offering the chance to make savings in the use of resources currently devoted to emergency care, which could be used to provide better services elsewhere, primary care involvement in the management of demand for emergency care could also benefit the wider NHS since rising emergency admissions were becoming a major problem in the 1990s. Figure 7.1 shows the increase in emergency medical and surgical admissions to NHS hospitals in England between 1989/90 and 1997/98. Medical emergency admissions increased by 32.3 per cent between 1989/90 and 1995/96, and surgical emergency admissions increased by 17.5 per cent over the same period. The consequent pressure on resources focused attention on the need to improve the management of hospital services (NHS Confederation 1997). Earlier research had shown that there was considerable potential for this (Audit Commission 1992).

While many factors influence the level of hospital activity, total purchasing gave GPs the opportunity both to directly manage their patients' emergency hospital use and to change service provision. Pilots were able to take steps to prevent emergency admissions to

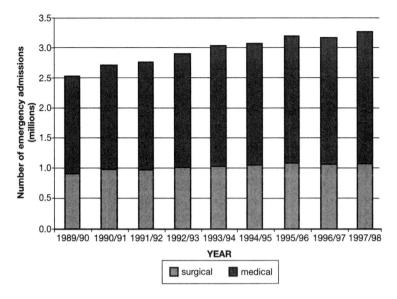

**Figure 7.1**   Emergency admissions to hospitals in England between 1989/90 and 1997/98

*Note*: The figures for 1996/97 and 1997/98 were provisional.
*Source*: Department of Health, Hospital Episode Statistics.

acute hospitals by developing services in alternative potentially more appropriate settings. In addition, as part of an aim to ensure that acute hospital beds were occupied only by patients who needed to be in an acute hospital, TPP GPs could take action to facilitate the timely discharge of their patients from acute beds.

It was expected that TPPs would purchase most, if not all, HCHS for their patients using budgets delegated to them by their local health authority and independent contracts. However, the first-wave TPPs did not all develop in line with this extended fundholding model and a diversity of commissioning models was apparent (Mays *et al.* 1998a). However, in the first live year, 31 TPPs (56 per cent) in England and Scotland did have main purchasing objectives relating to hospital services. Raftery and McLeod (1999) reported an analysis of HES and Scottish morbidity record 1 (SMR1) data for the 28 TPPs with complete activity data. This chapter focuses on the 16 TPPs (33 per cent) in England which pursued the objective of reducing acute hospital emergency admissions and/or length of stay to at least the end of the second live year, March 1998. Scottish

TPPs could not be included since the total purchasing initiative was abandoned in Scotland before the TPPs could complete their second live year. McLeod and Raftery (2000) provide further details of this study.

The hospital activity analysis was undertaken in order to establish whether the action taken by these TPPs to change hospital activity had had any impact. As 87 per cent (14 out of 16) of the TPPs attempted to influence both emergency admissions and length of stay, the change in the number of occupied bed days relating to emergency admissions in the targeted specialties and age group was chosen as an overall measure of impact. In recent years, emergency hospital admissions have increased while average length of stay has steadily decreased (Yuen 1999). In order to determine whether any change in the number of occupied bed days consumed by the patients of the TPPs could be attributed to their specific initiatives, rather than the product of these underlying trends, comparators for each TPP were used. The main comparator was all practices in the TPP's host health authority sharing the TPP's main provider.

The number of emergency admissions, the associated total number of occupied bed days and the average length of stay per finished consultant episode were analysed. Differences in the change in the number of admissions and the associated total number of occupied bed days between each TPP and its comparator were analysed assuming a Poisson distribution. Differences in the change in the mean length of stay per finished consultant episode were analysed using variances calculated directly from the data (Armitage and Berry, 1987; McLeod and Raftery 2000).

The analysis included activity from the medical and surgical specialties targeted by each TPP, and therefore varied depending on each TPP's objectives. The analysis included relevant activity from all NHS hospital providers. The TPPs' objectives, initiatives and hospital activity were explored using telephone interviews with the TPPs' project managers. The study was informed by other elements of the total purchasing national evaluation, including the surveys of contracting (Robinson *et al.* 1998; Robison *et al.* 1999) and budget-setting methods (Bevan 1997, and see Chapter 9), and the questionnaires used in the analysis of the set-up and organizational progress of the TPPs (Wyke *et al.* 1999b).

Activity in 1997/98 was compared to the comparable activity in the preparatory year, 1995/96. This approach allowed an overall assessment to be made of the progress made by the TPPs during their lifetime. However, comparisons were also made between

1995/96 and 1996/97, and between 1996/97 and 1997/98 (McLeod and Raftery 2000). Sixteen English TPPs pursued the objective of reducing acute hospital emergency admissions and/or length of stay for the whole duration of the TPP programme. Nine of the 16 TPPs were multi-practice and seven were single-practice TPPs. The mean list size of the multi-practice TPPs was 45,500 and the mean number of practices was 4.9.

## CHANGING ACUTE HOSPITAL EMERGENCY ACTIVITY

Table 7.1 shows that 11 of the 16 TPPs (69 per cent) experienced a reduction in occupied bed days which was greater than the reduction (or, in some cases, an increase) experienced by the comparator, and in each case the difference was statistically significant ($p < 0.05$).

How were these reductions in the use of hospital beds brought about? Three multi-practice TPPs reported that their main initiatives were to reduce both admissions and length of stay. Three TPPs concentrated on reducing admissions with length of stay a secondary focus, and the other three TPPs targeted length of stay while attempting to reduce admissions as a secondary objective. Generally their focus was on older medical patients, although the specialties and age groups targeted varied from geriatrics only (TPPs Cm13 and Cm4) to all medical and surgical specialties (TPP Cp2). The initiatives introduced by the nine TPPs varied in terms of scale, focus, resource requirements and start dates. Table 7.2 summarizes the action taken by these TPPs to reduce their use of acute hospital services.

Those multi-practice TPPs targeting admissions tended to increase their use of community hospitals or hospital-at-home services, while those TPPs targeting length of stay tended to introduce discharge liaison nurses or more comprehensive rehabilitation teams. In some cases, total purchasing provided a direct incentive for GPs to increase the care they provided to their patients via the use of GP beds at local community hospitals. Boxes 7.1 and 7.2 provide more information about two of the most ambitious TPPs: TPP Cm13 (Box 7.1) focused on reducing length of stay, and TPP Cm6 (Box 7.2) focused on reducing admissions.

Although the TPPs had a preparatory year, TPP Cm13 was unusual in being able to start its initiative at the beginning of the

**Table 7.1** Total purchasing pilots' targeted activity across all providers compared with local practices

| TPP type | | Comparison between 1995/96 and 1996/97 | | Comparison between 1996/97 and 1997/98 | | Comparison between 1995/96 and 1997/98 | |
|---|---|---|---|---|---|---|---|
| | | Number of TPs with relative change in the right direction[1] | Number and (%) of TPs with statistically significant change in the right direction compared to comparator | Number of TPs with relative change in the right direction[1] | Number and (%) of TPs with statistically significant change in the right direction compared to comparator | Number of TPs with relative change in the right direction[1] | Number and (%) of TPs with statistically significant change in the right direction compared to comparator |
| Occupied bed days | Multi-practice | 6 | 5 (55.6) | 6 | 6 (66.7) | 8 | 7 (77.8) |
| | Single-practice | 4 | 2 (28.6) | 6 | 6 (85.7) | 5 | 4 (57.1) |
| | All | 10 | 7 (43.8) | 12 | 12 (75.0) | 13 | 11 (68.8) |
| Admissions | Multi-practice | 6 | 0 (0.0) | 4 | 0 (0.0) | 8 | 1 (11.1) |
| | Single-practice | 3 | 0 (0.0) | 5 | 0 (0.0) | 3 | 1 (14.3) |
| | All | 9 | 0 (0.0) | 9 | 0 (0.0) | 11 | 2 (12.5) |

Note:
[1] The number of TPPs with a greater decrease, or smaller increase, in targeted occupied bed days or admissions compared to the comparator.

**Table 7.2**  Main emergency services initiatives introduced by the multi-practice total purchasing pilots with relevant main objectives

| Pilot | Cm13 | Cm15 | Cm5 | Cm6 | Cm2 | Cm4 | Cp2 | Cm18 | Cm11 |
|---|---|---|---|---|---|---|---|---|---|
| Increased use of GP beds at local community hospital | ✓ | | | | ✓ | ✓ | | ✓ | ✓ |
| Liaison nurse(s) facilitated early discharge/admission prevention | ✓ | | | ✓ | | | | | ✓ |
| Introduced dedicated rehabilitation team | ✓ | ✓ | | | | | | | |
| Increased use of community nurses or hospital-at-home care | | | ✓ | ✓ | | | | ✓ | |
| Improved out-of-hours GP cover | | | ✓ | | | | ✓ | | |
| Facilitated the introduction of a medical assessment unit at the main acute hospital | | | ✓ | | ✓ | | | | |

first live year. The other multi-practice TPPs generally initiated action in the second half of 1996/97.

Seven single-practice TPPs persisted with the objective of reducing acute hospital emergency activity for the duration of the two live years of the project. Their mean list size was 12,600. The focus of these TPPs divided between main initiatives to reduce admissions or length of stay. Compared to the multi-practice TPPs, the focus was not so frequently on older medical patients, although the specialties and age groups targeted varied from older medical patients only (TPPs Cm1 and Cm8) to all medical and surgical specialties (TPPs Cm9, Cm10 and Cm12). Table 7.3 summarizes the action taken by these TPPs to reduce their use of acute hospital services. The most frequently cited initiatives were the use of discharge liaison nurses and nursing home beds.

All nine multi-practice TPPs attempted to a greater or lesser extent to reduce both admissions and length of stay. Therefore the number of bed days was chosen as the principal measure of their

---

**Box 7.1    Case study of a total purchasing pilot with a main objective of reducing length of stay for acute hospital emergency admissions**

**Initiative**
In April 1996 the TPP appointed a utilization nurse who facilitated the early discharge of acute geriatric admissions at its main provider to a TPP-instigated local community hospital rehabilitation unit. The TPP funded 16 beds and the health authority funded two beds. The unit was seen as a collaborative venture between the TPP, health authority and both acute and community trusts. The team staffing the unit included two consultant geriatricians and two GPs from the TPP. In 1997/98, 199 TPP patients were admitted to the rehabilitation unit following early discharge from the main acute trust and 35 TPP patients were admitted to the rehabilitation unit as direct admissions. The latter would have been acute geriatric admissions in the absence of the community facility.

**Resource implications**
The TPP planned to fund early discharge to a community hospital rehabilitation unit by using length of stay-sensitive pricing at the acute provider. In 1996/97, the acute provider agreed to length of stay pricing bands for geriatric activity despite arguments with the TPP during the contract negotiations. The community hospital activity was covered by a simple block contract of £397,800 in 1997/98. The TPP estimated that it had reduced its acute hospital expenditure by at least £470,000.

**HCHS budgetary outturn**
The TPP reported that it stayed within its budget in 1997/98 and that its budget has been decreased towards a target capitation allocation.

---

impact in terms of the relative change over time between TPPs and comparators. Seven of the nine TPPs experienced a reduction in their total number of occupied bed days for the targeted activity between 1995/96 and 1997/98, such that the reduction compared favourably to the change experienced by the local comparator and the difference in change was statistically significant (Table 7.4).

**Box 7.2   Case study of a total purchasing pilot with a main objective of reducing the number of acute hospital emergency admissions**

**Initiative**
In August 1996 the TPP appointed a discharge planning coordinator who led an intermediate care team from January 1997. The team included dedicated nurses and GP involvement. Most intermediate care was purchased from a pre-existing health authority-wide hospital-at-home service. Nursing home beds were also used and access to the health authority's community nursing teams was maintained. In 1997/98, the number of beds purchased by the TPP increased from six to eight and the number of project nurses was increased to four. The TPP reported that 222 admissions were avoided in 1997/98. Most referrals to intermediate care were made by the TPP's GPs. An increase in intermediate care activity during the last quarter of 1997/98 was aided by the liaison/discharge planning nurses employed by the TPP's main two acute hospitals as part of winter pressures initiatives.

**Resource implications**
Funding for the initiative was planned from expected savings in acute hospital expenditure and growth funds. The TPP wanted to contract with the main acute trust using length of stay pricing. The initiative was intended to be cost-neutral in the short term. In the longer term, the TPP anticipated that some savings would be made from lower acute or intermediate care service utilization by 'revolving door' patients (i.e. those with repeat admissions over a long period). The TPP reported direct expenditure on the initiative of £350,673 plus £97,962 hospital costs for patients subsequently admitted to hospital in 1997/98. The TPP estimated a saving of £75,661 on acute hospital expenditure as a result of the initiative on the basis of average cost pricing. The TPP reported that it had not been possible to reduce hospital expenditure at average cost and that past spend at the main acute trust had been maintained. The TPP noted the importance of growth funds and that winter pressures funding had had to be used to pump-prime the initiative. In 1997/98, the main acute provider agreed to a small length of stay rebate for early discharged cases.

**HCHS budgetary outturn**
The TPP identified its success in having operated within a capitation budget in a health authority that was significantly over capitation, rather than in terms of the estimated saving for the specific initiative. The TPP reported an underspend of £390,000 (1.1%) on its budget, of which £300,400 was used to offset an overspend in the first live year. Growth funds came from the increase in the TPP's population of 2.4% between 1996/97 and 1997/98, and the fact that the TPP's budget was moved closer to its capitation target which was above the level of historical spend.

**Table 7.3**   Main emergency services initiatives introduced by the single-practice total purchasing pilots with relevant main objectives

| Pilot | Cp1 | Cm12 | Cm14 | Cm9 | Cm8 | Cm10 | Cm1 |
|---|---|---|---|---|---|---|---|
| Increased use of GP beds at local community hospital | | | | | | ✓ | |
| Liaison nurse(s) facilitated early discharge/admission prevention | ✓ | ✓ | ✓ | ✓ | ✓ | | |
| Introduced dedicated rehabilitation team | | | ✓ | ✓ | | | |
| Increased use of community nurses or hospital-at-home care | ✓ | | | ✓ | | | ✓ |
| Facilitated the introduction of a medical assessment unit at the main acute hospital | | | | ✓ | | | |
| Introduced a social care coordinator or social services link worker | | | | ✓ | | | |
| Introduced use of nursing home beds | ✓ | ✓ | ✓ | ✓ | | | ✓ |

An analysis of the number of relevant admissions found that eight of the nine TPPs experienced a greater reduction or smaller increase in admissions compared to the local comparators, but that, with one exception, the differences in change were not significant.

**Table 7.4** Multi-practice total purchasing pilots and local comparator practices: changes in the number of occupied bed days in the targeted specialities between the preparatory year and the second 'live' year

| Pilot | Total emergency occupied bed days in targeted specialities across all providers in 1995/96 | | % change in total occupied bed days in targeted specialities between 1995/96 and 1997/98 | | Difference in % change between TPP and comparator with 95% CIs |
|---|---|---|---|---|---|
| | TPP | Comparator | TPP | Comparator | |
| Cm13 | 4628 | 46226 | -27.1 | 2.9 | 30.0 (26.6 to 33.6) |
| Cm15 | 8578 | 120111 | -17.6 | 2.8 | 20.4 (17.7 to 23.1) |
| Cm5 | 22418 | 16042 | -7.0 | 11.1 | 18.1 (15.2 to 21.1) |
| Cm6 | 17171 | 35026 | -22.2 | -5.8 | 16.4 (14.1 to 18.7) |
| Cm2 | 11745 | 25744 | -11.7 | -0.8 | 10.9 (8.0 to 13.8) |
| Cm4 | 18624 | 23860 | -10.6 | 0.1 | 10.7 (8.1 to 13.3) |
| Cm18 | 16605 | 32175 | -8.6 | -2.6 | 5.9 (3.4 to 8.5) |
| Cp2 | 10109 | 157492 | -3.0 | -2.1 | 0.9 (-3.7 to 1.9) |
| Cm11 | 3430 | 10707 | 46.2 | 16.9 | -29.3 (-36.3 to -22.3) |

*Note:*
See McLeod and Raftery (2000) for comparisons between 1995/96 and 1996/97, and 1996/97 and 1997/98.

All nine TPPs and their comparators experienced reductions in the mean length of stay per finished consultant episode between 1995/96 and 1997/98 (McLeod and Raftery 2000). TPP Cm13 experienced the largest reduction in length of stay for the targeted specialty. The TPPs started from different positions relative to their comparators: for example, the mean length of stay for TPPs Cm15 and Cm5 was significantly higher than that of their comparators in 1995/96.

Although the differences in change in the number of targeted admissions and mean length of stay between TPPs and comparators were not usually statistically significant, the differences indicate the contribution made by changes in admissions and length of stay to the changes in occupied bed days.

Six of the seven multi-practice TPPs found to be successful in their targeted specialties were also successful when analysis was repeated for occupied bed days across all medical and surgical specialties.

Six of the seven single-practice TPPs attempted to a greater or lesser extent to reduce both admissions and length of stay. Five of the seven TPPs experienced a reduction in the total number of occupied bed days for the targeted activity, which in each case compared favourably to the change experienced by the comparator (Table 7.5). In four of these five cases the difference in change was statistically significant.

An analysis of the relevant admissions found that three of the seven single-practice TPPs experienced a reduction in the number of emergency admissions in the targeted specialties between 1995/96 and 1997/98 compared to the local practices. The difference in change in admissions was statistically significant for one of these three TPPs. Six of the seven single-practice TPPs and all seven comparators experienced reductions in the mean length of stay per finished consultant episode between 1995/96 and 1997/98. Five of the seven TPPs experienced a greater reduction in mean length of stay per finished consultant episode compared to the comparators, although in each case the differences in change were not significant.

### Resource implications of changes in hospital activity

Since NHS contracts vary in the degree to which total cost reflects activity (Raftery *et al.* 1996), the ability of the TPPs to reduce their expenditure on emergency services through reducing activity depended on their type of contract. Pilots with aims to change their

**Table 7.5** Single-practice total purchasing pilots and local comparator practices: changes in the number of occupied bed days in the targeted specialities between the preparatory year and the second live year

| Pilot | Total emergency occupied bed days in targeted specialities across all providers in 1995/96 | | % change in total occupied bed days in targeted specialities between 1995/96 and 1997/98 | | Difference in % change between TPP and comparator with 95% CIs |
|---|---|---|---|---|---|
| | TPP | Comparator | TPP | Comparator | |
| Cp1 | 2234 | 87397 | −29.8 | −4.6 | 25.2 (20.6 to 29.8) |
| Cm12 | 7141 | 87016 | −18.1 | −3.3 | 14.8 (11.9 to 17.8) |
| Cm14 | 2126 | 110793 | −12.0 | −1.2 | 10.8 (5.3 to 16.3) |
| Cm8 | 2598 | 20513 | −5.7 | 1.3 | 7.0 (1.5 to 12.6) |
| Cm9 | 2735 | 55788 | −6.1 | −4.9 | 1.2 (−3.9 to 6.4) |
| Cm1 | 3938 | 17400 | 5.1 | 1.4 | −3.7 (−8.7 to 1.4) |
| Cm10 | 5124 | 55788 | 19.9 | −4.9 | −24.8 (−20.2 to −29.4) |

*Note:*
See McLeod and Raftery (2000) for comparisons between 1995/96 and 1996/97, and 1996/97 and 1997/98.

use of hospital services typically wanted to use contracts with providers that would closely link changes in activity to changes in funding. The characteristics of emergency activity are such that the TPPs generally based their contracts on the 'cost and volume' or 'sophisticated block' contracts used by health authorities (Table 7.6), rather than the 'cost per case' contracts used by standard fundholders for elective activity (Robinson *et al.* 1998; Robison *et al.* 1999).

In general, cost and volume contracts (and to some extent sophisticated block contracts) allow for variances in forecast

**Table 7.6** Multi-practice total purchasing pilots contracting arrangements and budgetary outturn in 1997/98

| Pilot | Contracting status | Main acute contract: type | Main acute contract: currency | HCHS budget outturn |
|---|---|---|---|---|
| Cm13 | Independent | Cost and volume | Bed days | 1.1% (£390,000) underspent |
| Cm6 | Independent | Sophisticated block | Finished consultant episodes | Stayed with budget |
| Cm15 | Independent | Sophisticated block | Finished consultant episodes | 0.6% (£60,000) overspent |
| Cm2 | Independent | Cost and volume | Finished consultant episodes | Stayed with budget |
| Cm4 | Independent | Cost and volume | Admissions | 0.5% (£90,000) underspent |
| Cm5 | Independent | Simple block | Finished consultant episodes | Underspent |
| Cp2 | Joint with health authority | Sophisticated block | Finished consultant episodes | Budget not set |
| Cm18 | Independent | Cost and volume | Finished consultant episodes | 0.5% (£90,000) underspent |
| Cm11 | Independent | Sophisticated block | Bed days | Overspent (budget increased) |

activity to be accompanied by changes in funding, dependent on a marginal cost tariff applied to prices based on finished consultant episodes at average specialty cost (Raftery *et al.* 1996). The TPPs found it difficult to use this contracting mechanism to move resources away from acute hospitals in line with their expectations. In general, acute trusts sought to maintain their income and the TPPs found themselves unable to negotiate new contract currencies, such as those based on admissions or bed days, which would more closely relate changes in activity to changes in funding.

Eight of the nine multi-practice TPPs had delegated budgets and directly purchased care using independent contracts. Of the five multi-practice TPPs targeting admissions, the expenditure implications of changes in hospital activity and growth in non-hospital activity for TPP Cm4 were minimal (because the initiative was contained within one combined acute and community health services trust). None of the other TPPs funded their initiatives entirely from contracted reductions in expenditure on acute hospital activity. Pilot Cm6 utilized growth moneys (Box 7.2). Pilots Cm2 and Cm18 benefited from health authority winter pressures moneys, and TPP Cm5 received funds from its health authority and local authority social services department. These five TPPs reported that they stayed within their budgets, or made savings, in 1997/98.

TPP Cm6 was the most ambitious of these TPPs (Box 7.2). It employed new staff and purchased new intermediate care services. However, the TPP's ability to proceed with its plans depended on the availability of growth funding supplemented by winter pressures funds, and not on withdrawing sufficient funds from its acute providers through contract renegotiations. The TPP's project manager stressed that funds could not be released from acute hospitals without closing wards or making people redundant. The issue of whether to close acute beds had to be managed at a strategic level over a wider geographical area than that covered by the TPP and over a five- to ten-year horizon. Hence, finding funds that did not destabilize the hospital had been critical to the success of this TPP. Indeed, the TPP reported that the acute provider's reluctance to agree length of stay-sensitive pricing had contributed to its targeting admissions rather than length of stay.

Pilot Cm2 supported a health authority-led development to introduce a medical assessment unit (MAU) at its main acute provider. Following assessment, appropriate patients (whether or not they were covered by the TPP) were transferred to a local community hospital rather than being admitted to the acute hospital.

This extra community hospital activity was funded through winter pressures money. This money was also used to introduce a community health services trust-managed hospital-at-home service. As a result, the change in services used by the TPP was not funded through alterations to existing contracts.

Pilot Cm5 supported the introduction of a MAU at its main provider and contributed a third of the funding for a social services assessment worker. However, major initiatives to provide intermediate care services were not undertaken. The main acute contract was a 'simple block' since the TPP's strategy was to promote the best use of resources within the main provider, rather than to transfer funds from the hospital.

In 1997/98, the intermediate care project run by TPP Cm18 was funded in part by winter pressures resources. The TPP reported that its main acute hospital trust had supported the TPP's aims, but refused to introduce prices that were sensitive to length of stay. The TPP project manager expressed the view that its main acute trust would not necessarily have lost income by agreeing to length of stay-sensitive pricing, because the TPP's action would have released beds which could have been used for other funded work such as waiting list initiatives. The project manager stated that the TPP's inability to introduce length of stay-sensitive pricing meant that it had not been able to use the independent contracting mechanism as intended. The TPP's parent health authority was interested in the TPP, but not to the extent of being prepared to provide active support if this meant shifting resources out of the hospital.

Pilot Cm4 aimed to decrease hospital geriatric medicine admissions by agreeing to an increase in the financial incentive to the TPP's GPs to use community hospital GP beds. Both the acute and community hospitals were part of the same trust and the proposed change in activity was not intended to result in significant financial savings for the TPP. The potential for savings was limited both because of the increase in cost to the TPP of GP bed admissions (which covered the cost of the higher financial incentive to the GPs) and the relatively high marginal cost rate of 35 per cent applied to changes in activity. As noted above, activity did not change in the intended direction, presumably because of the non-availability of some GP beds for part of 1997/98.

Three multi-practice TPPs focused on reducing length of stay. Pilot Cm13 (Box 7.1) was the only one of the nine TPPs able to introduce length of stay-sensitive pricing, such that it could transfer substantial resources from the acute sector and operate as intended within a capitation budget. While TPP Cm11 also succeeded in negotiating the introduction of length of stay-sensitive pricing for targeted acute activity in the first live year, the experience was unsatisfactory. Although the TPP reported that it had secured a more favourable pricing arrangement with its main acute provider in 1997/98, it was unable to release enough resources to cover the increase in community hospital activity. The major source of funding for its early discharge initiative came from a negotiated increase in the TPP's budget, rather than a transfer of funds from its main acute provider. TPP Cm15 was unable to agree length of stay-sensitive pricing at its main acute provider in either live year, but had sufficient growth moneys available to fund its own intermediate care project.

TPP Cp2 did not receive a delegated budget, but attempted to influence health authority commissioning, and was therefore comparable to a level 1 English PCG. Although the TPP concentrated mainly on its work to reduce acute emergency admissions in 1997/98, its principal project (out-of-hours GP cover) was cut back in line with the health authority's wishes. The TPP reported frustration at not being able to negotiate a delegated budget as intended.

Five of the seven single-practice TPPs held 'cost and volume' contracts with their main acute provider in 1997/98. Table 7.7 shows that six of the seven TPPs received a budget in 1997/98 and five of these TPPs reported that they had stayed within their budget (after taking into account fundholder savings).

The saving of over £500,000 (5.7 per cent) on its HCHS budget reported by TPP Cm8 was exceptional. The TPP's project manager noted that its budget had not been too high, but that the TPP had been very efficient. However, the survey of 1997/98 budget allocations (see Chapter 9) indicated that this TPP's per capita allocation was the highest of the 34 TPPs for which data were provided.

**Interpreting the analysis**

The change in the number of occupied bed days relating to emergency admissions in the targeted specialties and age group, compared to a comparator, was chosen as the overall measure of the TPPs' impact. The use of relative change in occupied bed days provided a single overall measure of change, and is appropriate because most of the TPPs (14 out of 16) attempted to influence both emergency admissions and length of stay.

**Table 7.7**  Single-practice total purchasing pilots contracting arrangements and budgetary outturn in 1997/98

| Pilot | Contracting status | Main acute contract: type | Main acute contract: currency | HCHS budget outturn |
|---|---|---|---|---|
| Cp1 | Joint with health authority | Cost and volume | Finished consultant episodes | Budget not set |
| Cm12 | Independent | Sophisticated block | Finished consultant episodes | £8000 overspend offset by previous fundholder savings |
| Cm14 | Independent | Cost per case | Bed days | 1.2% (£35,000) overspend offset by fundholder savings |
| Cm8 | Independent | Cost and volume | Finished consultant episodes | 5.7% (£500,000) underspend |
| Cm9 | Independent | Cost and volume | Finished consultant episodes | Underspent |
| Cm1 | Independent | Cost and volume | Finished consultant episodes | 1.1% (£72,200) underspend |
| Cm10 | Independent | Cost and volume | Finished consultant episodes | Not known by TPP |

The use of local practices as the main comparator for each TPP was intended to control for differences in data quality between different hospital providers, and to provide a comparator population which, due to its proximity, could to some extent be assumed to be demographically similar. The TPPs tended to include practices from the early fundholding waves, and therefore tended to be relatively large and well organized (Audit Commission 1996). So while the TPPs may have differed from other local practices due to their fundholding experience, they shared hospital providers and had similar population characteristics.

The analysis included the activity targeted by each TPP, and consequently varied depending on the TPP's objectives. In order to assess the TPP's impact on aggregate emergency activity, a secondary analysis compared change in occupied bed days across all medical and surgical specialties. Six of the seven multi-practice TPPs, and three of the four single-practice TPPs found to be successful in the targeted analysis were also successful when the analysis was applied to all medical and surgical specialties. This finding suggests that although the TPPs generally focused attention on a subset of emergency activity, success in the targeted area was associated with a desirable impact at an aggregate level.

Using the same main outcome measure criteria – but with the comparison made with all other practices in the host health authority rather than just local practices – produced the same results. However, when all medical and surgical activity was substituted for the targeted activity, one additional multi-practice TPP was found to be successful. When the main outcome measure criteria were applied to activity at the TPP's main provider only, the analysis found that fewer TPPs were successful (56 per cent and 43 per cent respectively). However, this comparison is of limited value due the variation between the TPPs in the proportion of total activity taking place at their main provider (Raftery and McLeod 1999). Overall, these analyses show similar trends and support the other results.

### The impact of total purchasing pilot status

Unlike GP fundholding, which operated within a statutory framework, total purchasing had pilot status only and TPPs operated with little central guidance. While some TPPs were allowed desirable discretion to experiment, the price paid by others was considerable. This had a significant bearing on their ability to shift resources out of hospitals. The absence of central guidance relating to the budget-setting and contracting arrangements for the TPPs had serious consequences in some cases. Health authorities did not agree budgets in a timely manner (see Chapter 9), and budget-setting problems affected the agreement of contracts. The 1996/97 contracting survey found that 36 per cent (10 out of 28) of TPPs with independent contracts reported difficulties in obtaining agreement on all of their contracts because of budget-setting problems (Robinson *et al.* 1998). In the second live year, the proportion of TPPs in this position had only fallen to 22 per cent (6 out of 27) (Robison *et al.* 1999). The delays in agreeing budgets with health authorities were to some extent a consequence of the lack of obligation placed on health authorities for timely action. Similarly, NHS providers had no obligation to cooperate with the TPPs' aspirations to change the usual contract arrangements between health authorities and providers in order to link changes in activity more closely to changes in funding.

## The impact of the political climate

Chapter 5 described the many factors affecting the environment in which the TPPs operated. A key factor influencing the TPPs' ability to pursue their objectives of changing emergency hospital services was undoubtedly the fundamental change in political climate during the lifetime of total purchasing. In 1994, total purchasing was seen as a logical extension of the Conservative government's preferred purchasing model. But within a month of the beginning of the second live year there came a change in government and the inevitable end of fundholding, and this made the future of devolved budgetary responsibility seem bleak. This change in climate had a profoundly negative impact on the TPPs' ability to secure cooperation for change from both acute providers and host health authorities.

The story of how one single-practice TPP – active in promoting early discharge in 1996/97 – came off the rails in 1997 illustrates both the difficulties experienced by several TPPs due to the impact of political change and the loss of key impetus. The lead GP reported that in May 1997 its nurse coordinator had been 'poached' by the local acute trust as her work was seen as so valuable that the hospital wanted her to work for them. A new nurse coordinator was not appointed until October/November, and then, following the publication of the White Paper *The New NHS* in December 1997, the TPP resigned from total purchasing because it realized that single-practice fundholding and total purchasing would not survive. In contrast, another single-practice TPP which did pursue its objectives reported that the practice used fundholder savings to keep their discharge nurse in post during 1998/99, and that the TPP's experience and staff had been embraced by the successor PCG in 1999/2000.

## Contracting and resource implications

In order to reduce acute hospital activity, it was necessary for the TPPs to develop alternative services, such as community nursing teams or community hospital general practice beds facilitated by discharge liaison nurses. At the same time, the TPPs believed that it was necessary to fund this new activity by reducing their expenditure on acute hospital services. Consequently, in general, the TPPs attempted to negotiate contract prices based on admission numbers or length of stay, rather than finished consultant episodes, in order to link changes in activity more closely to changes in funding. The TPPs were usually unsuccessful in changing contract arrangements and, with a few exceptions, they reported that health authorities did not intervene to support them. This predicament constrained initiatives. In practice, most of the 16 TPPs obtained other sources of funding, such as winter pressures resources, to realize their goals. As noted above, the TPPs' project managers held differing views on the ability of acute hospitals to respond to the financial implications resulting from TPP-initiated changes in service use.

Total purchasers' contracts did facilitate quality improvements (Robison *et al.* 1999), and in this respect the TPPs came close to achieving the change 'in the power relationship between the fundholding GP and the provider' (Goodwin 1998), which was manifest in the shorter waiting times secured by fundholding practices (Dowling 1997). However, managing emergency activity is fundamentally different from elective activity. While fundholders had the potential to move activity and income away from hospital providers that would not cooperate, total purchasers were constrained by the characteristics of non-elective health care and the absence of a statutory framework to enforce their contracting objectives.

Even if total purchasing had existed within a statutory framework, it would still have been fundamentally different from fundholding, which was specifically designed for the purchasing of elective services. Emergency activity is different, and so total purchasing had to be different. Despite successful initiatives to reduce acute activity, ultimately GPs are not able to choose where or when most of their patients will be admitted in an emergency. For most emergency activity, the acute hospitals have a captive audience of patients and GPs. So the TPPs' ability to force change through straightforward contracting tactics, such as threatening to change provider, was limited.

It is not surprising, therefore, that the most common service development linked to independent contracting reported by TPPs in 1996/97 was a change to discharge arrangements, 'which hinges on the use of "length of stay" . . . sensitive contract currencies to permit [a] shift of resources' (Robinson 1998: 19). However, in practice, the hospitals had no obligation to agree to change from the common NHS practice of pricing activity on the basis of finished consultant episodes at average specialty cost.

### Implications for primary care groups

Both fundholding and total purchasing provided opportunities for GPs to change their use of hospital services. PCGs are intended to offer similar opportunities. However, the total purchasing and fundholding experience was that most TPPs did not attempt to change hospital activity, and many PCG GPs may choose not to follow in the footsteps of the innovators discussed in this chapter. The new financial incentives are intended to be 'sufficiently attractive to health professionals and PCGs members to provide motivation to perform well' (NHS Executive 1998c: 22). While their effectiveness based on the fundholding experience remains equivocal, the use of incentives is itself contentious (Majeed and Malcolm 1999) and the burden it will place on setting budgets at practice level is formidable (Smith 1999).

Therefore, the difficulty experienced by some TPPs in using contracts to manage a transfer of resources away from secondary care may exist into the future. Guidance for the new longer term service agreements to be used in the NHS allows for the development of complex contracts. These could be service-based at sub-hospital level and use health care resource groups (a British version of diagnosis-related groups) rather than finished consultant episodes for pricing. In addition, financial incentives for both providers and commissioners to manage activity levels could be incorporated. For example, 'It might be agreed that up to a given threshold the PCG would bear the cost of higher than expected [emergency] referrals, while the NHS Trust would bear the cost of higher than planned Accident and Emergency admissions' (NHS Executive 1998a: 17). The TPPs would have welcomed this approach to service agreements, because they commonly wanted to strengthen the link between activity and funding levels.

However, the overall strategy is to combine a 'large element of confirmed core funding' (NHS Executive 1998a: 16) over a number of years with sufficient financial flexibility at the margin to enable the operation of incentives and penalties. This compromise is problematic. Financial contract negotiations are mainly concerned with marginal resources, whether they are focused on the allocation of growth funds, or the consequence of initiatives to change hospital activity (Dawson and Goddard 1998). So the allocation of core funding is irrelevant to these negotiations (Dawson and Goddard 1998). At the margin, hospital providers may still find that their interests (in terms of, say, reference cost league tables) are best served by increasing or maintaining activity (Dawson and Street 1998), rather than agreeing to release resources related to PCGs' plans for activity changes. In the long term, cost-effective commissioning requires decreases in hospital activity to be matched by reductions in funding at average cost. The advent of longer-term service agreements may not create incentives for NHS hospitals to take the long term action required to bring about change to average costs.

## CONCLUSIONS

*The New NHS* White Paper acknowledges total purchasing as one of the models on which PCGs have been developed (Secretary of State for Health 1997). The experience of the TPPs is important because, to some extent, their role anticipated PCGs. The total purchasing initiative showed that it is possible for GPs to work successfully on one of the most intractable problems in the NHS: how to manage emergency hospital demand. Total purchasing 'commissioning' resulted in a change in the use of acute hospital emergency services in the minority of TPPs that chose to make it a sustained priority. In general, this entailed the introduction of alternative care arrangements for elderly patients, which in turn reflected the use of locally available facilities. In principle, this suggests that PCGs/PCTs with relevant priorities could make an important contribution to managing rising emergency hospital use in the NHS.

However, given that most TPPs did not attempt consistently to influence hospital activity, many GPs may be content to function at PCG level 1 (i.e. simply advising the health authority), rather than take on the challenging responsibilities of managing hospital use. Although level 2 PCGs are similar to the TPPs discussed in this chapter with regard to their budgetary responsibility for a proportion of hospital services, they are not volunteer groups of experienced fundholders. In addition, total purchasing was demanding for GPs who had to devote considerable time and energy to it, and be prepared to accept new responsibilities for the local health system. Therefore, even if PCGs have clear objectives relating to secondary care, it will take time for them to change hospital use.

The total purchasing experience suggests that the range of intermediate services initiated by the TPPs may only be sustainable if appropriate resources are released from the acute hospital sector. The extent to which PCGs beyond level 1 will emulate the early changes to hospital service use made by the TPPs in this chapter will be greatly influenced by the level of cooperation they receive from acute hospitals and health authorities.

Purchasers wishing to transfer activity from acute hospitals should aim to release funds at average cost. However, in the short term, such as the life of total purchasing, hospitals tend to argue that they can only be expected to lose income at marginal cost, unless they use released capacity to generate additional income. In practice, most of the successful TPPs obtained other sources of funding which enabled them to make changes without taking money out of their local acute hospitals. It remains to be seen whether the current planning arrangements in the English NHS – in which health authorities lead the development and implementation of health improvement programmes – will facilitate appropriate funding arrangements for initiatives to reduce emergency activity at acute hospitals.

# 8

# THE MANAGEMENT AND TRANSACTION COSTS OF TOTAL PURCHASING

## Andrew Street, Michael Place and John Posnett

Fundholding was designed to increase general practitioner aware-ness of the opportunity costs of the resources they used when they referred their patients or prescribed for them. It was hoped that, if budgetary and clinical responsibility could be combined, GPs would contain treatment costs and use resources more efficiently. A primary care-led NHS, in which decisions about the purchase and provision of services were taken as close as possible to patients, was expected to be more effective and responsive than a system domi-nated by health authority purchasing (NHS Executive 1995). By 1996, fundholding had covered more than 50 per cent of the popu-lation in England (Department of Health 1996a). However, despite periodic revisions to the eligibility criteria for fundholding, it was unlikely that it would cover the entire population. It was introduced with considerable additional funding, which both encouraged par-ticipation in the scheme and opposition to it, on the grounds of the inequity as a 'two-tier' service and the costs of devolving budgetary responsibility to practices (Dixon 1994; National Audit Office 1995; Bevan 1998). Efforts to encourage increased GP participation in the commissioning process would have to consider forms of involvement acceptable to those GPs opposed to fundholding. And in the context of general concern about management costs in the NHS, less costly alternatives to fundholding were desirable.

Total purchasing was the most ambitious of the proposals for extending GP-based commissioning. Since they were mostly organ-ized on the basis of groups of practices, TPPs had greater potential than fundholders to take on more of the commissioning responsibilities that had traditionally resided with health authorities. Furthermore, by combining responsibility across practices, it was possible that TPPs would be able to operate more effectively and efficiently than single-practice fundholders. In particular, it was hoped that by sharing management functions, TPPs would require lower management support than the mixed model of fundholding alongside health authority commissioning which had preceded them.

However, when the TPPs were created there was little on which to assess their likely management costs. The problem was compounded by the formal separation of fundholding from the additional functions associated with total purchasing. Within TPPs, responsibility for purchasing services covered by the fundholding budget, including elective surgery and outpatient care, remained with the individual practices. Fundholding management allowances were supposed to cover the costs of commissioning these services. At the TPP's discretion, total purchasing covered potentially all the rest of the hospital and community services, including A&E care. The cost of managing this additional responsibility was funded from a total purchasing management allowance awarded directly to the TPP, rather than to its individual practices. Allowances for these costs were negotiated between TPPs and their local health authority. But, in the absence of formal guidance and faced with uncertainty about the cost associated with managing the particular services devolved from the health authority to the TPP, there was no reason to believe that the allocation would reflect the true management input required. As part of the national evaluation of the total purchasing experiment, it was considered important to assess this input directly, by detailing and costing the management activities involved in running TPPs.

The research aimed to answer two policy questions. First, would there be sufficient incentive for GPs to cooperate fully with the aims of the TPP? Practice-based fundholding had incorporated a clear incentive: any savings realized from managing the fundholding budget could be reinvested to make improvements to the practice. In contrast, because any savings arising from total purchasing would be distributed among a group of practices, the incentive to collaborate may have been diluted. This question is addressed more fully in Chapter 10.

Second, would it be possible to reduce overall management costs by encouraging practices to act jointly as purchasers? This second question is the main topic of the current chapter. However, because of the way TPPs were established, only a partial answer could be provided through empirical research into how TPPs operated. The reason for this was that, as mentioned, the management of services covered by fundholding remained outside the responsibility of the TPP and separately funded. Hence, the incentive and opportunity for sharing management resources across practices was constrained. It was only with the advent of PCGs and the attendant elimination of the artificial separation of fundholding from total purchasing that a common pool, comprising all primary care management support, was likely to be observed. Nevertheless, evidence about the costs of managing TPPs provides a solid basis for considering the likely management costs of PCGs. The majority of this chapter describes the management and transaction costs associated with total purchasing. The analysis identifies the main cost drivers associated with co-operative working across practices. This forms the basis for considering the likely costs of organizing commissioning at PCG level, taking into account the pooling of practice-based purchasing activity and the transfer of functions from health authorities.

## MANAGEMENT AND TRANSACTION COSTS OF TOTAL PURCHASING PILOTS

Total purchasing management allowances were negotiated to cover the additional managerial infrastructure, over and above that of fundholding, such as a total purchasing management team, office facilities, and compensation to GPs to cover their absence from general practice. However, the costs of total purchasing were not borne by the TPP alone. The local health authority had to commit resources both to establishing the projects and to monitoring their progress. Furthermore, costs were incurred as a result of the contracting process. These 'transaction costs' were borne by the TPP and the providers with which they negotiated contracts. The evaluation was designed to capture these wider costs wherever they fell.

Data were collected from seven projects, including a second-wave TPP. Reflecting the organizational diversity among all first- and second-wave TPPs, the sample included single-practice and multi-practice projects, a mix of projects with and without a total purchasing manager, and projects with between one and four NHS providers in the vicinity (Table 8.1). Full details of the method and

**Table 8.1**   Sample total purchasing pilots in the transaction costs study

| TPP | Number of practices | Project-specific manager | Nearby NHS providers |
|-----|---------------------|--------------------------|----------------------|
| A | Multiple | Manager | 4 |
| B | Single | Manager | 2 |
| C | Single | No manager | 1 |
| D | Multiple | Manager | 2 |
| E | Multiple | Manager | 3 |
| F | Multiple | No manager | 1 |
| G | Multiple | Manager | 4 |

results are provided elsewhere (Place *et al.* 1998) while a summary of the findings is provided here.

### Total incremental costs

Details of the total management and transaction costs of total purchasing over and above (i.e. incremental to) fundholding are presented in Table 8.2. In the preparatory year, the average total incremental cost per project amounted to £111,000 and to £2.68 per capita. Costs increased in the first live year to £116,000 per project and £2.85 per capita, but fell in the second live year to £91,000 per project and £2.23 per capita.

Per capita costs converged over time. In the preparatory year, these ranged from £1.38 to £4.88, with the highest cost project incurring costs three and half times those of the lowest cost project. By the second live year, the difference was less extreme, with the lowest cost TPP incurring per capita costs slightly more than half those of the highest cost TPP. Interestingly, convergence came from both directions, with the highest cost TPPs reducing their costs as lower cost TPPs increased theirs.

There is no simple explanation for the change in costs over the three-year period. The increase in the first live year was relatively uniform, with only one TPP having lower costs than in the preparatory year. This pattern reflected a change in emphasis from establishing the TPP to operational activities, best exemplified by running clinical subgroups, which drew on a greater number of people than had been involved in the preparatory year. In the second live year many of these activities were scaled back. In some cases, the intensity of effort witnessed in the first live year was no longer considered necessary, either because the group's purpose

**Table 8.2** Total incremental transaction costs of total purchasing over fundholding

| TPP | Population | Preparation year 1995/96 Total £ | Preparation year 1995/96 Per capita £ | First live year 1996/97 Total £ | First live year 1996/97 Per capita £ | Second live year 1997/98 Total £ | Second live year 1997/98 Per capita £ |
|---|---|---|---|---|---|---|---|
| A | 31,804 | 79,197 | 2.49 | 79,609 | 2.72 | 50,247 | 1.75 |
| B | 30,000 | 76,854 | 2.56 | 101,900 | 3.07 | 87,793 | 2.62 |
| C | 12,943 | 63,182 | 4.88 | 45,581 | 3.52 | 37,265 | 2.87 |
| D | 70,000 | 100,366 | 1.43 | 113,898 | 1.56 | 121,956 | 1.60 |
| E | 66,643 | 250,767 | 3.76 | 274,183 | 4.18 | 274,187 | 2.39 |
| F | 46,113 | 164,290 | 3.56 | 135,833 | 3.59 | 104,954 | 2.93 |
| G 2nd wave | 33,535 | 46,404 | 1.38 | 61,385 | 1.83 | 80,152 | 2.37 |
| **Average** | **41,577** | **111,580** | **2.68** | **116,056** | **2.85** | **91,083** | **2.23** |

*Note:*
Population figures relate to preparatory year. Per capita costs are based on population figures for their particular year.

had been served or because GPs were happy to delegate responsibility to the TPP management team.

This observation might suggest that costs incurred in the second live year most accurately reflect those which might be expected once the TPP is fully established. However, such an inference may be mistaken, because the situation was confused by policy changes to primary care during the second live year and which culminated in the introduction of PCGs (see Chapter 1). A number of TPPs reduced their activities in the expectation that total purchasing would be short-lived and in anticipation that they would soon be working within a different model of health care commissioning.

**Costs by sector**

The involvement of individuals in activities relating to each TPP was summarized according to the organizations they represented in order to gain an understanding of the distribution of costs across different sectors. This information is presented in Table 8.3 as an average for the seven projects. Not surprisingly, most of the cost (around 85 per cent) was borne by the TPP itself, this proportion remaining reasonably constant over the three years. The bulk of these costs related to the TPP management team, but a substantial burden (upwards of 24 per cent) fell on GPs involved in the scheme. It was apparent that GPs' time input was not fully compensated for financially. Where locum payments were made, there were concerns that cover, even if obtainable, was a poor substitute. This may partially explain the reduced input by GPs observed at most of the TPPs in the second live year.

The costs of the TPP management team also fell in the second live year, from £1.73 per capita to £1.35. However, this fall was not universal, and the bulk of the reduction occurred in a single TPP (project E) which more than halved the input of its TPP management team. This TPP comprised ten fundholding practices and had inherited a considerable administrative complement. While in the first two years of the TPP the duties of these staff included total purchasing, it was subsequently decided that there was insufficient work to keep them all occupied. This suggests that there may be economies of scale in having practices work together, although because this experience was not repeated elsewhere, such an extrapolation should be made with caution. In addition, although total purchasing did not require the staffing complement inherited by project E, it proved difficult to make redundancies and generate savings. While a

**Table 8.3** Transaction costs by sector

| Sector | Preparation year 1995/96 | | First live year 1996/97 | | Second live year 1997/98 | |
|---|---|---|---|---|---|---|
| | Per capita £ | % | Per capita £ | % | Per capita £ | % |
| TPP | 2.25 | 84 | 2.42 | 85 | 1.94 | 87 |
| GPs | | 24 | | 24 | | 26 |
| Management | | 59 | | 61 | | 61 |
| Health authority | 0.34 | 13 | 0.33 | 12 | 0.14 | 6 |
| Acute trusts | 0.04 | 1 | 0.03 | 1 | 0.03 | 1 |
| Community trusts | 0.04 | 1 | 0.07 | 2 | 0.09 | 4 |
| Other | 0.01 | 0 | 0.01 | 0 | 0.02 | 1 |
| **Total** | **2.68** | **100** | **2.85** | **100** | **2.23** | **100** |

redundancy plan was proposed, individual practices were unwilling to lose staff or to divest responsibility to a central unit. In fact, TPPs had little incentive to reduce their management costs. They were not formally subject to the management cost targets imposed on health authorities and, once they had secured their management allowance, there was no reason for them to reduce expenditure.

On average, the input provided to the TPPs by health authority staff fell over the three years, from 13 per cent of per capita costs to 6 per cent in the second live year. In part, this reflected a reduction in activities associated with establishing the TPP, such as determining their formal status and setting their budgets, and an early desire by health authorities to have close involvement with their TPP, from which they subsequently felt able to withdraw.

The transaction costs falling on local providers related to the time of senior managers and clinicians involved in negotiations or contract monitoring with the TPP. Additional costs incurred by acute trusts were relatively low – indeed, in one pilot, the introduction of total purchasing is estimated to have reduced costs to the acute provider as a consequence of a fall in the number of meetings previously held with practices operating independently as fund-holders. The impact on community mental health trusts was greater, and increased over time. The level of costs is explained, primarily, by the need to improve inadequate information systems so that they could provide the activity and financial detail required by general practice-based purchasers.

## Costs by level of managerial control within the total purchasing pilot

There were three main levels of managerial activity within a typical TPP:

- level 1, or the TPP project board, represented the formal mechanism by which the health authority discharged its responsibility to monitor and, in some cases, to guide the development of the TPP, and so held the governance role;
- level 2, or the TPP executive board, was the decision-making group of the TPP, responsible for the management and operation of the pilot;
- level 3, or the TPP subgroups, reflected day-to-day activities in support of the pilot's operation, including clinical and contracting activity.

These levels are set out diagrammatically in Figure 3.1 in Chapter 3. Meetings were coded according to their appropriate managerial tier, with level 3 meetings further subdivided according to the parties involved. Costs summarized by these levels are shown for the three years of the TPPs in Table 8.4.

Reflecting their formal status as subcommittees of their parent health authority, structures were developed in each TPP so that the health authority could ensure that the TPP was performing satisfactorily. The TPP project board (level 1) was the main forum in which relations between the health authority and TPP were administered and typically featured a mix of representatives from the two organizations. These meetings varied among projects in frequency and in the extent of involvement by GPs and senior health authority staff. In general, senior health authority managers regarded their own direct involvement as essential in order to discharge their responsibilities towards the TPP. Meetings typically took place quarterly, although in one pilot the group met monthly. In some cases, the meeting included all or some of the GPs involved in the TPP, and the range of health authority representatives varied considerably. It is self-evident that costs were increased the more GPs and senior health authority staff were involved and the more frequently the group met.

Typically, TPP executive group meetings (level 2) were held monthly, although in three of the projects these meetings took place approximately each week. In most cases, meetings were attended by the GPs nominated to take the lead in total purchasing, by the TPP manager, and by representatives of the health authority. Managers and clinicians from local providers were invited periodically. As with TPP project board meetings, the per capita cost of these meetings remained reasonably constant over the three years.

Level 3 typically involved a weekly meeting between the lead GP(s) and the TPP management team, as well as meetings with external bodies. Generally, regular executive group meetings were supplemented with meetings of practice staff, meetings with providers, clinical subgroups, training and other activities. Internal TPP meetings accounted for the highest proportion of these costs. Meetings with the health authority were reduced once decisions about roles and responsibilities had been made. The range and frequency of level 3 meetings appeared to depend on how active the TPP was in promoting service change. GPs tended to be more heavily involved when the project was active in promoting service development, and less so if the emphasis was simply on contracting.

**Table 8.4** Costs by level of managerial control

| Level of TPP managerial control | Code | Preparation year 1995/96 Per capita £ | % | First live year 1996/97 Per capita £ | % | Second live year 1997/98 Per capita £ | % |
|---|---|---|---|---|---|---|---|
| TPP project board | 1 | 0.11 | 4 | 0.09 | 3 | 0.09 | 4 |
| TPP executive group | 2a | 0.51 | 19 | 0.53 | 18 | 0.56 | 25 |
| TPP core management | 2b | 1.34 | 50 | 1.47 | 52 | 0.95 | 42 |
| Internal TPP meetings | 3a | 0.35 | 13 | 0.44 | 16 | 0.30 | 14 |
| Health authority meetings | 3b | 0.17 | 6 | 0.10 | 3 | 0.08 | 4 |
| Providers' meetings | 3c | 0.14 | 5 | 0.15 | 5 | 0.16 | 7 |
| Public meetings | 3d | 0.03 | 1 | 0.03 | 1 | 0.06 | 3 |
| Training | 3t | 0.02 | 1 | 0.04 | 1 | 0.01 | 0 |
| Other | 3x | 0.01 | 0 | 0.01 | 0 | 0.01 | 0 |
| **Total** | | **2.68** | **100** | **2.85** | **100** | **2.23** | **100** |

**Costs by function**

A functional breakdown of the transactions costs of total purchasing is given in Table 8.5. Functions are subdivided according to whether activities took place between the health authority and TPP (HA-TPP), within the TPP itself, or between the TPP and providers (TPP providers).

Interaction between the health authority and TPP was rarely confined to the formal TPP project board meetings. Health authority staff often sat in on internal TPP meetings, and provided public health, contracting and computing support. Some health authorities also held their own internal meetings to ensure strategic coordination of the TPP. The extent of health authority involvement may have had much to do with local politics and with the extent to which it had confidence in the TPP. In two of the projects, the TPP project board was disbanded after the development period. Instead, the projects were monitored through regular reports submitted by the TPP executive group and through the normal line management structure. In contrast, another health authority substantially increased its input into running the TPP.

Most of the costs (some 50 per cent or more) associated with total purchasing were devoted to managing internal relations within the TPP. Much time was spent in involving individuals in the management process, coordinating their views and communicating these throughout the organization. These internal coordination costs included steering group meetings and other management meetings involving GPs, nurses and practice staff along with members of the TPP management team. Involving GPs, in particular, was seen as important in encouraging them to accept financial responsibility for clinical decisions. However, in some projects, participating GPs appeared content to delegate most of the routine responsibility for the TPP to the management team and the lead GP, and this tendency became more apparent as the TPP became more established. The extent to which such delegation occurred was dependent on local factors. In TPPs with no prior history of collaboration, GPs had to develop working relationships with one another and devise effective lines of communication. These activities proved time-consuming.

Other costs internal to the TPP derived from activities bracketed as 'search and information' to support the commissioning process. These included clinical subgroups, health needs assessment and development of purchasing plans. These activities were undertaken

**Table 8.5** Transaction costs by function

| Function | Preparation year 1995/96 | | First live year 1996/97 | | Second live year 1997/98 | |
|---|---|---|---|---|---|---|
| | Per capita £ | % | Per capita £ | % | Per capita £ | % |
| HA-TPP | 0.80 | 30 | 0.65 | 23 | 0.61 | 27 |
| Coordination | | 22 | | 15 | | 15 |
| Information | | 2 | | 2 | | 3 |
| Monitoring | | 5 | | 6 | | 8 |
| Internal TPP | 1.37 | 51 | 1.40 | 49 | 1.29 | 58 |
| Coordination | | 28 | | 29 | | 46 |
| Information | | 24 | | 21 | | 12 |
| TPP providers | 0.51 | 19 | 0.79 | 28 | 0.32 | 15 |
| Information | | 2 | | 10 | | 4 |
| Negotiating | | 11 | | 6 | | -1 |
| Monitoring | | 6 | | 11 | | 12 |
| **Total** | **2.68** | **100** | **2.85** | **100** | **2.23** | **100** |
| Coordination | 1.33 | 50 | 1.23 | 43 | 1.38 | 62 |
| Information | 0.74 | 28 | 0.92 | 32 | 0.41 | 18 |
| Negotiation | 0.31 | 12 | 0.32 | 6 | -0.01 | -1 |
| Monitoring | 0.28 | 10 | 0.50 | 18 | 0.45 | 20 |

to inform the TPP about its population's needs and priorities and to provide guidance on how these should best be met.

The final group of activities (TPP providers) arose from meetings between the TPP and local providers that were directly related to the contracting process. These transaction costs reached a peak in the first live year, amounting to £0.79 per capita before falling to a low of £0.32 in the second live year. One reason for the initial increase in costs was that TPPs did not begin contracting independently until the first live year. In the preparatory year, to gain familiarity with the contracting process, TPP staff often sat in on negotiations between the health authority and providers. Subsequently, rather than merely negotiating a contract, TPPs participated with providers in service developments or regular quality assurance meetings.

One reason for the reduction in transaction costs in the second live year was that GPs, who had usually accompanied the TPP manager to meetings in the first live year, no longer felt it necessary to attend. Indeed, contract negotiation costs appeared negative in the second live year. This was influenced by a single project (E) that combined the negotiation of fundholding and total purchasing activity, thereby reducing the total number of contracting meetings. The required formal separation of fundholding and total purchasing budgets may explain why savings of a similar magnitude were not realized in other TPPs.

## Costs and features of total purchasing pilots

The management and wider transaction costs observed in the sample projects varied considerably. Despite convergence in the second live year, costs ranged from £1.60 to £2.93 per capita. It is relevant to consider the possible determinants of differences among projects. Analysis of the management allowances failed to indicate any statistically significant correlation between per capita direct management expenditure and whether the project had a specialist total purchasing manager, the number of practices in the project or the organizational complexity of the project (Posnett *et al.* 1998).

Table 8.6 shows the relationship between management costs borne directly by the TPP (i.e. excluding costs to the health authority and providers) and the size of the TPP, expressed both in terms of population served and the practices involved. The only clear relationship was that average total costs per practice were higher in

**Table 8.6** Transaction costs borne by each TPP and its features

| Project code | Number of practices | Number of practitioners | First live year | | Second live year | |
|---|---|---|---|---|---|---|
| | | | Average per practice £ | Average per 1000 patients £ | Average per practice £ | Average per 1000 patients £ |
| C | 1 | 7 | 37,358 | 2,886 | 30,496 | 2,346 |
| B | 1 | 12 | 60,627 | 1,826 | 59,957 | 1,789 |
| F | 5 | 25 | 18,626 | 2,461 | 20,017 | 2,792 |
| A | 5 | 20 | 15,001 | 2,560 | 8,659 | 1,504 |
| G | 7 | 23 | 8,195 | 1,708 | 8,660 | 1,789 |
| D | 8 | 36 | 12,417 | 1,361 | 13,474 | 1,418 |
| E | 10 | 35 | 26,655 | 4,060 | 15,286 | 2,352 |

single-practice pilots. Beyond this, there was no obvious correlation between costs and the number of practices. Perhaps a more relevant adjustment for size is the cost per capita. If there were economies of scale to be gained, one would have expected per capita costs to be lower in TPPs covering larger populations. There was some evidence of lower costs as the size of the TPP increased in the first live year, but in the second live year no relationship was apparent.

There were likely to have been two opposing determinants of the observed relationship between TPP size and the costs of total purchasing. First, the cost of *managing budgets* was dependent on the size of the budget, where size of budget was a proxy for the level of activity of the pilot. If the management input was not perfectly divisible (i.e. if some costs were fixed up to a capacity constraint), there would have been economies of scale. Management costs per capita should have declined as the size of the budget increased up to the point at which management capacity needed to be increased. Second, the cost of *coordination* depended on the number of GPs and the number of practices. Other things being equal, for a given number of GPs the cost of coordination should have been lower in a single-practice TPP than in a pilot with multiple practices, simply because coordination within a practice was likely to have been less costly than coordination across practices. Similarly, the cost of coordination was expected to be higher as the number of GPs (and the budget) increased.

These observations suggest two general conclusions. First, if the population covered by a TPP was large enough to achieve economies of scale in the management function, a single-practice pilot was likely to have had lower costs than a multi-practice TPP of the same size. This is because of the additional cost of coordination in a multi-practice TPP. Second, if the population was too small to capture available economies of scale, combining a number of single practices into a multi-practice TPP might reduce overall costs, but the extent of this benefit might have been eroded if the number of practices became too large.

## LESSONS FOR THE ORGANIZATION AND DEVELOPMENT OF PRIMARY CARE COMMISSIONING

There are marked similarities between total purchasing and PCGs in England. Ultimately, a totally devolved commissioning system is envisaged with PCGs having responsibility for virtually all NHS care. Although this devolution will, inevitably, be staged over time, PCGs now involve all GPs in England. This has significant implications for management costs.

It would be wrong to infer that the eventual costs of NHS primary care commissioning will be the same as the costs of total purchasing. In part, this is because costs will depend on the precise way in which PCGs and primary care trusts (into which PCGs will develop) are organized. Further, estimates of the TPP costs relate to a situation in which total purchasing operated for a limited section of the population in parallel with general practice fundholding and health authority commissioning. In addition, the average size of PCGs (covering a population of approximately 100,000) is larger than that of most of the TPPs.

The expected management costs associated with universal primary care commissioning depend on the average size of a typical PCG, and on two other factors:

- the perceived aims of the scheme and the extent to which budgetary responsibility is to be delegated to practice level;
- the extent to which the current functions of health authorities can be reduced or transferred to local commissioners.

**The aims of primary care commissioning**

The future management costs of primary care commissioning in the NHS will depend, to a significant extent, on the aims of the scheme. In general, primary care commissioning has been rationalized either as a means of improving patient access and service delivery through the inclusion of a primary care perspective in the commissioning process or as a means of making GPs directly accountable for the resource consequences of their clinical decisions.

If the main aim is simply to include a primary care perspective in the commissioning of services, the need for the direct involvement of all GPs may not be substantial. This limited objective could have been achieved by extending locality-based commissioning, in which nominated GPs acted in an advisory capacity to the health authority (Balogh 1996). Under this model, the health authority retained budgetary responsibility, but GPs provided advice on the contractual process. In particular, this helped to ensure that health authorities placed contracts with the providers to which GPs were likely to refer patients.

However, in addition to facilitating locally sensitive commissioning, PCGs are intended to encourage all GPs to consider the financial implication of their clinical practice. In due course, all PCGs are expected to manage budgets. But, unlike fundholding, the practices must act *collectively* rather than individually in managing a common budget. Within this framework, the referral and prescribing behaviour of any individual practice may have consequences for the whole group. It is difficult to see how the group can be successful in maintaining expenditures within budget unless each practice accepts its collective responsibility and agrees to be bound by the decisions of the group.

In many multi-practice TPPs, GPs appeared content to delegate financial responsibility to the lead GP and the TPP management team. This reduced costs, but it also diluted the extent to which GPs faced direct incentives to alter their own behaviour (see Chapter 10). Experience suggests that influencing the behaviour of GPs as providers and as gatekeepers depends on the extent to which they are actively engaged in the management of a budget. Unless peer pressure is strong, the aim of engaging all GPs within a local group will probably require notional budgets set at practice level, even if budgets are aggregated for management purposes.

In order to make GPs financially responsible, they must be sufficiently motivated to work with their colleagues in the PCG towards developing and realizing common organizational objectives. All GPs are obliged to participate in a PCG of one form or another. However, the incentive for these independent (and generally individualistic) contractors to cooperate with one another and accept interference in their decision making is less obvious than it was for fundholding (Butler and Roland 1998).

For those who were not opposed to fundholding on ideological grounds, there were clear incentives to taking on fundholding status, as it promised GPs greater leverage and autonomy about where, when and how their patients were treated and the prospect of generating savings to plough back into the practice. As much larger conglomerations of GPs, former fundholders and non-fundholders, now in the same PCG, will have to reconcile their differences and come to a shared vision about overall objectives. Compared to fundholding, it is likely to prove more difficult to reach consensus and to ensure that all GPs consider the wider interests of the PCG when making clinical decisions that have financial implications. GPs may resist attempts to make them participate in a scheme that has the prospect of reducing their own autonomy.

Furthermore, the potential costs of securing GP involvement in commissioning and the collective management of resources should not be underestimated. In many of the TPPs, GPs were not fully reimbursed for their time. They accepted this situation because total purchasing was a high-profile experiment and because they saw themselves as pioneers. Universal primary care commissioning may require significantly higher expenditure to compensate GPs for their time since many will be less motivated than were the volunteer participants in TPPs.

**Transfer of health authority functions**

It is reasonable to assume that under a model in which responsibility for most health care commissioning is progressively devolved to PCGs, some of the functions of the local health authority will be reduced. The impact on management costs depends on three factors: the functions of the health authority devolved to PCGs; the functions of the health authority no longer required in the absence of fundholding; and any new or enhanced functions relating to PCGs.

None of the TPPs reduced the costs of their host health authority. In most cases, additional costs were evident. However, this was not surprising since total purchasing existed alongside fundholding and health authority commissioning. The relevant question is the extent to which costs may be expected to change in the long run under a system of compulsory universal primary care commissioning in the English NHS.

In principle many of the existing functions of health authorities could be devolved to PCGs. For example, it has been estimated that up to 60 per cent of the former functions of health authorities were also functions of general practice-based commissioners (Griffiths 1996). Some of the functions of health authorities were eliminated after fundholding disappeared in 1998. Particular examples include allocation of fundholding budgets, financial audit and general assistance to GPs in the purchasing role. But other functions are likely to be enhanced over time, including allocation of budgets to PCGs, and audit and performance management of PCGs. More significant may be the increased demands from PCGs on the public health, finance and information capacity of health authorities. The effect of these conflicting factors on overall management costs is difficult to quantify, but since the assumption is that many activities will be transferred rather than eliminated, the net impact could be neutral.

However, cost neutrality may not be realized for two reasons. First, transferring functions from the health authority may involve additional costs because there is more than one PCG per health authority. Overall costs are more likely to increase the smaller the PCGs, the greater the diversity in their development process, and the greater the extent to which functions are transferred from the health authority and duplicated across PCGs. In order to contain costs, groups might work together to create a 'purchaser support agency' to share the costs of common functions (Smith *et al.* 1999).

Second, the time period over which change can be implemented will influence the level of management costs. The level of responsibility accepted by different PCGs and primary care trusts (PCTs) will vary for quite some time. A health authority containing a fully autonomous PCT will be unable to reduce its overall level of support while it retains responsibility for level 1 or 2 PCGs. As a result, there will be an interim period in which costs are increased as primary care commissioning is expanded without any corresponding reduction in the functions of the health authority.

## CONCLUSIONS

A number of themes emerge from the analysis reported in this chapter. First, most of the additional costs associated with total purchasing fell on the TPP itself, on GPs and on the host health authority. The bulk of costs were associated with budget management and with coordination among practices and between the TPP and the health authority. Relatively little was expended directly on the contracting process: additional costs to providers were relatively low, although this was partly a reflection of the relatively low level of direct engagement between TPPs and providers, and the selective nature of TPPs' purchasing.

Second, the *laissez faire* approach to the pilots led to a wide range of interpretations of what constituted total purchasing (Mays *et al.* 1997a). In turn, this was reflected in the wide range observed in the level of management costs. Facilitating the involvement of GPs in the commissioning process cannot be achieved without a significant investment in organizational development. Those projects that invested in developing organizational and managerial infrastructure tended to make greater changes in new total purchasing service areas such as mental health, emergency admissions, A&E, and community care for the elderly (see Chapters 5 and 6).

Third, the relationship between TPP size and cost was not straightforward. Economies of scale in managing the budget were expected to lead to lower per capita costs in larger organizations. But any economies may have been more than offset by increased coordination costs. There was evidence that a significant determinant of the differences among TPPs in the level of management spending was the extent to which individual GPs were actively engaged in the activities of the project and were reimbursed for their time. In multi-practice primary care organizations, the costs of coordinating GPs across different practices can be expected to rise as the size of projects increases.

Fourth, there were substantial total management and transaction costs associated with the addition of total purchasing to the models of commissioning which existed in the NHS in the mid-1990s. Most of these costs were generated by the need for coordination among GPs and managers within a TPP, and by the need for the health authority to offer strategic leadership to TPPs. A significant part of the cost was borne by GPs participating in the scheme, for which they were not always fully compensated. The future success of primary care commissioning may depend on the continued willingness of GPs and other primary care professionals to make this commitment. However, the costs of compensating GPs and other primary care professionals should not be underestimated, particularly if one of the aims of primary care commissioning is to secure the involvement of *all* local professionals in the commissioning process. This may prove difficult if GPs perceive the aims of the PCG to differ from the interests of their own practices.

The larger PCGs which replaced both fundholding and total purchasing are expected to be more efficient (that is, to have lower per capita management costs) than the previous mixed system in which fundholders, total purchasers and the health authority operated in parallel. However, because PCGs involve an extension of the coverage of primary care commissioning, it is difficult to see how long-run costs will be lower in aggregate. As Chapter 5 demonstrated, progress will be slow and achievements poor if management costs are restrained unrealistically. It remains to be seen if the benefits flowing from the ability of PCGs to link clinical decision making and budget management at local level, and to develop a clinically informed perspective on commissioning hospital and non-hospital services, justify the costs.

# 9

# BUDGET SETTING AND ITS INFLUENCE ON THE ACHIEVEMENTS OF TOTAL PURCHASING PILOTS

## Gwyn Bevan and Hugh McLeod

Budget setting proved highly controversial under standard fund-holding. It was suspected by some that the reason why fundholders were better able to secure gains for their patients than health authorities was simply that fundholders had been more generously funded. If it were to emerge that TPPs were more effective purchasers than health authorities, then this might simply be because TPPs had more money. Differences in funding might also explain why some TPPs were more effective purchasers than others. Therefore, it was important to examine how budgets were set and the resulting relative funding level of each TPP. However, the early experience of TPP budget setting for TPPs raised two quite different research questions.

The first-wave TPPs reported in their preparatory year (1995/96) that agreeing budget-setting methods and allocations caused the greatest strain on the relationship between the TPPs and their health authorities. Two pilots withdrew because of problems in setting budgets. The original research objective, which was to examine the relative funding of TPPs, assumed that most TPPs would know their budgets and begin to negotiate service changes with providers well before the start of the financial year. (Official guidance was that purchasers ought to indicate to providers in September any major changes that they proposed to make for the financial year beginning the following April.) Yet, in their first 'live' year (1996/97), only a minority of TPPs had a budget formally agreed before the start of the financial year. So the first main research question raised by studying the setting of budgets was: why was this so problematic and what approaches might overcome these problems so that budgets could be set earlier for the following year?

The second wave of TPPs had a similar experience in their first live year: only a minority of TPPs had a budget agreed before the financial year began. However, surprisingly, in the second live year of the first-wave pilots again only a minority of TPPs had a formally agreed budget before the financial year began. Chapter 5 shows that TPPs continued to cite agreeing budgets as one of the most serious obstacles to achieving service changes. The peculiar budgetary status of most TPPs turned out to be not a transient difficulty, rather for most a defining characteristic of being a TPP. The second main research question was: why did this status persist and what were its consequences?

This chapter argues that these two questions emerged because the development of TPPs was played out as a struggle between three transactors in the NHS market: TPPs, the more powerful health authorities, and hospital providers. Lead general practitioners in TPPs saw total purchasing as a means of extending the benefits they had secured for their patients through fundholding. Indeed, some GPs hoped that by being pioneers of total purchasing they would recreate the kinds of opportunities available to the pioneers of fundholding. On the whole, these hopes were not realized. Since total purchasing, in principle, covered the whole of HCHS, the two other transactors in the local quasi-market sought to ensure that total purchasing did not recreate on a larger scale the difficulties that fundholding had created for them.

Most health authorities sought to avoid the difficulties that had been created by funding fundholders on the basis of historic allocations. If, like fundholding, the first wave of total purchasing were to be extended through subsequent waves to cover a significant proportion of the authority, then funding solely on a historic basis would reveal inequities in resource use in relation to need, but with no easy way of reducing them. Consequently many health authorities saw the need to begin total purchasing with some kind of capitation formula to assess whether historical levels of spending were too high. However, this created technical and distributional difficulties in setting budgets for the first 'live' year of both the first- and second-wave TPPs.

The technical difficulties were in working out what the TPPs' spending had been, and in developing and applying a capitation formula. Health authorities and TPPs had no official guidance on how to resolve these difficulties, because the process of setting budgets was deemed to be part of the local pilot's activity. The distributional difficulties arose because applying the results of a capitation formula typically meant that either the health authority gained resources and the TPP lost resources or vice versa. This was because each TPP's budget was created by deduction from the authority's allocation. Typically, there were differences between the estimate of what a TPP would actually spend and its target which represented a fair share. Thus, for example, if a TPP's estimated level of spending was lower than its target fair share, this would imply an increase in resources for the pilot and a cut for the rest of the health authority's population.

As discussed in Chapter 7, TPPs with aims to change their use of hospital services typically wanted to use provider contracts which would closely link changes in activity to changes in funding. The characteristics of emergency activity are such that the pilots generally based their contracts on the 'cost and volume' or 'sophisticated block' contracts used by health authorities, rather than the 'cost per case' contracts used by fundholders. However, the pilots aimed to link activity and funding closely by changing the contract currency away from episodes of care to admissions or bed days. Most hospitals sought to avoid the difficulties which had previously been created for them when fundholders used their budgetary power to take money out of hospitals at an average cost (say £1000) per case. The provider could typically make savings at marginal cost only (say £250) per case. This may explain the position towards the end of fundholding in which health authorities had financial deficits (of, say, £8 million) while fundholders were sitting on unspent savings of similar magnitude. Health authorities shared providers' concerns because they would have to finance the difference between income lost by providers at average cost and savings made by providers at marginal cost. Authorities wanted to avoid financing the gains to TPP patients, which they could only do by reducing services for other patients in the authority. For this reason, health authorities had an incentive to be cautious over the extent to which they supported their TPP's attempts to change historical funding levels.

Thus total purchasing was a replay of the old struggles of fundholding with two crucial differences: TPPs were pilots, not statutory organizations, and were (at least officially) subcommittees of health authorities. This helps explain why so few TPPs had the freedom fundholders had had to use real money to make changes in hospital services. The rest of this chapter discusses the principle of finance by capitation and its implications, together with the problems of measuring risk and of developing formulae for populations defined by general practices. It reviews the experience of setting budgets for TPPs, the problems encountered, the methods used, and the results in terms of resources per capita. It also examines how budgets and budget setting related to whether TPPs had independent contracts, and their success (or the lack of it) in making changes to hospital services (see Chapter 5 for a broader discussion of the determinants of more and less successful TPPs). And it considers the lessons from total purchasing for new primary care organizations in the UK in using population-based budgets to make changes to hospital services, and setting budgets both for the organization as a whole and for smaller populations within these new organizations.

## SETTING BUDGETS FOR ENROLLED POPULATIONS RATHER THAN GEOGRAPHIC POPULATIONS

### The logic of finance by capitation

There are three main methods which insurers and governments use to pay for health care:

- basing future budgets on past expenditure;
- paying providers by future volume;
- creating organizations defined by the populations they serve and paying them by capitation.

The first method lacks any long-term justification and most insurers now favour fairer ways to offer incentives for efficiency by providers, or equity for populations. Insurers in the USA have tried the second, but found that it resulted in escalating costs. Paying providers by volume is also likely to perpetuate inequities in the distribution of supply because, as the report of the Resource Allocation Working Party (RAWP) observed (Department of Health and Social Security 1976), there is ample evidence that supply fuels demand. Therefore, there are two reasons for introducing finance by capitation: to contain costs, as in the USA, and to promote equity, as in the UK.

For insurers in the USA, the family of health maintenance

organizations (HMOs) is a particularly important example of 'managed care' (Starr 1982; Reinhardt 1997; Robinson and Steiner 1998). HMOs are funded by capitation. A leading organizational form of HMO is that in which primary care physicians act as gate-keepers to specialists.

In the UK, capitation methods were introduced to remedy inequities in the availability of resources per capita since a ration-ale for creating the NHS was that access to health care would no longer depend on where people happened to live (Bevan *et al.* 1980). From the formation of the NHS, as GPs were paid on the basis of their list size, there was a policy of distributing GPs more equitably (Webster 1998). Little was done, however, about equi-table allocations to HCHS until health authorities were created in the mid-1970s and spending on these services could be related to populations (Mays and Bevan 1987). A year after these health authorities had been created, the Department of Health commis-sioned the Resource Allocation Working Party (Department of Health and Social Security 1976) to address inequity between health authority areas. Other UK countries commissioned their own working parties with similar terms of reference. Each country has since distributed resources to health authorities with reference to capitation formulae (Bevan *et al.* 1980). In addition, there was evidence of territorial injustice *within* health authorities from studies of variations in hospital admissions at small area level (Department of Health and Social Security 1988) and general prac-tice rates of referral (Crombie and Fleming 1988). However, noth-ing was done directly to address the intra-authority problem until the development of fundholding and total purchasing. Once small area inequities were revealed by these developments, pressure came to bear on the government and health authorities to remedy them.

As discussed in Chapter 10, a weakness of financing health authorities by capitation was that GPs were, in principle, given clinical autonomy to refer patients to any hospital and, until the advent of fundholding and total purchasing, did not bear the cost consequences of their decisions. The logic of finance by capitation implies the integration of purchasers' responsibilities with GPs' decisions on referrals, and hence organizing purchasing and budget management in some way around general practice. The experience of TPPs is therefore directly relevant to the development of primary care organizations in the UK, and to other countries developing finance by capitation.

## Lessons for total purchasing budgets from fundholding

It was originally intended that fundholding budgets would be derived using a capitation formula (Secretaries of State for Health, Wales, Northern Ireland and Scotland 1989). This would have been consistent with the way health authorities' budgets are set, namely, with reference to past levels of spending, and target levels of fair spending derived by a formula based on capitation. Because of methodological problems, no capitation formula was used initially for fundholding budgets, which were based solely on estimates of past use of services at current prices. Setting budgets in this way revealed considerable variations in spend per capita at practice level, which suggested inequities between fundholding practices. Although past spending is a reasonable starting point for setting budgets, the lack of capitation targets to address these inequities created problems in deciding future allocations (both between different fundholders, and between fundholders and non-fund-holders). In particular, there were:

- accusations that fundholding had introduced a 'two-tier' NHS, and undermined equity (Dixon 1994; Dixon *et al.* 1994; Glennerster *et al.* 1994);
- technical problems over accounting for changes which had occurred since budgets had originally been estimated (for example, in inflation, growth money and increases in emergency admissions, which lay outside fundholding);
- problems over setting future budgets to generate appropriate incentives; if GPs made changes that resulted in savings, then this raised the question of how much of those savings they should be allowed to keep in the following year's budget.

In contrast, deriving a capitation target based on the population served helps set future budgets in ways that promote equity, by applying the same principles across different purchasers, and also efficiency, by providing a benchmark for future allocations which is independent of past use, or of subsequent changes in future allocations.

Because of the many difficulties created by setting budgets for fundholders based on their estimated past use of services, the NHS Executive (1996a) eventually issued guidance on developing capitation benchmarks for fundholding. Although health authorities were free to choose their own methods of setting budgets for TPPs, most were influenced by this guidance and, in order to avoid some of the difficulties generated by setting budgets for fundholding, sought to develop capitation target allocations for TPPs alongside estimates of their past levels of expenditure.

## PROBLEMS IN APPLYING CAPITATION FORMULAE TO TPPS

A capitation formula requires three sets of statistics:

- *populations*: sizes, age structures and other measures of risk;
- *risk rating*: how age and other measures of risk produce changes in use of volumes of services;
- *costs or prices*: how to translate data on volumes of different types of care into resources.

Each set of statistics poses problems, but there is a tendency in developing formulae to focus on problems of risk rating (additional to age), and to neglect the difficulty of obtaining good data on populations and problems caused by variations in provider costs.

Administrative areas defined health authorities' populations. There were three problems created by having to define TPPs' populations in terms of the patient lists of general practices:

- *list inflation*: indicated by the estimates of populations registered with general practices in an authority being greater than estimates of the health authority's population derived from the census. Reasons for these differences include problems with general practice lists being out of date, through not taking account of patients who have died, or moved, or had babies, and under-recording by the census;
- *overlapping health authorities*: practice populations may be drawn from more than one health authority;
- the population in census areas (wards) may be registered in different practices, creating an *attribution problem* in using data on risk (for example, socio-economic indicators) by wards to estimate risks by practices.

Most TPPs also posed a problem because of their *small* populations. Martin *et al.* (1997) showed that applying the capitation formula used for health authority budget setting to populations of less than 30,000 produced estimates of fair shares subject to large errors. Some TPPs had populations that were much lower than 30,000 patients (see Chapter 3).

In turn, risk rating has been well described as being 'essentially contested' (Sheldon *et al.* 1993). The root of the problem is that the risk of populations contracting illnesses for which there is effective care cannot be directly measured. Hence, the debate in risk rating is decided by which proxies are the best measures. As the debate is about proxies, it cannot be resolved (if direct measures were available these would be used and not proxies). Pilots posed an additional problem to health authorities in risk rating because they were delegated purchasing responsibility for a *subset of services* (see Chapter 4). These might require to be rated differently from the entire range of HCHS (Bevan 1997).

Finally, national formulae have sought to compensate health authorities for variations in costs that are beyond the control of providers of health care, but not to finance other variations in costs, which would generate perverse incentives towards inefficiency. Where there are significant variations in costs between different providers in a health authority, ignoring these means that different areas within the authority will be given different purchasing power. It would be a mistake to fund purchasers within a health authority in ways that guarantee extra funding for inefficient providers. But, in the short run, it may well be necessary to allocate extra money to a locality which has to use a provider with high costs caused by inefficiencies. It would be appropriate to set a time limit, after which allocations would be reduced, to allow a reasonable time for the provider to make its services more efficient.

## THE EXPERIENCE OF SETTING TPP BUDGETS

### The budgetary process: methods

Health authorities used three main methods of determining TPPs' allocations:

- historic – based on estimated past expenditure only;
- capitation – estimating the TPP's share of the health authority's allocation by applying some kind of capitation formula;
- a mix of both methods, in which the TPP's allocation was set between its estimated past level of spending and its estimated target level derived from a capitation formula.

Data on 37 first-wave TPPs were collected in the health authority surveys of both live years. Sixteen pilots used historical only, 5 capitation only, and 16 a mix of both methods in the first year. In the second year, 13 continued to use historical, 8 capitation only, and 16 a mix, showing a small shift away from using historical methods. However, in the second year, there was an important difference between those TPPs that had negotiated their own independent contracts and those that had not. Budgets of 84 per cent (21 out of 25) of the TPPs with independent contracts were set using a capitation formula, in contrast to 17 per cent (2 out of 12) of those without independent contracts. Budgets of 9 of the 12 without independent contracts were set using estimates of historical expenditure only. Thus, where TPPs had potential to make changes independently, health authorities sought to include a capitation estimate in setting budgets. For other TPPs, historical estimates were deemed sufficient.

Of the health authorities responsible for the 16 pilots using a mix of methods, in 1996/97, 12 reported an agreed pace of change over which allocations would move towards a fair share target: 4 agreed a period of two years; and 3 a period of five years or more. By 1997/98, 9 had reported an agreed pace of change, and only 1 reported a period greater than two years.

For the second wave TPPs, which began a year later, 13 used historical only, 7 capitation only, and 21 a mix. Of this 21, 11 agreed a pace of change, and 3 of these agreed a period of longer than two years over which allocations would move towards target.

Table 9.1 gives results for both waves of TPPs, for health authorities that supplied details on their capitation method. Although practice varied, they normally followed national formulae in risk rating of populations for both first- and second-wave TPPs. Local prices were used by 62 per cent of health authorities for first-wave TPPs, and 51 per cent of health authorities for second-wave TPPs.

**Table 9.1** Use of national methods and provider prices in formula

|  | First wave 1996/97 | | First wave 1997/98 | | Second wave 1997/98 | |
|---|---|---|---|---|---|---|
|  | *Yes* | *Total* | *Yes* | *Total* | *Yes* | *Total* |
| National formula for risk | 13 | 23 | 21 | 23 | 23 | 28 |
| Variation in provider prices | 18 | 29 | 20 | 37 | 21 | 41 |

## The budgetary process: problems

Sixty five per cent (40 out of 62) of TPP lead GPs surveyed in 1996/97 had replied by the end of August 1996. At that time, only 65 per cent (26 out of 40) of those pilots had been formally offered and agreed their allocation for the year, so over a third of TPPs were four months into the 1996/97 financial year without an agreed allocation. Indeed, only a quarter (26 per cent) stated that they had known their budget before the start of the financial year. Just over half (54 per cent) the lead GPs thought that the method of setting budgets was fair and a third (34 per cent) thought the method was unfair. The dissatisfied minority included GPs who indicated that the allocation method chosen by their health authority (capitation or historical) had produced a lower allocation for the TPP than the alternative would have done.

Eighty-three per cent of GPs reported that they had found the process of setting budgets difficult. At its bleakest, one GP described the process as 'a recipe for disaster, failure and disillusionment'. Another highlighted problems caused by the TPP being a subcommittee of the health authority, and hence lacking independence. This lead GP wrote; 'The health authority won't "let go" of their budget easily and have been very difficult to deal with.' The pilots needed to have support from NHS Executive Regional Offices for budget setting (as they had for fundholding), but this was not forthcoming. Unlike fundholding, there was no deadline by which budget offers for TPPs had to be made. Nor was there a formal process for resolving disputes between the TPP and the health authority over what the budget ought to be. These factors contributed to delays in setting TPP budgets.

On the other hand, some health authorities had handled this difficult process with openness and skill, so that GPs understood the difficulties and had confidence in the way their allocations had been decided. Thus one GP observed; 'The good rapport that we have with officers and directors at our health authority has enabled us to pick our way through these complexities.' Indeed, the main lesson from a series of workshops organized by the NHS Executive and Regional Offices with the research team was that health authorities ought to be open about the process, including the difficulties to be tackled. This appeared to matter much more than technical sophistication.

Table 9.2 summarizes the problems reported by health authorities in setting first-wave TPP budgets for 1996/97, and first- and

**Table 9.2** Problems in setting budgets

| | First Wave 1996/97 | | First Wave 1997/98 | | Second Wave 1997/98 | |
|---|---|---|---|---|---|---|
| | Problems | Total | Problems | Total | Problems | Total |
| Method for capitation target | 10 | 25 | 4 | 21 | 2 | 16 |
| Data for capitation | 9 | 26 | 4 | 21 | 2 | 16 |
| Estimating spend | 25 | 28 | 15 | 21 | 14 | 16 |
| Accounting for standard fundholding | 12 | 27 | 3 | 19 | 6 | 16 |
| Accounting for blocked back | 18 | 27 | n/a | n/a | n/a | n/a |

second-wave budgets for 1997/98. These problems contributed to delays and, in some cases, to no budget being set. The two most common and persistent problems were estimating actual expenditure – in particular for A&E and community health services for which there were no data on activity at practice level – and estimating costs of services that the TPP had 'blocked back' to the health authority (i.e. those services that the TPP did not purchase directly).

Only a minority of authorities reported serious problems in producing the required estimates of the population (total, and its distribution by age, or by age and sex): 18 per cent (5 out of 28) with first-wave TPPs in 1996/97. Twenty eight per cent (8 out of 28) said that they had excluded the population covered by other authorities; that is the TPP acted as purchaser for only the majority of its population resident in one health authority. As few first-wave TPPs were in cities, 'list inflation' was not a common problem. Where list inflation was more than 2 per cent, health authorities tended to take this into account.

### Outcomes of the budgetary process: delays and failure in agreeing budgets

The findings on delays and failure in agreeing budgets are based on the 70 per cent (37 out of 53) of first-wave TPPs for which data are available for both 1996/97 and 1997/98, from 34 health authorities and health boards; and 66 per cent (21 out of 32) of the second-wave TPPs in 1997/98.

Figure 9.1 gives the distribution by month when budgets were agreed for 1996/97 and 1997/98. This shows that 19 per cent of TPPs

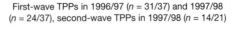

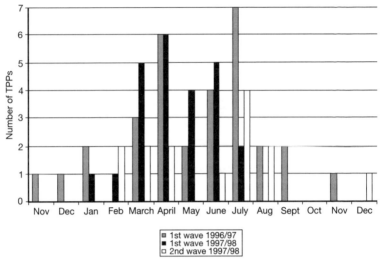

**Figure 9.1**   Distribution by month over which budgets were agreed for 1996/97 and 1997/98

agreed a budget before the start of the financial year in April (for both years of the first wave and the single year of the second wave). More first-wave TPPs went on to agree a budget after the start of the financial year in 1996/97 (65 per cent; 24 out of 37) than in 1997/98 (46 per cent; 17 out of 37).

Agreeing a TPP budget mattered more if the TPP was able to make contracts independently of the authority. In 1996/97, 62 per cent (33 out of 53) of first-wave TPPs held independent contracts (Robinson *et al.* 1998), and this compares with 68 per cent (25 out of 37) of first-wave TPPs included in the surveys of both years which held independent contracts. Figure 9.2 shows that most TPPs with independent contracts in 1996/97 agreed budgets for 1996/97 during the nine-month period to September 1996, compared with a four-month period to June 1997 for the second live year.

Although only a minority of TPPs had budgets before the start of each financial year, most health authorities believed that delays in setting budgets would not have impaired what the TPPs were trying to achieve. For first-wave TPPs, only 26 per cent (9 out of 34) of health authorities stated that delays in determining the TPP

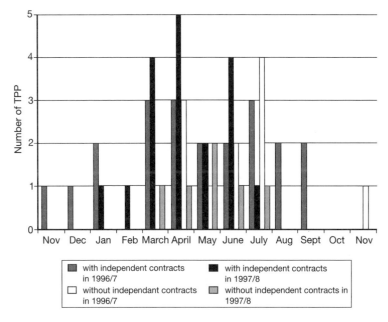

**Figure 9.2**   Distribution by month over which budgets were agreed for 1996/97 and 1997/98 for first-wave total purchasing pilots with and without independent contracts

allocation would have been likely to have limited what the TPP was aiming to achieve in 1996/97; and this fell to 6 per cent (2 out of 34) in 1997/98. For second-wave TPPs, only 14 per cent (3 out of 21) of health authorities stated that delays in determining the TPP allocation would have been likely to have limited what the TPP was aiming to achieve in 1997/98. This is in stark contrast to results reported by TPP respondents themselves who saw delays in setting budgets as a serious impediment to achieving change (see Chapter 5).

**Outcomes of the budgetary process: resources per capita.**

To estimate the budget available to a TPP, it was necessary to determine three components of its expenditure on HCHS:

- the total resources available;
- the element for fundholding (which was meant to be managed separately);

- the percentage of the HCHS' allocation which was 'blocked back' by the TPP to the health authority.

To compare TPPs, it is essential to take account of the size of population, because TPPs varied from 8000 to 100,000. Ideally, variations in a populations' age composition and their risk additional to age ought to be taken into account, but it was not possible to do so because health authorities used different methods of accounting for these differences.

Table 9.3 gives an analysis of data on expenditure on HCHS per capita for the first-wave TPPs for 1997/98, classified by the method used to determine their allocation. It shows that using capitation methods of allocation alone resulted, on average, in TPPs having about £40 per capita more than the £360 per capita produced by the other methods. This suggests that practices that became TPPs had been making lower than average use of HCHS for their populations. Table 9.3 also shows, surprisingly, that the capitation method generated greater variation in allocations than the use of historic estimates. Figure 9.3 shows that this is because two TPPs were given very high estimates of their target allocations – in excess of £500 per capita (this compares with an average of £470 per capita for HCHS in England in 1997/98; NHS Executive 1996b). Table 9.3 indicates that, on average, TPPs 'blocked back' about a quarter of the total HCHS allocation. Thus, the move from fundholding to total purchasing meant that practices increased their spending power per capita from about £100 to about £350.

## RELATIONSHIP BETWEEN OUTCOMES OF THE BUDGETARY PROCESS AND TPPS' ABILITY TO CHANGE HOSPITAL SERVICES

This section shows how the presence of a delegated budget was important for those pilots aiming to change the use of hospital services – although there was little relationship between the results of the budgetary process (i.e. whether or when the budget was formally agreed, or the level of the budget) and whether the TPP was able to make changes in acute hospital services.

Chapter 7 reported on 16 TPPs whose main purchasing objectives were to change their use of acute hospital services by reducing emergency admissions or length of stay in 1997/98. Fourteen of these TPP sites had independent contracts and two had joint

**Table 9.3** Average budgets of first-wave total purchasing pilots

| Method | Total HCHS per capita | Standard deviation | N | SFH HCHS per capita | Standard deviation | N | % blocked back to HA | Standard deviation | N |
|---|---|---|---|---|---|---|---|---|---|
| Capitation | 408 | 90 | 6 | 113 | 13 | 5 | 33 | 19 | 4 |
| Historic | 362 | 66 | 11 | 109 | 17 | 8 | 19 | 11 | 2 |
| Mixture | 366 | 70 | 17 | 119 | 22 | 16 | 23 | 13 | 12 |
| All methods | 372 | 72 | 34 | 116 | 20 | 29 | 25 | 14 | 18 |

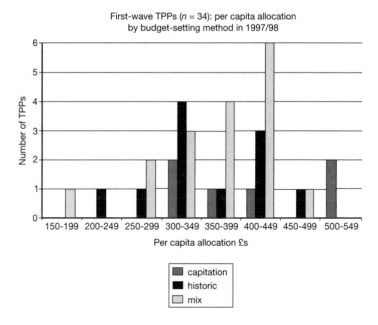

**Figure 9.3**    Distribution of budgets of first-wave total purchasing pilots in 1997/98

contracts with their local health authorities. The survey of health authorities in the second live year found that for the 14 TPPs with independent contracts, three had formally agreed a budget in March 1997, six agreed their budgets between April and July 1997, and five did not indicate an agreement date. The relevant health authorities provided data on the allocations made to 13 of these 14 TPPs. The budgets for 62 per cent (8 out of 13) of the pilots were calculated on the basis of historical spend and a capitation target. These TPPs received a wide range of per capita budgets. However, the TPPs that were successful in changing hospital services, in terms of the outcome measure described in Chapter 7, did not necessarily have relatively large per capita allocations.

As noted in Chapter 7, in general pilots that pursued objectives of changing emergency activity at acute hospitals utilized extra funds, such as winter pressures resources. It is not possible to determine to what extent the budget levels, actual payments made to acute providers and the presence of winter pressures funds together resulted in a change in overall expenditure on the services targeted by the TPPs.

The two TPPs that had joint contracts with their local health authorities had originally wanted to contract independently. One which was unable to agree a budget in either year reported that this was because the health authority was unwilling to risk any potential loss of income to local providers, following the disaggregation of health authority contracts. The other TPP intended to have its own independent main acute contract in 1997/98, but was unable to do so because the health authority wanted to maintain control of resource flows to its main providers. In both these cases, the health authorities provided the TPPs with *extra* funds to finance their changes.

### How did TPPs function without timely budgets?

In 1996/97, setting budgets proved difficult, time consuming and frustrating for first-wave TPPs. If TPPs had wanted to indicate to providers their intentions to make major shifts in services in September 1995, few, if any, would have had adequate financial information on which to base such indications. Because of technical problems over data and methods, and the distributional implications of deriving capitation targets, it is not surprising that budget setting proved so problematic for first-wave TPPs in 1996/97 and for second-wave TPPs in 1997/98. The 1997/98 survey showed that the number of first-wave TPPs encountering problems with setting budgets had decreased as they gained experience. However, the problem caused to TPPs from delays in setting budgets was little better in the pilots' second live year. There are two explanations for this paradoxical finding.

First, it appears that some TPPs and health authorities had 'given up' total purchasing in 1997/98. This was probably because they realized that they had made little progress in 1996/97 and saw little prospects for their pilots beyond 1997/98. The second live year, compared with the first, was a mix of progress, regression and abandonment of effort. It had become increasingly apparent that the new Labour government, elected in May 1997, was determined to abolish all forms of budget holding by individual practices. For large geographically concentrated TPPs in England and Wales, total purchasing offered a launching pad into the new primary care purchasers. However, for single-practice TPPs, there was no such prospect. Only short-term gains could be secured, mainly within primary care. There was no scope to take total purchasing forward in terms of changing secondary care. This meant that, whilst single-practice TPPs had tended to be the more successful in 1996/97, by 1997/98 larger TPPs had begun to make gains as the effort required to make these complex organizations work began to pay off. Moreover, this investment could be carried forward to the development of the new PCGs in England. (The importance of the political context in which TPPs developed is explored more fully in Chapter 5.)

Although TPPs seeking to make changes in their second live year, had greater potential, since they had larger budgets, to change HCHS than fundholders, in practice they were largely working in the dark since they did not know the level of resources available to them before each financial year. Health authorities believed that this would not impair the TPPs' capacity to make changes, but TPPs consistently reported this to be a serious handicap. These findings can be understood by seeing total purchasing as both an extension of, and reaction to, fundholding. Fundholders were given real budgets and considerable freedom to move resources between providers within and outside the NHS, since they had a separate legal identity from health authorities and had access to relatively small amounts of hospital resources. The extension of fundholding into total purchasing was a response to grass-roots pressure from a small number of innovative fundholders, with encouraging support from ministers, for GPs to be able to manage a greater proportion of HCHS resources. However, unlike fundholding, total purchasing was non-statutory and not seen as the brainchild of the Secretary of State. Although health authorities were to encourage total purchasing, each authority had considerable discretion over the development of its TPP(s). In addition, unlike fundholding, there was no statutory requirement for TPPs to have a separate budget, no deadline by which budgets were to be set, nor any means of arbitration for disputes between health authorities and TPPs over budgets (see Chapter 1).

Total purchasing was thus very different from fundholding. Whereas in fundholding, GPs could act largely independently from the health authority, in total purchasing there tended to be a tripartite process of negotiations between the TPP, provider and health authority. The health authority had a veto in some sense over changes being proposed. This explains the failure to find a simple relationship between budgets and TPP performance. Neither when budgets were set, nor their level, nor the size of budget taken by the TPP seemed to matter. What did matter was that a budget was available in order to facilitate change. This required three enabling characteristics: the drive of the lead GP, the support of the health authority, and the willingness of providers to explore service change. Without the first to originate ideas for change, nothing would happen. Without the second, the resources required for these ideas to be implemented were unlikely to be made available. Without the third, all changes could be rejected outright, or be presented to the health authority as having adverse impacts on the rest of the health authority's population. This might also encourage the health authority to oppose these changes. Furthermore, if a TPP did not have a budget, or lacked the freedom to use it, this was likely to be because the authority, or its providers, or both, had reservations about the effect of the TPP using its budget to change services. This was more likely to be the explanation than difficulties in setting the budget.

TPPs typically wanted to reduce their patients' use of acute in-patient services and to use the resources thus released to finance developments outside acute hospitals. Their aim to move resources out of an acute hospital by reducing expenditure, mainly at average cost, when providers claimed they could only make savings at marginal cost, was controversial. Its immediate effect would have been to make services worse for non-TPP patients using the same hospital. Furthermore, the new Labour government, elected in May 1997, was antipathetic to the risk that market trading would create short-term instability. Indeed, the election result was widely anticipated in the NHS. As a result health authorities and providers were able to resist TPPs' contracting objectives more easily. A consequence of allowing TPPs to release resources from acute hospitals only at marginal cost was to constrain drastically their ability to finance significant developments outside acute hospitals.

## RESOURCE ALLOCATION AND BUDGET SETTING IN THE 'NEW NHS'

Primary care groups beyond level 1 in England are required to manage a global cash limit across what have hitherto been three separate budgets: HCHS, general practice prescribing costs; and the cash-limited element of the general medical services (largely the costs of employing practice managers and practice nurses) (Secretary of State for Health, 1997). There are likely to be few major problems in using a capitation formula to set fair share target allocations for these new primary care purchasers. This is because PCGs have fairly large populations (around 100,000) and are defined geographically. There will be problems in cities caused by list inflation (see above), and general problems in determining actual expenditures for some services at practice level. The main problem will relate to the implications of using the capitation targets.

The first problem is that using a capitation target will mean changes in budgets for the primary care purchasers, which are likely to bring about significant changes in provider incomes. Those purchasers gaining resources may want to invest in developing services outside acute hospitals, and those losing resources will have to cut their spending in these hospitals. This raises the same problem encountered by the TPPs, namely that in the short term these hospitals are likely to be able to make savings only at marginal costs, and therefore will require changes in budgets and services to be regulated over the medium term.

The second problem will also impact on providers where a purchaser's spend is higher than its fair share target because its provider has higher than average unit costs. It would be appropriate to set a pace of change in reducing allocations to allow the provider a reasonable time to make its services more efficient.

The third problem is where a purchaser's spend is higher than its fair share target because its population has higher than average rates of use of services. This should be tackled by analysis of clinical behaviour and resource allocation at practice level. It is likely that variations in resources per capita between practices within the same purchaser will be due to differences in the volume of services (not their price, as they will typically be using the same provider). The question is whether these variations are caused by the formula underestimating relative risk, or variations in medical discretion (Bevan 1997).

Using information on discretionary admissions, derived from studies of small area variation in admission rates, it is possible to assess whether practices with high admission rates are likely to be justified by population need or are manifestations of medical discretion. If a practice has higher admissions than indicated by a capitation formula which allows for age and risk, in which categories are these high volumes concentrated? Are they in discretionary categories of admission that are likely to be inappropriate (such as tonsillectomy and disc surgery); or are they in categories of admission known to exhibit low variation and are likely to be appropriate (such as acute myocardial infarction and hip fractures)? If a practice with high admission rates has these concentrated in discretionary categories, this suggests that these volumes ought to be reduced. Indeed, reducing spending on these admissions is likely to mean that resources are available for redistribution to more effective treatment. If, on the contrary, higher admission rates are concentrated in low variation categories, this suggests that the indicative capitation formula may be underestimating risk for that practice.

## CONCLUSIONS

The experience of the TPPs has demonstrated the following lessons for the new primary care purchasers in the NHS:

- Setting budgetary targets against past estimates of expenditure for the new primary care purchasers is not a purely financial exercise. It is fundamental to the performance of the NHS, since targets provide important benchmarks for understanding causes of variations in per capita spend that create inequity.
- To make sense of these benchmarks, it is necessary to investigate the differences in prices and volumes of hospital services brought about by different purchasers and practices. This should indicate priorities for action: to reduce inefficiencies in providers; or in discretionary referrals by GPs; or in discretionary admissions by hospital doctors. In these ways, primary care purchasing has the potential to deliver greater equity and efficiency.
- Health authorities will also need to develop means of regulating purchaser-induced changes, while also encouraging local providers to develop the capacity to make savings of more than simply marginal cost.

# 10

# MANAGING BUDGETS AND RISK

## Gwyn Bevan, Kate Baxter and Max Bachmann

Enthoven's proposed model of an NHS internal market (Enthoven 1985) was one in which district health authorities continued to run hospitals, took on new responsibilities by employing general practitioners, and were able to trade hospital care in a competitive market. A key organizing principle was that of managed care by one type of health maintenance organization (HMO), which offers health insurance to individuals based on monthly premiums and employs primary care physicians to act as gatekeepers to specialists (Starr 1982; Weiner and Ferris 1990; Enthoven 1995; Reinhardt 1997; Robinson and Steiner 1998). The growth of managed care is designed to tackle the problems created by insurance of 'moral hazard': as people no longer have to worry about costs, this encourages increased expenditure. A common way for insurers to tackle this problem is by user charges, but there are two problems with these (Evans 1987). Doctors rather than patients typically make decisions, and it is difficult to design user charges so that they only deter frivolous use of services rather than deterring patients from seeking timely and appropriate treatment. It therefore makes more sense to put economic pressures on doctors, rather than patients, in framing demands for health care. This is what the various forms of managed care aim to do. Enthoven's model for the NHS implies that GPs would face budgetary constraints on the volume of their referrals to specialists, who in turn would be subject to market competition on the price of services that they supplied.

The 1991 NHS reforms of health authorities (Secretaries of State 1989) followed only one part of Enthoven's model by introducing an internal market. Health authorities were transformed from being managers of HCHS into insurers who relied on contracts, but GPs remained independent contractors rather than health authority employees and, in principle, were free to refer. The problem of moral hazard remained for GPs' referrals. Furthermore, hospital doctors' decisions were now free of direct health authority control. Although health authorities were officially described as 'purchasers', they only fulfilled the unattractive part of what is normally understood to be that role: they paid the bills. GPs and hospital doctors still largely shaped demand. Health authorities were best described not as 'purchasers' but as insurers who practised 'unmanaged care', in US terms. A consequence of health authorities' weak structural position as insurers was the recurrent problem of clinicians' 'overperformance' against contracts – trusts tended to achieve contracted volumes before the end of each financial year, yet GPs and hospital doctors continued to identify cases that needed care. Authorities had no extra money to pay for these cases.

Given health authorities' general lack of control over the demands for health care shaped by GPs and hospital doctors, standard fundholding and TPPs were fascinating innovations in the NHS, because they experimented with the HMO model. Each offered the potential for GPs to integrate their traditional roles of providing primary care and acting as gatekeepers to specialist care with a new role of manager of resources (and by implication that of insurer for their populations). One reason for GPs to volunteer to do this under fundholding and total purchasing was because they recognized that rationing of access to health care has to be done, and that they would rather do this themselves than have this done for their patients by others, such as bureaucrats. Standard fundholding was carefully designed to enable GPs to become insurers specifically for those services that they could influence by their own prescribing and decisions on elective referrals. Over recent years, however, the most serious problems for authorities of overperformance have been caused by explosive increases in emergency (or non-elective) admissions (Round 1997); this explains the interest in extending standard fundholding.

Total purchasing is highly relevant to the 'new NHS', in which the purchasing of health care is organized around PCGs defined by general practices for local populations (Secretary of State for Health 1997). PCGs are intended to replace the two purchasing models introduced by the internal market based on districts and general practices (Secretaries of State 1989). PCGs have a cash limit for their populations' share of resources. The *New NHS* White Paper (Secretary of State for Health 1997) and ensuing guidance (NHS Executive 1998b, 1998c and 1998d) emphasized that PCGs will need adequate management arrangements and risk management plans for their budgets. They will have to manage their spending on both routine and rare costly admissions within these cash limits. These issues, crucial for the future of PCGs, are explored in this chapter.

## OBJECTIVES OF THE ANALYSIS

This part of the evaluation aimed to discover whether and how TPPs had assessed their financial risk due to rare costly referrals; what risk management arrangements they had made; the eventual outcomes of these arrangements in terms of over/underspending; and whether concerns about the expense of rare costly referrals had influenced the process of deciding whether to make such referrals.

In terms of managing spending, GPs in a single-practice TPP might be more likely to accept peer review of the resource consequences of their decisions, and find it easier to reach agreements over how to manage spending, than GPs in a TPP based on a large number of practices. This is because GPs in a single practice are already working within a partnership. However, in terms of managing the risk from rare costly referrals, the advantage in budgetary management was expected to lie with the large multi-practice TPPs, since they had access to a larger risk pool. Therefore this chapter tackles two related issues:

- *Containing the costs of routine care within a fixed budget:* the extent to which GPs in TPPs and as standard fundholders integrated their clinical and financial roles of gatekeeper and insurer. Did all GPs get involved in budgetary management, or was it just the lead GP? In initial interviews with TPPs, some standard fundholding practices had said that they did not involve other GPs when expenditure was projected to exceed the budget for the financial year. Instead, they acted just like a health authority: they contacted the hospital and asked for admission of their patients to be deferred. Where all GPs were involved, it was relevant to find out whether they did have information in time to avoid year-end spending crises.
- *Managing rare costly referrals:* US commentators, drawing on the experience of HMOs, argued that populations of at least 50,000

were necessary to avoid bankruptcy of primary care-based purchasers due to random variation in costs (Scheffler 1989; Weiner
and Ferris 1990). This suggested that only multi-practice TPPs,
with larger patient populations, would be able to manage the risk
from rare costly referrals that were not covered by contracts with
hospitals and for which the pilot has to pay (that is, those which
were not blocked back to the health authority). However, even if
a large population was a necessary condition for risk management, it would not be sufficient in itself, for two reasons. First,
although increased size would mean that smaller financial provision would have had to be made to manage risk, this still
required a proper assessment of that financial provision. A small
TPP that made adequate provision based on a proper assessment
of risk was likely to be less vulnerable than a large TPP that did
not. Second, there would still be a problem of managing expenditure on rare costly referrals even if apparently adequate
arrangements had been made. If GPs believed, for example, that
they had only to be concerned about expenditure on routine
admissions, because rare costly referrals were covered by insurance, this would simply reintroduce the problem of moral hazard
for rare costly referrals. GPs ought not to have been insulated by
insurance from responsibility for the consequences of their
decisions. Such insulation ought to have been confined only to
referrals over which GPs had relatively little discretion (for
example, forensic psychiatry or severe trauma). Where GPs had
discretion, risk management arrangements needed to be
designed so that the TPP was liable for part of the costs. This
again raises the problems of involving GPs in budgetary management, in which small TPPs might have been found to have the
advantage.

Data on management of budgets were returned by 45 of the 49
available TPPs (92 per cent), 32 of 35 (91 per cent) multi-practice
and 13 of 14 (93 per cent) single-practice pilots. Eight projects did
not hold a live budget and so gave information only on standard
fundholding. For budgetary management of total purchasing, the
maximum response rate was 37 out of 49 TPPs (11 single- and 26
multi-practice pilots). Questions on risk management for rare costly
referrals were relevant to some of the TPPs that did not answer
questions about budgetary management. The maximum response
rate for the section on rare costly referrals was 42 out of 49 TPPs.
Missing data for different questions gives various denominators;

results for each question are therefore reported with both percentages and the total number of responses.

## MANAGING BUDGETS

### Scope of budgetary responsibility

A key determinant of each pilot's exposure to financial risk and budgetary management responsibilities was how much of its total purchasing budget remained its own responsibility, and how much was 'blocked back' to its health authority; 'blocking back' means that the health authority retained responsibility for purchasing specified services. Thirty-two pilots reported both their budgets and the amounts blocked back to health authorities. Four blocked back their entire budgets and therefore carried no risk. Seven blocked back between half and all of their budgets. Eight blocked back between a quarter and a half. Ten blocked back under a quarter. Three blocked back none of their budgets. Eighty-seven per cent (28 out of 32) carried at least some financial risk and budgetary responsibility.

### Integration of financial and clinical roles

TPPs were asked about their earlier experience of managing a budget as standard fundholders. The aim was to find out if GPs had been involved in financial decisions under standard fundholding, to see if this involvement had continued into total purchasing, and to note any differences.

All practices claimed that as standard fundholders, they had tried to manage expenditure to ensure continued activity throughout the financial year. However, two in three (29 of 44, 66 per cent) thought that at some stage they might have been heading for an overspend. One in three (15 of 44, 34 per cent) had to restrict admissions to urgent cases only, leaving routine cases until the next financial year. So although almost all practices as standard fundholders intended to contain costs, not all were able to do so, and one of their methods of curtailing expenditure was the same as that employed by health authorities.

Although in their time as standard fundholders, practices had had some problems in managing expenditure, most had developed ways of controlling demand and monitoring individual GP referral rates. Table 10.1 lists the most common methods used to try to

**Table 10.1** Methods of controlling expenditure as a standard fundholder

|  | Yes (n = 44)[1] | % |
|---|---|---|
| Were GPs aware of the financial position? | 43 | 98 |
| How were GPs made aware of the financial position? |  |  |
| – by receiving information on expenditure against budgets? | 42 | 96 |
| – receiving information on referral levels? | 37 | 84 |
| – other methods? | 12 | 27 |
| How were referrals controlled? |  |  |
| – through peer pressure to reduce expenditure? | 29 | 66 |
| – by imposition of referral ceilings? | 9 | 21 |
| – other methods? | 22 | 50 |

*Note*:
[1] One pilot did not feel able to answer questions relating to standard fundholding due to the different coverage of total purchasing and standard fundholding budgets.

ensure GPs' awareness of standard fundholding expenditure and to control demand. Almost all GPs (96 per cent) had received information on their expenditure against budgets. Eighty-four per cent had received information on their referral levels. Other methods to make GPs aware of the financial position were providing details on budgets at the same time as in the previous year; providing details of case-mix changes; monitoring prescribing; and making available referral costs by individual GPs. In more than half of the practices, referrals were controlled through peer pressure. Few practices had imposed referral ceilings. Other methods of controlling referrals included imposing financial ceilings; encouraging the use of preferred providers; auditing the outcome of referrals; and using in-house waiting lists or slowing the release of referrals.

In contrast, although about half of the TPPs (18 of 32, 56 per cent) stated that they used methods similar to those in standard fundholding to control demand, some did not see total purchasing activity as being as amenable to GPs' control as standard fundholding services. Consequently they found these questions difficult to answer. However, many pilots had introduced innovations to control their total purchasing expenditure. Eighteen pilots gave details of the methods they employed. Some used the same methods as for standard fundholding and others had introduced new methods. Table 10.2 summarizes these methods and gives the number of pilots using each. One common method was to monitor the activity of providers carefully and to impose penalties for

**Table 10.2**    Methods used to control total purchasing expenditure

| | No.[1] |
|---|---|
| Contract penalties for providers or more intensive monitoring, and more involvement of TPPs in monitoring, of provider activity | 8 |
| GPs hold group discussions of cases, particularly extra-contractual referrals | 7 |
| Low-technology facilities are used as an alternative to acute facilities | 6 |
| Regular financial reporting and forecasting, or flexible budgets, facilitate control | 6 |
| Practice protocols are followed | 3 |
| GPs change referral patterns if necessary | 2 |
| Other methods (working to agreed levels of activity; education of GPs on the costs of referrals; working closely with practice-based social worker) | 3 |
| Control not possible or not necessary | 3 |

*Note*:
[1] More than one response was given per TPP.

under/overperformance. This is in contrast to the methods used in standard fundholding in which practices concentrated on controlling their *own* demand (for example, through peer pressure and referral ceilings), rather than imposing contract penalties and passing the responsibility for controlling demand to providers. Total purchasing practices also worked together to control their demand, by discussing individual cases and following practice protocols.

**Level of involvement of general practitioners**

Creating organizational integration through joint budgets between practices does not of itself result in individual GPs integrating their financial and clinical roles. What proportion of the GPs in a TPP were informed of expenditure by the TPP, and genuinely involved in monitoring this expenditure and in making decisions to control it? Table 10.3 analyses all TPPs (single and multi-practice) together. It shows which GPs were routinely in receipt of relevant monitoring information and involved in decision making in order to manage budgets. In most TPPs, only the lead GPs were involved in financial decision making, but about 30 per cent of pilots involved all their GPs in such decisions.

More multi-practice than single-practice pilots relied on the lead

**Table 10.3**   General practitioners involved in reviewing and decision making for managing budgets in total purchasing pilots (% of pilots)

|  | Lead GP only | Some but not all GPs | All GPs |
|---|---|---|---|
| Receive information on expenditure to date | 17/37 (46) | 7/37 (19) | 13/17 (35) |
| Review/discuss expenditure against budgets | 20/36 (56) | 10/36 (28) | 6/36 (17) |
| Review/discuss expected annual spend | 17/36 (47) | 8/36 (22) | 11/36 (31) |
| Decide on actions to adjust expenditure | 14/35 (40) | 10/35 (29) | 11/35 (32) |

GP alone to review expenditure against budgets and discuss this with TPP managers (17 out of 25 (68 per cent) versus 3 out of 11 (27 per cent); p = 0.006). This is an important difference between multi-practice and single-practice pilots in how they integrated their roles as gatekeeper and insurer. There was no difference between single- and multi-practice TPPs in any of the other categories.

**Methods of managing budgets**

Table 10.4 shows the methods of managing budgets used by single- and multi-practice TPPs. Few TPPs monitored individual GP referral rates (about a third of single- and multi-practice pilots). Almost two-thirds of multi-practice pilots monitored referrals at practice level and it can be assumed that single-practice TPPs monitored practice-level referrals. Over 80 per cent of TPPs had some kind of protocol for sharing information about activity and financial data, both between GPs and practices. However, half the single-practice TPPs, but only a fifth of multi-practice pilots, had a protocol for making modifications to activity or expenditure, if necessary. This important difference is not, however, statistically significant (p = 0.08). This may be linked to the later finding that multi-practice TPPs had more difficulty adapting their expenditure within the financial year (Table 10.5). It may be that some TPPs were hoping that, simply by giving their GPs information about expenditure, they would automatically make modifications to their referral patterns if necessary, negating the need for protocols. Where TPPs had the facility to vire funds between total purchasing and standard fundholding budgets, or between the TPPs and their

**Table 10.4**   Methods of managing budgets: differences between single- and multi-practice pilots (%)

|  | *Total* | *Single practice* | *Multi-practice* |
|---|---|---|---|
| Were individual GP referral rates monitored? | 11/37 (30) | 3/11 (27) | 8/26 (31) |
| Were individual practice referral rates monitored? | 16/25 (64) | N/A | 16/25 (64) |
| Is there an agreed protocol for sharing information between GPs on activity and financial data? | 30/35 (86) | 8/10 (80) | 22/25 (88) |
| Is there an agreed protocol for sharing information between practices on activity and financial data? | 20/24 (83) | N/A | 20/24 (83) |
| Is there an agreed protocol for making appropriate modifications (in GP/practice performance)? | 10/34 (29) | 5/9 (56) | 5/25 (20) |
| Were funds vired between | | | |
| – standard fundholding and TPP elements of the fund?[1] | 13/24 (54) | 5/8 (63) | 8/16 (50) |
| – health authority and TPP?[2] | 12/20 (60) | 1/5 (20) | 11/15 (73) |

N/A: not applicable.
*Notes*:
[1] A further 10 TPPs did not have the facility to vire funds between total purchasing and standard fundholding budgets.
[2] A further 14 TPPs did not have the facility to vire funds between themselves and the health authority.

health authorities, over half did so. The exception was that only one of five single-practice TPPs vired funds between the TPP and the health authority. This was from the TPP to the health authority.

All except two TPPs monitored spending against budgets for all their contracts. The two that did not do so monitored only a selected number of contracts. No single-practice but one in three multi-practice pilots (8 of 24, 33 per cent) accounted for expenditure at the time of referral (p = 0.02). One pilot accounted both at the time of referral and when an invoice was received. The remainder (23 of 32, 72 per cent) accounted for expenditure when the invoice was received from the hospital. Relying on invoices is inadequate: by the time it is clear that the project is heading for an overspend, it is likely to be too late to do anything about it. The problem created by expenditure committed but not reported was a common cause of bankruptcies of HMOs in the USA (Weiner and Ferris 1990).

## Success and satisfaction in managing budgets

Table 10.5 gives measures of success in, and satisfaction with, financial management. It was more likely in single than multi-practice pilots for actual expenditure to follow planned expenditure in 1996/97. Almost nine in ten multi-practice pilots found actual spending differed from planned spend. The proportion for single-practice TPPs was only three in ten ($p < 0.01$). This could have been both under- and overspending. However, by the financial year-end, only 3 per cent of TPPs had any large unplanned savings, whereas 31 per cent had experienced some kind of financial difficulty. Five (14 per cent) TPPs had to stop admitting non-urgent patients as a result of financial difficulties. More (76 per cent) reported that they were not able to maintain activity at the desired level throughout the year.

**Table 10.5**   Success in managing budgets: differences between single- and multi-practice pilots (%)

|  | *Total* | *Single practice* | *Multi-practice* |
|---|---|---|---|
| [1]Was there a variation in actual compared to planned spend? | 26/37 (70) | 3/11 (27) | 23/26 (88) |
| Was there a large unplanned saving? | 1/37 (3) | 0/11 (0) | 1/26 (4) |
| Was there any kind of financial crisis/difficulty? | 11/36 (31) | 1/11 (9) | 10/25 (40) |
| Did you stop admitting non-urgent patients? | 5/37 (14) | 1/11 (9) | 4/26 (15) |
| Did the TPP maintain continued activity at the desired level throughout the year? | 28/37 (76) | 7/11 (64) | 21/26 (81) |
| Was the performance of GPs satisfactorily monitored? | 16/32 (50) | 5/8 (63) | 11/24 (46) |
| Was the performance of practices satisfactorily monitored? | 17/25 (68) | N/A | 17/25 (68) |
| *Was the performance of GPs satisfactorily adapted?[1] | 12/34 (35) | 6/10 (60) | 6/24 (25) |
| Was the performance of practices satisfactorily adapted?[2] | 7/24 (29) | N/A | 7/24 (29) |
| *Has the system changed for 1997/98? | 11/35 (31) | 0/11 (0) | 11/24 (46) |

N/A: not applicable.
* $p < 0.05$
*Notes*:
[1] 11/34 (33%) TPPs considered this unnecessary.
[2] 9/24 (38%) TPPs considered this unnecessary.

More single-practice TPPs appeared to have difficulty maintaining the desired level of activity, although this difference was not statistically significant. This may have been because single practices were more easily able to use TPP money to finance standard fundholding shortfalls, therefore problems in standard fundholding impacted on total purchasing. Each practice in a multi-practice TPP usually managed its own standard fundholding budget entirely independently of the total purchasing budget, making virement from total purchasing to standard fundholding more difficult (and such transfers in either direction were technically prohibited).

A third of TPPs were planning to change their financial management systems in 1997/98. These were all multi-practice pilots ($p < 0.01$). In half or more TPPs, the project manager believed that the performance of GPs and/or practices had been satisfactorily monitored. However, differences arose between single- and multi-practice pilots in their satisfaction with adapting their financial performance, if this was necessary. Whereas 60 per cent of single-practice pilots were happy with their ability to adapt GP performance within the year, the corresponding figure for multi-practice pilots was only 25 per cent ($p < 0.05$).

TPPs reporting that they had changed their budgetary and monitoring system for 1997/98 were more likely to have experienced a financial crisis than those which reported no such change (6 out of 11 (55 per cent) versus 4 out of 23 (17 per cent); $p = 0.04$). Projects which either experienced a financial crisis or changed their budgetary management system for 1997/98 were those in which project managers believed that GP performance had not been satisfactorily adapted within the year, or where it had been difficult to do so.

Table 10.6 shows that most TPPs (83 per cent) reported that the degree of clinical freedom allowed to the GPs allowed was 'about right'. Fewer were satisfied with financial management. A third found it insufficiently sophisticated. There were no differences between single- and multi-practice pilots.

**Table 10.6**   Satisfaction with budgetary management systems and degree of clinical freedom ($n = 35$) (%)

|  | Too bureaucratic/ complicated | About right | Too flexible/ not sophisticated |
|---|---|---|---|
| Clinical freedom within the system | 3 (9) | 29 (83) | 3 (9) |
| System of financial management | 4 (11) | 20 (57) | 11 (31) |

PCGs aim to integrate GPs' responsibility for clinical and financial management by requiring them to manage their clinical decisions and their consequences within a hard budget constraint. This creates fundamental tensions for GPs about where their loyalties lie: with the individual patient, all their patients, or the NHS as a whole? For TPPs, there was no similar constraint. Project managers reported that they believed that GPs in TPPs were, on the whole, satisfied with the degree of clinical freedom they were afforded. This implies that for TPPs there were few or no constraints, such as referral and financial ceilings, and suggests only a limited degree of integration of GPs' roles as both insurer and gatekeeper.

## Concerns about financial risk

Two-thirds of pilots (28 out of 32) were worried that rare costly referrals might make them exceed their budgets. The types of rare costly referrals that pilots were most worried about were specific types of psychiatric referrals and intensive care admissions (Table 10.7). Most types of case required specialized services that were not usually available in every district.

**Table 10.7** Types of rare costly referrals that worried total purchasing pilots at the outset

|  | Number of TPPs[1] |
| --- | --- |
| Mental health (including eating disorders, forensic, long-stay, specialist in-patients) | 16 |
| Intensive care (including paediatric and neonatal) | 11 |
| Transplants | 5 |
| Haematology, leukaemia | 4 |
| Renal | 4 |
| A&E, emergency admission | 3 |
| Cardiothoracic, or cardiology procedures | 3 |
| Spinal injuries and operations | 2 |
| Rehabilitation | 2 |
| Cancer, including chemotherapy | 2 |
| Hyperbaric treatment | 1 |
| Cochlear implant | 1 |
| Burns | 1 |
| Paediatric surgery | 1 |
| *In vitro* fertilization | 1 |

*Note*:
[1] 25 of 28 pilots that were worried provided at least one example.

## Risk assessment and risk-pooling methods used

Few pilots had assessed their financial risk thoroughly during or before 1996/97 (Table 10.8). About 60 per cent of pilots had made some attempt by examining their practice populations' previous referral rates or hospital prices. Half calculated the expected cost of rare costly referrals. One in three pilots examined referral rates from the rest of the district and one in five modelled risk using computer simulation methods. Smaller and single-practice pilots were more likely than larger and multi-practice pilots to have used each risk assessment method, but differences were not statistically significant.

Various risk-pooling methods were used by TPPs. Three in four shared risks with their health authorities. This was done by paying health authorities a portion of their budget in return for health authorities covering the costs of rare costly referrals, defined clinically or by cost. In this way the health authority acted as reinsurer. More than one health authority acted as insurer for three pilots, by means of inter-district consortia. One in ten (4 out of 40) pilots had changed the premiums for their insurance funds for the second live year (1997/98). A third of pilots spread risk from year to year, thus effectively increasing their risk pools. A third used other methods including monitoring referrals and costs, peer review of referrals,

**Table 10.8**    Risk assessment methods used

|  | $n/N(\%)$[1] |
| --- | --- |
| Have you assessed the financial risk posed to your pilot by rare costly referrals? | 25/42 (60) |
| Did you ever |  |
| – look at previous referral rates for your practice, or practices in your pilot? | 27/42 (64) |
| – look at previous referral rates for practices in your district? | 15/42 (36) |
| – look at hospital prices for rare costly referrals? | 24/42 (57) |
| – calculate the expected cost of rare costly referrals (that is, multiply the number of referrals expected by the price of each referral)? | 21/42 (50) |
| – undertake computer simulation to explore the expected cost of rare costly referrals? | 8/42 (19) |

*Note*:
[1] $n$ = number who responded positively to this question
$N$ = number who responded in total.

and keeping unallocated funds in a contingency fund. None reported using private insurance.

**Decision making about referrals**

A key question was whether concerns about costs influenced GPs' decision making about referrals. GPs consulted various people or organizations before making rare costly referrals (Table 10.9). In 86 per cent (36 out of 42) of pilots, GPs consulted someone else before making such a referral – usually the health authority or other GPs in their practice. GPs in multi-practice or larger pilots were twice as likely to make the decision without consulting anyone else (8 out of 29 (28 per cent) versus 2 out of 13 (15 per cent) respectively), but these differences were not statistically significant. GPs were significantly more likely to decide without consulting anyone else in pilots with more than 20 GPs than in pilots with fewer than 20 GPs (7 out of 16 (44 per cent) versus 3 out of 26 (12 per cent); p = 0.03).

**Avoiding an expected overspend**

Several methods of avoiding overspending on rare costly referrals were described (Table 10.10). One in four pilots chose a less costly option for managing patients, one in six refused to allow a referral, and one in seven asked the health authority to help financially. The six pilots that made explicit rationing decisions by refusing to allow costly referrals because the expected cost exceeded their budget

**Table 10.9** Consultation with colleagues about rare costly referrals

|  | $n/N(\%)$[1] |
|---|---|
| Who decides about whether to make an extra-contractual rare costly referral (%): |  |
| – the patient's GP in consultation with other GPs in the practice? | 23/42 (55) |
| – the patient's GP in consultation with the health authority? | 21/42 (50) |
| – the patient's GP in consultation with GPs from other practices in the pilot?[2] | 10/29 (34) |
| – the patient's GP alone? | 10/42 (24) |

*Note*:
[1] $n$ = number who responded positively to this question
 $N$ = number who responded in total.
[2] Not applicable to single-practice projects.

**Table 10.10**   Methods of dealing with projected overspends

|  | $n/N(\%)^1$ |
| --- | --- |
| Did you defer any referrals to next financial year? | 2/35 (6) |
| Did you choose a less costly option for managing patients? | 8/35 (23) |
| Did you refuse to allow costly referrals? | 6/35 (17) |
| Did you ask the health authority to help financially? | 6/35 (17) |
| Did you use any other method to avoid an overspend? | 9/35 (25) |

*Note*:
[1] $n$ = number who responded positively to this question
 $N$ = number who responded in total.

(Table 10.10) were behaving like health authorities. These specific
rationing decisions might have been based on careful prioritization,
or been *ad hoc* responses to inadequate risk management.

### Problems experienced due to overspending on rare costly referrals

Five pilots (5 out of 37 (14 per cent)) reported problems because
the cost of rare costly referrals exceeded the provision made for
them, but follow-up telephone interviews found that only four of
these had overspent. Problems were experienced for a wide range
of population sizes and per capita budgets. The specific problems
experienced by the four pilots were in each case due to between one
and three exceptionally costly patients, mainly due to the costs of
psychiatric or intensive care. One pilot had to spend £40,000 on a
paediatric intensive care admission, £60,000 on a cardiac referral,
and over £100,000 on a long-stay patient. Another spent over
£200,000 on two psychiatric admissions to private secure facilities.
A third spent £89,000 on an intensive care admission following an
emergency operation, and a third (with a 13,000 population) spent
£80,000 on a patient with an eating disorder and £30,000 on an
intensive care admission. There were no differences in the probability of reporting problems between single- and multi-practice
pilots, or between pilots with more or fewer than 30,000 population.
These problems can be attributed to inadequate provision for risks.
An earlier paper (Bachmann and Bevan 1996) suggested suitable
risk management arrangements for 15 categories of rare costly
referral. The 15 types of referral included all of the cases that had
led to overspending by TPPs, and most of the cases that worried
pilots (Table 10.7). The expected costs of these 15 types of referral,
based on costs and rates from one district, are about £12 per capita.

The risk premiums required to cope with year-to-year variations are about £24 for a population of 10,000, and £16 for a population of 30,000 (Bachmann and Bevan 1996). In comparison, the budgets for rare costly referrals in the four pilots that overspent were all set too low (range: 88p to £9.58 per capita). More careful planning could have avoided such problems.

Despite this, relatively few pilots reported problems due to overspending on rare costly referrals. This was surprising, considering that most were worried, but few had fully investigated this risk or taken steps to avoid it. The infrequency of problems was not primarily due to pilots blocking back responsibility for rare costly referrals to their health authorities, as most pilots retained this responsibility. Nor was it due to pilots receiving exceptionally generous allocations: the reported per capita budgetary allocation for all HCHS was £368 for the pilots, which was less than the national average of £440 for health authorities (Office of Health Economics 1995).

A lack of good information could have been one explanation for problems being reported infrequently. Many pilots did not have accounts itemizing their expenditure on rare costly referrals and did not know whether they had overspent or underspent. Only 15 pilots were able to estimate what they had spent in 1996/97 on rare costly referrals (over and above their contributions to risk-sharing schemes). Only 14 could state what they had expected to spend during this period, and only 10 provided both estimates. An explanation for the lack of information, aside from the logistical difficulties of collecting and analysing the data, could have been a lack of serious concern by pilots about whether there would be any penalties from overspending caused by rare costly referrals. There may have been an assumption that, as they were subcommittees of health authorities, any overspending would have to be made good by the health authority. Therefore, in practice, the ultimate risk was borne not by TPPs but by health authorities. Other possible reasons for the lack of problems reported due to rare costly referrals could have been good risk management, which was not identified in this research, or simply good luck.

### Savings from spending less than was budgeted for rare costly referrals

One in four pilots (10 out of 40) spent less than their budget for rare costly referrals during 1996/97. Nearly one in two single-practice pilots underspent their budget compared with one in seven multi-practice pilots (6 out of 13 versus 4 out of 27; p = 0.03). One in two small pilots (with less than 30,000 population) underspent their budget compared with 1 in 19 larger pilots (9 out of 21 versus 1 out of 19, p = 0.009). This could have reflected the greater ability of smaller or single-practice pilots to manage demand for rare costly referrals. Alternatively, it could have been due to chance, because smaller risk pools would have led to more random variation in referral rates and therefore a greater probability of underspends as well as overspends. If the latter explanation were true then smaller practices would still be at higher risk of overspending in the following year, and savings should have been kept for that purpose.

Of the ten pilots reporting savings, four held the savings over to the next year in case of overspending in the future, and six spent the savings. Only one pilot returned its savings to the health authority, compared to six which asked the health authority to help financially with an expected overspend. This suggests an asymmetry in implicit risk sharing, with pilots that made savings keeping them, but the health authority (and non-total purchasing practices) bearing the risk of TPP overspends.

## IMPLICATIONS FOR PRIMARY CARE GROUPS

The *New NHS* White Paper envisages PCGs developing through stages over a ten-year period (Secretary of State for Health 1997). The ability of PCGs to balance their income and expenditure is critical to their evolution and should be a key consideration in their structure and function. Like TPPs, PCGs are subcommittees of their health authorities, and the experience of TPPs provides the best evidence yet in guiding their development.

The evidence from total purchasing in the first live year (1996/97) was that integration of clinical and financial roles was more likely to happen within single-practice TPPs than in multi-practice organizations. Unfortunately, we do not have evidence on their development in their second live year. In 1996/97, single-practice TPPs were more likely to involve GPs other than the lead in decision making; found it easier to adapt GP performance within year; and were more often able to keep their spending in line with what had been planned. During their first live year of total purchasing, multi-practice TPPs were new organizations in which practices and their GPs were in the early stages of developing coherent organizations.

Their capacity to manage budgets and involve all GPs was likely to improve, had they been allowed a number of years to develop. In 1996/97, smaller and single-practice TPPs were not more likely to report problems due to overspending on rare costly referrals. This could have been due to prudent or opportunistic risk sharing with health authorities. Alternatively it could have been due to luck, or a lack of timely information about financial problems.

The NHS reforms introduced in 1991 (Secretaries of State for Health 1989) divided GPs into two groups: fundholders and non-fundholders. The study of TPPs has identified an important third kind: non-fundholding GPs in fundholding practices. This third type may be seen as 'free-riders' who were happy to accept the benefits of fundholding and total purchasing for their patients (for example, more practice-based services) provided that this did not interfere with their clinical autonomy. This third kind offers an explanation for the problems experienced, particularly by multi-practice TPPs, in managing their budgets. As the impact of each GP on the whole organization is relatively small, each GP has an incentive to 'free-ride' in the absence of personal sanctions to the contrary.

Integration of GPs' insurance and gatekeeping roles may be encouraged within PCGs by developing internal budgeting at practice level, or by small subgroups of GPs volunteering to work together. Department of Health guidance stresses that PCGs governing arrangements should promote financial control by supporting the effective management of devolved budgets. Groups starting at level 2 would 'take devolved responsibility for managing the budget for health care in their area, formally as part of the health authority . . . [and] maintain financial control by managing the deployment of budgets devolved to them, including monitoring expenditure against indicative practice-level budgets' (NHS Executive 1998c). Budgets in PCGs should be set at the level of individual practices because 'budgets should be managed at the same level as spending decisions are made' (NHS Executive 1998b). Correspondingly, 'incentives at practice level will be a feature of the primary care group financial framework', and 'could take the form of contributions towards service development, practice development [or] professional development' (NHS Executive 1998b). It is unclear what, in practice, the sanctions might be against individual GPs who free-ride, or the incentives to integrate their traditional role with that of insurer.

Developing practice-based budgets within larger groupings is certainly an advance on the experience of total purchasers, and should mitigate opportunities for free-riding. But the total purchasing experience suggests that the logistics of information management may make this aim difficult to achieve for some years. Indeed, managerial capacity is likely to be a key limiting factor in the devolution of HCHS budgets from health authorities to PCGs, and within PCGs. Organizing financial management at PCG level may appear to offer economies of scale in managing budgets compared with doing so at practice level (Posnett *et al.* 1998). But if effective budgetary management by PCGs requires budgetary management at practice level, then such savings are illusory. It suggests that savings in management costs may only be achieved by loss of budgetary control by PCGs.

Department of Health guidance recognized that budgetary allocations to PCGs will be affected by 'the risk management arrangements established between the health authority and the primary care group or primary care groups in question' (NHS Executive 1998c). Department of Health guidance recommended that 'primary care groups will need to work together with their practices to develop suitable risk management strategies to avoid overspends (or significant underspends) against their budgets. The strategies that they adopt should also be based on the existing approaches used by their parent health authorities. Some risks may require establishment of a contingency reserve' (NHS Executive 1998b). Research on TPPs suggests that existing approaches will typically be inadequate as few health authorities or TPPs had assessed the relationship between population size and random fluctuations in costs of rare costly referrals (Bachmann and Bevan 1996). One explanation for this was that TPPs expected health authorities to pay for any overspending (but to allow TPPs to keep savings from underspending).

Nevertheless, PCGs ought to find risk management easier than TPPs because they will cover larger populations (about 100,000, against a TPP mean of 33,000) and annual contracts between purchasers and providers will be replaced by longer term service agreements, in principle, covering three-year periods. These two changes effectively increase the size of PCGs' risk pools compared with TPPs, where this is conceived in terms of person-years at risk. New arrangements specifically for rare costly referrals could also make risk management easier for PCGs. Extra-contractual referrals have been replaced by service agreements for low-volume, high-cost specialist services, at health authority level. This could make the future costs of such referrals more predictable and beyond the scope of PCGs. At regional level, it is intended that consortia for funding even more specialized services will be arranged in and between regions. Therefore, PCGs are currently exposed to few risks (Department of Health 1998c). On the other hand, this raises again the question of whether such arrangements will introduce a moral hazard for rare costly referrals by blunting incentives for GPs to consider their costs. As argued in the introduction, such insurance arrangements ought to be restricted to the types of referral over which GPs have little discretion rather than in terms of the rarity of the risk.

In summary, from the perspective of the management of risk and budgets, together with developing incentives for the efficient use of resources, there are trade-offs in choosing the scale at which GPs should be encouraged to take on their new role of insurer. Groups of practices covering larger populations will have less financial risk due to random variation, but their GPs will be less able to work together and consequently less willing to change their clinical practice to seek efficiency gains in the face of budgetary constraints. However, experience of TPPs and a theoretical model of risks suggest that the risk from rare costly referrals for small populations is less of a problem than was originally anticipated. Indeed, the new arrangements seem to have been designed to the point of overkill to reduce a problem that small TPPs could manage quite well. Such overkill is likely to be counterproductive since it ensures that no GPs need worry about the costs of these referrals.

More generally, to justify moving budgets from health authorities to PCGs, GPs ought to take some responsibilities for the management of risks with *some* sanctions on individual GPs for overspending budgets. Experience of TPPs suggests that GPs are more likely to work together in managing clinical decisions against budgets in small groups. So PCGs should monitor and act on practice-level budgets and expenditure if they want GPs to help them balance their budgets. However, it is difficult to see how this can be achieved if the 'new NHS' is to reduce transactions costs. Jonathan Weiner, in a personal communication, has observed that an efficient, not-for-profit, HMO spends about £300 per capita per year on management costs! Can PCGs really be serious about managed care with an approximate management cost of £3 per capita?

# 11

# HOLDING TOTAL PURCHASING PILOTS TO ACCOUNT

Jennifer Dixon, Nick Goodwin and Nicholas Mays

All organizations that handle public money are accountable for the way in which those funds are spent. Key questions about the accountability of these organizations include:

- Who are they accountable to?
- What are they accountable for?
- What are the mechanisms to ensure and demonstrate accountability?
- Are these mechanisms followed appropriately?

Like the general practitioner fundholding scheme before it, the total purchasing experiment allowed general practices to take direct responsibility for public funds to purchase HCHS on behalf of their registered patients. The *New NHS* White Paper (Secretary of State for Health 1997) extended this responsibility to all general practices in England (rather than volunteer practices as in the case of GP fundholders and TPPs) through PCGs established in 1998. GP fundholders and TPPs were accountable for the management of the significant sums of public funds they employed.

Since the NHS came into being in 1948, GPs have worked as independent practitioners, under contract to the near monopoly purchaser of care – the NHS. Until the advent of fundholding, GPs were not accountable directly to the state (the NHS) for managing NHS funds (since they did not hold a budget) or for their overall performance to any great degree. GPs were accountable mainly for their clinical competence to the General Medical Council. GP fundholding and total purchasing changed all that. GPs and their staff became directly responsible for millions of pounds of tax-payers' money. As budget holders, they became explicitly account-able to the state for the first time. As independent practitioners, fundholders were unused to the mechanisms set up to ensure accountability. When fundholding was extended on a pilot basis to total purchasing, accountability arrangements had to be developed still further.

This chapter explores the adequacy of these mechanisms through the experience of the first-wave TPPs. It begins by briefly defining accountability and sketching the intended mechanisms to ensure accountability of fundholders and later TPPs. It then examines the extent to which these mechanisms were followed in the case of total purchasing. The chapter ends by discussing the lessons from the total purchasing initiative, which are relevant to developing effec-tive accountability for PCGs.

## WHAT IS ACCOUNTABILITY?

Accountability has been defined as:

> The construction of an agreed language or currency of dis-course about conduct and performance, and the criteria that should be used in assessing them.
>
> (Day and Klein 1988)

In political science terms, public accountability is normally thought of as the process of giving an account of performance by those who administer institutions on the public's behalf. Two main dimensions of public accountability are usually identified: *political account-ability*, which concerns the relationship between the elected repre-sentatives and the people; and *administrative accountability*, which concerns the relationship between the administrative agencies that implement law and policy (New 1993).

In a health care context, clinicians are also accountable for their clinical competence to the relevant professional body, for example, the General Medical Council in the case of doctors and the United Kingdom Central Council for Nursing in the case of nurses and health visitors. However, this aspect of accountability is not discussed in this chapter since total purchasing made little or no difference to it.

### Administrative accountability

NHS bodies are administratively accountable by statute to the Secretary of State for Health, and ultimately to Parliament, for the management of resources allocated to the NHS and the performance of the service. Management of resources includes the financial probity with which funds are spent; NHS organizations are accountable to the House of Commons Public Accounts Committee in this respect. NHS organizations are also accountable to the Parliamentary Commissioner for Health in cases where maladministration is suspected.

### Political accountability

In 1988, Day and Klein neatly noted that political accountability for the NHS could be described as being directed 'formally upwards', but 'informally downwards'. 'Formally upwards' meant to the Secretary of State for Health, who is accountable to Parliament and ultimately to voters. 'Informally downwards' meant to the public; this form of accountability was informal because there were no means for the public to, for example, vote out the managers of local health services, since the board members of health authorities are not democratically elected (unlike councillors in local authorities). Furthermore, health authorities are not required to act directly in response to the wishes of the populations they serve. Although mechanisms to ensure downward accountability to the public are not strong in the NHS, a range of channels exist:

- NHS trusts must hold an annual public meeting and publish an annual report;
- health authority board meetings must be open to the public;
- there is a statutory responsibility for each health authority to ensure that a community health council is functioning in its area, which represents the public interest and must be consulted when there are major plans by the health authority to alter local services;
- PCGs are required to publish annual accountability agreements setting out their future plans and past performance.

Furthermore, recent policies have encouraged health authorities to consult the public directly, for example, via the *Local Voices* initiative (Department of Health 1991a) and *Promoting Patient Partnership* (Department of Health 1996c). In addition, in 1998 the Labour government took the unprecedented step of setting up a regular national survey of patients' and users' experiences of the NHS.

## ACCOUNTABILITY ARRANGEMENTS

### Health authorities

Health authorities are accountable to the NHS Executive, and to the Secretary of State for their financial management and overall performance. They must take account of central government policies – for example, as set out in the planning and priorities guidance published annually by the NHS Executive (NHS Executive 1996d) and in health service circulars – when developing local policies and commissioning health services.

A corporate 'contract' is agreed each year by the health authority and the local NHS Executive Regional Office setting out the goals of the health authority for the year against which its performance is to be reviewed. There is no national template for the corporate contract, and management objectives are likely to vary by NHS region and by health authority

Some of the aspects of the corporate contract, such as management costs, waiting times and provider productivity, are quantifiable. In many other areas, quantification is not possible or less meaningful. In these areas, health authorities are usually asked to demonstrate progress, and the process of reviewing performance takes the form of a discussion of progress rather than the achievement, or not, of specific targets.

## FUNDHOLDERS AND TOTAL PURCHASING PILOTS

Fundholding and total purchasing gave GPs and their staff the responsibility for managing NHS resources directly to purchase specified treatments provided outside primary care, for example community health services and secondary care. Standard fundholders were legally responsible for a budget for elective in-patient and day case services, outpatient care, prescription drugs, diagnostic tests and practice staffing. These funds were managed independently of the health authority by the fundholding practice. Fundholders enjoyed significant autonomy.

A different arrangement existed for the TPPs, which had only informal status as pilots and were not recognized in legislation. Unlike fundholding, the budget for these services was not assigned to the TPP to manage independently, but was managed jointly by the TPP and the health authority. TPPs were made subcommittees of the health authority and, therefore, directly accountable to the health authority for the funds managed beyond the scope of the fundholding scheme. The health authority remained legally responsible for the TPP's funds and was in a strong position to influence how the funds were used.

There was no prescribed list of goods and services that TPPs could purchase, as there was in fundholding. In theory, a TPP could, in addition to holding a separate fundholding budget, hold a budget for *all* the rest of its patients' HCHS. In practice, most TPPs chose to take the responsibility for purchasing only a limited selection from the services not covered by the fundholding scheme. Typically, these included emergency admissions, general medicine, care of the elderly, and paediatrics (Robinson *et al.* 1998). The responsibility for purchasing services such as A&E services, services for people with a learning disability and many tertiary hospital services typically remained with the health authority, although the TPP was able to exert some influence over the purchasing process (Robinson *et al.* 1998).

In 1995, guidelines were issued (NHS Executive 1994a) outlining in what ways health authorities should hold standard fundholding practices accountable. In 1996, despite the informal status of the TPPs, the NHS Executive indicated that this framework should also apply to TPPs in the absence of anything having been developed specifically for the TPPs (NHS Executive 1996c). The accountability framework covered four main areas: management accountability and financial accountability (i.e. administrative accountability); accountability to patients and the wider public (i.e. political accountability); and professional accountability (not discussed in this chapter).

## MANAGEMENT ACCOUNTABILITY OF FUNDHOLDERS AND TOTAL PURCHASING PILOTS

Fundholding practices (and, by extension, TPPs) were each required to publish an annual practice plan and submit it to the health authority. The plan was to set out how the practice (TPP) intended to use its fund and management budget over the year and demonstrate the practice's (TPP's) contribution to national targets and priorities as well as any locally agreed objectives. As part of their annual planning, fundholders (and TPPs) were required to announce major shifts in their purchasing intentions in the same way as health authorities. Health authorities were required to confirm that fundholders' (and TPPs') plans were consistent with national priorities, and 'in aggregate, meet national targets and objectives set out in the annual planning and priorities guidance'.

Fundholders (and TPPs) were required to submit a brief annual report to the health authority setting out performance against their plan and highlighting significant developments. Fundholders (and TPPs) and health authorities were required to hold regular review meetings to identify areas for development and planning in future.

### Accountability to patients and the wider public

Fundholders (and TPPs) were required to publish documents that related to the management of their fund, for example major shifts in purchasing, annual practice plans and performance reports. These documents were to be sent to the health authority and local community health council and a copy or summary was to be made available at the practice for consultation by patients. While the accountability framework encouraged practices to involve patients in service planning and review, no specific requirements were made. Fundholders (and TPPs) were required to have appropriate systems for handling complaints.

## FINANCIAL ACCOUNTABILITY OF FUNDHOLDERS AND TOTAL PURCHASING PILOTS

Fundholders (and TPPs) were required to prepare and make available annual accounts for independent audit by the Audit Commission. Expenditure and activity by fundholders (and TPPs) was to be monitored by the health authority on a monthly basis. The use of any savings was also to be approved by the health authority/NHS Executive Regional Office. Furthermore, fundholders were required to specify in their annual practice plan how they intended to deliver their contribution to the local efficiency targets set by the NHS Executive.

The guidance was described by the NHS Executive as a 'framework' for accountability. How mandatory some of the more specific requirements were, whether or not specific hard targets should be achieved, and the mechanisms which the health authority could use to influence the fundholders' (and TPPs') practice were not made so clear despite the apparent formality of the framework. Unlike the system of performance review between health authorities and NHS Executive Regional Offices, there was no mention of the need for a corporate contract between the health authority and its devolved purchasers. In a technical sense, it was not clear whether or not the health authority could have a corporate contract with itself (since the TPP was a subcommittee of the health authority). In practice the approach adopted by the NHS Executive was to give fundholders and TPPs more autonomy and scope to innovate than their health authorities.

## ASSESSING THE ACCOUNTABILITY OF TOTAL PURCHASING PILOTS

### Managerial accountability

*Formal structures of accountability*

By the autumn of 1995, almost all the TPPs had formed a project board to oversee the development and activities of the TPP on which health authority staff were represented (see Chapter 3). Just under half of the project boards had been made formal subcommittees of the health authority by autumn 1995, and all had by April 1996. The project board typically included the lead GPs in each practice involved in the TPP, the total purchasing manager and various health authority representatives (for example, a non-executive director of the health authority). In many, voting rights had been made explicit. The project boards met regularly (typically monthly) to oversee development of the TPP and report to the health authority. The majority of TPPs had also formed executive boards comprising TPP practice staff (typically GPs and the total purchasing project manager) which met typically weekly to discuss day-to-day operational matters.

*Decision-making autonomy*

If all TPPs had developed formal structures of management and accountability, how did they work in practice? In the preparatory year, 1995, almost all TPP respondents reported that key decisions relating to the development of the TPP were taken at the level of the TPP, and ratified by the project board. Key players in this process were the lead GPs. This remained unchanged in 1997 – a year after the TPPs went live. While there was significant involvement of health authority staff at most projects (and relations were regarded as far closer than under fundholding), in most cases health authority staff did not appear to play a key role in decisions affecting the development of the TPP. In a small minority of TPPs, health authority staff were represented on clinical subgroups reviewing specific services.

In 1995, TPPs' priorities for purchasing tended to be based on GPs' views of local service issues, influenced by their own experience of treating patients. While the health authorities' purchasing plans were available to the TPPs to review when designing their own plans, obtaining information on past service delivery patterns (in order to put together a business or purchasing plan) had not been straightforward since health authorities and providers had difficulty disaggregating information for TPP patients. Such difficulties also led to widespread problems for budget setting (see Chapter 9). Information problems caused great frustration and, as a result, as one TPP GP put it, business plans were often informed by the 'gut feelings of the general practitioners'. In a minority of instances, the TPP simply followed the same plans as the health authority for the services that they were purchasing. Formal consultation with patients over these plans appeared to be rare, although approximately half the TPPs had involved health authority public health medicine staff in an attempt to assess needs to inform purchasing. The majority of TPPs had shared and discussed their purchasing intentions with health authority representatives on the project board, and in several pilots the TPP's purchasing intentions were published in the same document as the health authority's.

The high degree of freedom perceived by the TPP staff as to what to purchase was reflected in responses by health authority lead managers in 1995 when asked about the degree of autonomy afforded to the TPPs in decision making. Thirty-six per cent reported that the TPPs had been given total autonomy (response rate 92 per cent). Fifty-five per cent aimed to give the TPPs as much freedom as possible, but with qualifications. These were typically that the TPP should work within the framework of health authority strategy, and should not act to the detriment of local health services used by other practices. A typical response was:

The TPP is given total autonomy to spend the health commission's [health authority's] resources. However, the TPP will be asked to justify purchasing decisions if it diverts from those laid out in the Health Investment Plan.

Only 9 per cent of respondents reported that the TPP had little or no autonomy in decision making.

The high degree of autonomy that the health authorities claimed to give to TPPs in 1995 was confirmed by the responses in 1997 from the TPP manager and lead GP. The vast majority (95 per cent) of responses revealed that key decisions over the development of the TPP occurred at practice/TPP level, but were generally ratified by the health authority subcommittee and/or project board.

A typical method developed by a TPP for agreeing its objectives with the health authority was as follows:

The TPP[s] decide on strategies and then decide[s] who are the key players for each strategy and then go and lobby the key player to get them on board. It is then taken to the Director of Primary Care as a *fait accompli*.

However, a minority of TPPs reported that they had little room for manoeuvre:

The health authority comes with instructions as to what can and cannot be done. We should have been given total freedom.

It [total purchasing] has been under the control of civil servants, who don't know what is going on and who will put a brake on any idea so that nothing drastic happens.

### Reviewing and reporting performance

In 1995, almost all TPP GPs thought that they would be held to account through regular review at the TPP project board or health authority subcommittee (a view that proved accurate in the first live year, 1996/97). Many also thought that they would be held to account through their purchasing plan/intentions. But most acknowledged that not all the rules of engagement had been fully worked out with the health authority in the preparatory year. At the same time, approximately two-thirds of health authorities reported that they had no plans to develop a corporate contract with the TPP akin to that between the health authority and the NHS Executive Regional Office. Typically, such a contract was believed to add 'too much red tape'. Yet, one-third of health authority respondents reported plans to develop a separate corporate contract with their TPP, and one health authority had developed a constitution, specifying criteria by which the TPP would be held to account.

In 1995, the lead GPs were asked what they believed the health authority would expect them to achieve with respect to notable national policy objectives, including: the *Health of the Nation* strategy (Department of Health 1992), the *Local Voices* initiative (Department of Health, 1991a), the *Patient's Charter* (Department of Health 1991b), the *NHS Efficiency Index* targets for hospital activity in relation to resource inputs (Appleby 1996) and the recently issued guidelines for sharing continuing care responsibilities between the NHS and the local authority social services departments (NHS Executive 1995). They were also asked whether or not they thought they would have to work towards the local strategic objectives of the health authority. The results, shown in Figure 11.1, categorize the responses according to whether the lead GPs understood they were required to achieve any hard or specified targets, whether they believed that they were expected to work generally towards policy objectives, or whether no expectations had been raised by the health authority.

The responses show that six months before the TPPs went live, the GPs reported that they had not been asked to deliver on hard targets in any area, with the exception of financial targets (they were expected to balance the TPP's budgets; see below), and *Patient's Charter* standards. Significant numbers of lead GPs thought that they would be expected to achieve the same targets as the health authority, although these had not been made explicit to them. In the majority of cases, GPs did not know what the expectations of the health authority were.

In most cases, the lead GPs expressed willingness to work towards the same targets as the health authority. Some TPPs had been doing so in any case (e.g. *Health of the Nation* targets), and a few were attempting to involve the public or patients via the community health council or through patient focus groups. Many noted that targets set out in the *Patient's Charter* and the *NHS Efficiency Index* were being addressed through their fundholding work and that the health authority had made no further requirements. A notable proportion had difficulty with two specific policies: the *NHS Efficiency Index* – comments included 'it is rubbish'; 'it fundamentally goes against total purchasing'; 'we are going to have

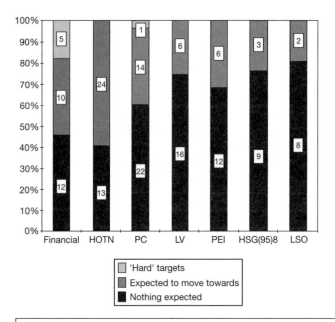

Key: Financial = financial management; HOTN = *Health of the Nation* targets; PC = *Patient's Charter* targets; LV = *Local Voices*; PEI = *Purchaser Efficiency Index* targets; HSG(95)8 = meeting guidelines for NHS and social services continuing care responsibilities; LSO = local strategic objectives.
Note: The numbers in the bars refer to the number of TPPs that responded to this question.

**Figure 11.1** Lead general practitioners' understanding of what the total purchasing pilot would have to achieve with regard to financial management and key national policy objectives, 1995

difficulty getting agreement [with the health authority] over this one') – and *Local Voices* – many thought that it was difficult to involve patients meaningfully. In general, the responses indicated that the lead GPs expected that measured achievement against targets would not be a formal and explicit requirement: 'Whether or not we achieve them will be in the lap of the Gods'; 'We have a "mature and mutual understanding" with the health authority over the targets'; 'We will be expected to comply, but we will not lose sleep over [attainment of] the targets.'

In 1997, health authority leads were asked about how they intended to hold TPPs to account for the funds that they had spent during 1996/97, and what the TPPs were expected to achieve in key national policy areas: *Health of the Nation*, the *Patient's Charter*, the *NHS Purchaser Efficiency Index*, *Local Voices*, breast and cervical cancer screening (as an example of a recent national policy development), and other local strategic objectives. Most of the health authority leads reported that the mechanism for reviewing TPP performance was through regular meetings of the project board. Figure 11.2 shows whether there was an expectation that the TPPs would achieve hard targets, a formal expectation of progress, an informal expectation of progress towards targets, or no expectation in each policy area.

Most respondents had a formal expectation that the TPPs would work towards national and local policy objectives, but there was little or no explicit monitoring of the TPP in place. Typically, it was assumed by many health authority leads that some targets (such as cervical cancer screening and those set out in *The Health of the Nation*) were being worked towards by the practices in the course of their routine delivery of general medical services (GMS). Breast cancer screening was typically left by the TPP to the health authority to purchase. *Patient's Charter* standards and the *NHS Efficiency Index* targets were thought to be more relevant to fundholding than total purchasing, and, typically, health authority leads reported that they monitored these in aggregate across the entire health authority population with any identified problems investigated at practice level. There was a common implicit assumption that the TPPs comprised 'good' practices, which were performing better against targets than other practices in the health authority. Therefore they could, and should, be left alone as far as possible. Several health authorities pointed out the difficulty of monitoring targets at TPP level because of the poor quality of available data. Indeed, since health authority leads expressed difficulties in achieving the same policy objectives themselves, some had taken a lenient approach to such achievement in TPPs. For example, regarding *The Health of the Nation,* one manager said: 'We struggle with that as a health authority, never mind the TPPs [having] to demonstrate that.'

The responses by the TPP managers in 1997 revealed a very similar picture: they were willing to work towards most targets, with the exception of the *NHS Efficiency Index* and the expectations set out in *Local Voices*. The TPP managers also confirmed that health authorities were generally ambivalent about whether TPPs needed to demonstrate progress towards the targets, and only a minority of TPPs had been required to do so.

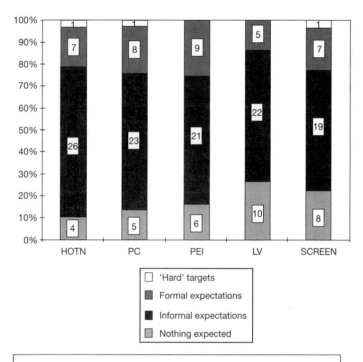

*Key*: HOTN = *Health of the Nation* targets; PC = *Patient's Charter* targets;
PEI = *Purchaser Efficiency Index* targets; LV = *Local Voices*; Screen =
National breast and cervical screening targets.
*Note*: The numbers in the bars refer to the number of TPPs that responded to
this question.

**Figure 11.2**   Health authority leads' expectations of what total
purchasing pilots should deliver against key national policy objectives,
1997

In 1997, the health authority leads were also asked about the
extent to which they thought the TPP could destabilize local
services, and whether or not the local impact of purchasing by TPPs
on non-TPP patients had been monitored. In the majority of
responses, the health authority leads thought that there was *potential* for destabilization. The minority (typically those whose TPPs
were small) thought not. Most thought that this danger was more
theoretical than real, on the grounds that their TPP was deemed to
be 'responsible'.

## FINANCIAL ACCOUNTABILITY

In the overwhelming majority of TPPs, the requirements and approach to financial monitoring were similar across the country. As indicated in the responses above, TPPs and health authority leads reported that monitoring of financial performance occurred regularly (monthly or quarterly) through meetings of the project board. Typically the board monitored expenditure and activity against budget, attempting to explain variances, and took action to avoid overspends. However, in some cases even straightforward monitoring of activity and expenditure could not be accomplished because of severe deficiencies in the health authority and/or TPP information systems – a few TPPs had to monitor expenditure using paper records.

At TPP level, monitoring tended to occur more frequently, often weekly, at the meetings of the TPP's executive board. Typical activities at this level included validating the provider activity data that generated invoices to ensure that the TPP was not being over-billed.

Every health authority indicated that, although details had not been finalized, the TPP accounts would be audited in the same way as the health authority's accounts – by external auditors. However, there was next to no activity by health authorities to query or investigate the *rationale* for expenditure on specific NHS services by TPPs – only six health authority leads mentioned monitoring the quality of services purchased, but none gave any details of how they were doing so. None mentioned investigating the *appropriateness* of the services purchased. The strong tendency was to adopt either the approach taken for fundholders, or to treat the TPP as an integral part of the health authority as the NHS Executive Regional Offices chose to do (Strawderman *et al.* 1996). The result was that monitoring and audit were dominated by accounting concerns and almost never with quality or cost-effectiveness. This is also reflected in the modest extent to which health authorities required TPPs to demonstrate achievements against national policy targets, as discussed earlier.

On the management costs of TPPs, the health authority leads reported auditing the management cost accounts of the TPP in a similar ways to those of fundholders. Again, the prime focus of such audits was on whether the money spent had been devoted to the intended purpose and/or had been spent legally. There was no mention of, say, comparing the management costs of the TPP with other similar pilots. Given the large range of variation in direct management costs per capita for first-wave TPPs (from £0.26 to £8.05, mean £3.00; Mays *et al.* 1997a and see Chapter 3), it might have been expected that health authorities would have been concerned to ensure that the management costs of their local TPPs were appropriate.

## ACCOUNTABILITY TO PATIENTS AND THE WIDER PUBLIC

The total purchasing initiative was part of a wider effort in the mid-1990s to move towards a more primary care-led NHS (NHS Executive 1994b). In addition, total purchasing developed in a national context in which 'working towards a well informed public' was one of the five strategic objectives for the NHS as set out in the Conservative government's White Paper, *The National Health Service: A Service with Ambitions* (Department of Health 1996b). In practical terms, accountability of TPPs to the public, like fundholders, was based on the requirement to make key documents publicly available (see above). While the active involvement of patients in service planning and review was encouraged, there were no explicit requirements for patient involvement (NHS Executive 1994b).

During interviews towards the end of the first 'live' year (1996/97), each lead GP was asked the following question: 'What efforts have been made by the TPP to consult the practice population over the range of services purchased by the TPP, or any major changes in contracts?' (Prompt: has the TPP involved the community health council (CHC) and, if so, how?).

In interpreting the responses of the lead GPs to this question, the analysis focused on the extent to which different levels of patient accountability had been reached, as outlined in the consultation document *Involving Patients: Examples of Good Practice* (NHS Executive 1997a). Specifically, the responses of the lead GPs were classified as follows:

- neither informing nor consulting patients;
- informing patients;
- consulting patients.

### Neither informing nor consulting patients

Forty-six per cent of lead GPs (24 out of 49) reported that the TPP had done nothing either to inform or consult patients on the development of the project or any changes that the pilot wished to make to local services. Most of the respondents held the view that there was little or no need for any formal consultation with patients since a high level of awareness of patients' needs and wants was already available through GPs' day-to-day contact with their patients. In addition, these GPs expressed scepticism about the value of patients' views as follows: '[Patient consultation] would be a waste of effort since patients are not in the best position to give an informed and constructive opinion.'

These GPs appeared not to have followed the requirements set out in the accountability framework for fundholding and total purchasing (NHS Executive, 1994b) which mentions making key documents, such as annual practice plans and purchasing intentions, available at practices for consultation by patients. Most GPs in this group either assumed that patients were unlikely to be interested in any of the developments, or that the dissemination of information directly to patients was inappropriate.

**Informing patients**

Fourteen per cent of lead GPs (7 out of 49) reported that patients had been informed of developments at the TPP, rather than consulted about them. The main mechanisms used were practice newsletters or leaflets, posters attached to surgery notice boards, or more detailed waiting room displays. Although most GPs in this group felt that informing patients was necessary and would be likely to stimulate patient interest, there was a common disappointment that the information provided to patients had not necessarily been taken up with any enthusiasm. The following observation was a typical response: '[The TPP informed patients] through a practice leaflet, poster and a press release ... but there have been no enquiries from any patient.'

**Consulting patients**

By contrast, the remaining GPs (21 out of 49) had attempted actively to consult patients through patient participation groups, patient fora or by conducting patient satisfaction surveys and, occasionally, through consulting patient interest groups (where a proposed change to a service was discussed at length between a wide range of interested parties including the TPP, health authority, providers and patients). However, even in this group the GPs typically took the view that there was little or no need for any formal consultation – one, for example, felt that the TPP had been coerced into a consultation process: 'We only organized a public meeting [on total purchasing] because it was felt 'politically correct' to do so.'

While 30 members of the public attended this meeting, a far lower level of public participation was more usual. Indeed, the ability to engender public and patient involvement in consultation groups proved to be difficult, and several patient participation groups had been disbanded because of this. The following examples were typical:

> At our last forum group only three people turned up . . . one of whom left when he realized he was in the wrong meeting.

> We had to cancel our forum meetings because numbers decreased to the point where participants were usually just practice employees and health service workers rather than patients.

However, there were instances of more successful approaches to patient involvement. For example, one single-practice TPP set up a 'Friends' group to discuss purchasing priorities for the patients of the town. This process culminated in a decision that the TPP would not purchase *in vitro* fertilization treatment. In another TPP, 1500 patients attended four public meetings before the project went live on the basis of which a newsletter and patient participation group were established at the public's request. But the experience of most TPPs highlighted the difficulties faced in routinely generating any significant public interest or patient participation in purchasing decisions.

### Informing and consulting community health councils

The accountability guidelines made explicit reference to the expectation that copies, or summaries, of relevant documents be sent to CHCs, and that closer relations with CHCs would occur (NHS Executive 1997a). However, the responses from lead GPs suggest that formal links with CHCs were rare – most TPPs reported no contact at all. Only 2 out of 53 projects had a CHC representative on the project board in 1995, rising to only 5 out of 52 projects by 1997. In only one of these cases did the CHC and TPP cooperate closely.

## WERE TOTAL PURCHASING PILOTS ADEQUATELY ACCOUNTABLE?

A generally loose, relatively informal framework of accountability existed between health authorities and TPPs during the first live year of the scheme. This was a deliberate response to the pilot and informal status of the TPPs. The pilots posed a conceptual problem for the NHS because they were neither fully GP organizations unlike standard fundholders, nor fully part of the NHS bureaucratic hierarchy. They also depended on the health authorities for their management budgets. By and large, health authority respondents believed that the practices involved in total purchasing were experienced, 'good' practices which could generally be trusted to behave responsibly. Health authorities kept track of TPP activities and plans through the meetings of each project board, but, with the exception of conventional financial monitoring, did not generally require TPPs to demonstrate achievement against hard performance targets. The main requirement was that the TPPs should stay within budget, while showing the potential of GP-led purchasing in whichever ways they saw fit.

There were, however, more general expectations of performance – for example, that the TPPs would work towards achieving national policy goals – although progress towards them appeared to be monitored superficially, if at all. Indeed, there was a widespread reluctance by health authorities to hold the TPPs more formally to account through, for example, a corporate contract. This may reflect the difficulty, noted by several health authorities, of monitoring progress meaningfully at TPP or practice level given the data available. Health authority staff also tended to believe that a corporate contract was appropriate only between legally separate bodies, not between a subcommittee and the health authority. So a common approach taken by health authorities was to monitor activities across the whole health authority, and only if there were problems to investigate further at TPP or practice level. This may have reflected a realistic appraisal of how difficult it would be for the health authority to influence TPP behaviour, given the scepticism expressed by some GPs towards initiatives such as the *NHS Efficiency Index* and the measures designed to improve health authority accountability to the public, such as *Local Voices*.

Relatively informal accountability measures may also have reflected pragmatism since it would have been time-consuming to develop and implement more formal procedures. The impression given by health authority leads was that they were stretched enough, coping with implementing a variety of policy initiatives as well as fulfilling their own purchasing role, while at the same time experiencing high staff turnover. In many ways, the fact that the TPP was a subcommittee of the health authority (rather than, for example, a go-it-alone fundholding practice) made it convenient for the health authority to monitor the TPP less explicitly, given other pressures on managers' time. As with fundholding, total purchasing was designed to develop at the grass roots, thereby allowing innovation to occur. The prevailing view at the centre and the NHS Executive Regional Offices appeared to be to let the TPPs get on with minimal interference (Strawderman *et al.* 1996). In any case, under the pilot arrangements GPs could simply withdraw from total purchasing with impunity if excessive demands were made upon them.

A legitimate question raised by the study is whether it would have been appropriate or necessary, given the TPPs' legal status as subcommittees of their local health authorities, to performance manage TPPs any differently from other parts of the authority's activities. Similar questions could be raised over the extent to which it would have been appropriate for locality commissioning groups (with or without delegated budgets from the health authority) to demonstrate accountability separately from their parent health authority.

The answer to these questions depends upon the extent to which health authorities and the NHS Executive envisaged specific national policy initiatives being implemented at TPP level. The results of this study raise questions about the extent to which centrally designed performance measures and policy goals, such as the *NHS Efficiency Index* and *Local Voices*, can be applied at local level. The potentially conflicting nature of policies is likely to be thrown into sharper focus at practice/TPP level than at the level of the larger population of a health authority. Lead GPs were very quick to point this out and freer than health authorities to reject the policies. For example, it was commonplace for GPs to criticize the *Purchaser Efficiency Index* for the fact that it recognized activity only within acute hospitals, whereas the TPPs were in many cases attempting to shift patient care from hospital to primary and community settings with the encouragement of the NHS Executive (see Chapters 4 to 6). Therefore, holding TPPs to account for implementing policies might have demonstrated these policy weaknesses more clearly.

Turning to 'downward' accountability, it is clear that informing, consulting or involving patients in developing or implementing plans and in reviewing the progress of projects was not a high priority for TPPs. Most lead GPs did not place a high value on formal patient input, preferring to trust their own experiences of patient care. Instead they highlighted the difficulties of involving patients directly. Consequently, accountability to patients and the wider public remained unfulfilled in most TPPs.

These conclusions are similar to those presented in previous work examining the level of accountability to patients and the wider public developed through fundholding (Goodwin 1998). Generally, the internal market reforms of the first half of the 1990s did little to alter the traditional position of patients and the public either in terms of their involvement in decision making ('voice') or their ability to choose between primary and secondary care purchasers ('exit'). Indeed, both fundholding and total purchasing cast the GP as the informed agent acting on behalf of his or her patients.

## IMPLICATIONS FOR THE ACCOUNTABILITY OF PRIMARY CARE GROUPS

The evidence on 'upward' and 'downward' accountability of TPPs has obvious relevance to PCGs in the English NHS (Secretary of State for Health 1997). Ultimately, PCGs will be responsible for purchasing almost all primary and secondary care on behalf of their populations. Health authorities will largely lose their purchasing role (with the exception of mental health services), but retain and enhance their role in developing strategy, and in monitoring and holding PCGs to account.

Compared to TPPs, PCGs face much clearer arrangements for upward accountability as the basic building blocks of the English NHS at local level. They are formally accountable to their host health authority through locally negotiated 'accountability agreements'. These agreements set out, far more clearly than for fundholding and total purchasing, the criteria against which performance is measured so that national standards can be attained. In addition, each PCG is required to contribute to and work within the health authority's health improvement programme (HImP, i.e. the local health strategy). Each health authority has the power to withdraw all or some of the devolved responsibility from PCGs if they do not meet its targets.

However, the exact nature of the accountability mechanisms to be employed by health authorities in relation to individual PCGs differs according to the level at which the PCG operates. Level 1 PCGs, the least ambitious, advise the health authority on its commissioning, while level 2 groups take on responsibility for commissioning a range of HCHS using a devolved budget in much the same manner as the TPPs. Level 3 groups, however, are more radical departures from the TPPs since they are free-standing commissioning organizations with their own budgets, accountable to the health authority for commissioning almost all HCHS for a registered population. Level 4 PCGs will do the same, but have the added responsibility for the delivery of all community health services and all GMS activity and other payments previously determined by the national GP contract.

Both level 1 and level 2 PCGs are formal subcommittees of their health authorities, while levels 3 and 4 are truly distinct entities: level 4 PCGs (known as primary care trusts) are NHS trusts in their own right (NHS Executive 1998c). As a result, accountability mechanisms become progressively more formal from level 1 to level 4 because responsibility for the management of funds and commissioning of services will increase and require far greater scrutiny. However, as Mays and Goodwin (1998) point out, the autonomy of level 3 and 4 groups may be highly constrained in practice through requirements to work within central and local strategic guidance, including a range of new national service frameworks. In addition, it remains unclear whether PCGs will be allowed to manoeuvre resources significantly between NHS trusts with the same degree of freedom that was enjoyed under fundholding and, to a lesser extent, in total purchasing. Indeed, it is possible that the greater managerial autonomy offered through more advanced forms of PCG may be offset by stricter central strategic guidelines, policed through stronger upward accountability. The combination of greater financial delegation to PCGs and stricter central control from the NHS Executive over the content of services and the attainment of targets (typical of Labour's 'third way' in health care; Ham 1999) suggests a potential for tension where local needs and national policy initiatives conflict. PCGs are likely to be less compliant in responding to the large volume of central requirements than health authorities since they are led, in the main, by independent contractor GPs.

While more formal upward accountability appears to be a significant part of the 'new NHS', the lack of downward accountability to patients observed in TPPs is likely to be little changed in future. All PCGs are required to involve the public (and also the local authority) in their decision making, but the mechanisms for this involvement are not spelled out except for lay representation on their boards. Since most previous attempts at greater patient involvement appear to have been both difficult and unsuccessful without major effort (Mays and Goodwin, 1998), it is unlikely that PCGs will succeed where their predecessors failed.

Finally, the advent of PCGs raises the issue of clinical accountability *within* PCGs, which the TPPs by and large ignored in favour of their purchasing role. Fundamental to the PCG concept is the idea that GPs and practices act collectively, rather than individually, to manage a common budget, which includes part of their GMS and prescribing expenditures as well as resources for purchasing services, delivered by others. However, the potential rationing implications of this make it unlikely that all practitioners will easily accept this collective responsibility. It is likely that some GPs will refuse to be bound by the decisions of the collective, since their traditional personal decision-making autonomy will be reduced as a result. Some GPs may 'free-ride' (see Chapter 3) on the collectivity, claiming that their patients' interest should come first (Street and Place 1998). As Mays and Goodwin (1998) point out, while information feedback and well-structured peer review within the PCG may be able to reduce inappropriate variations in the performance of professionals, in some cases there may be need for sanctions where embedded and unjustifiable differences of opinion and performance exist which have significant resource implications. It is feasible that such sanctions could be imposed by the management of a level 4 PCG if it set the terms and conditions of practitioner employment, but the mechanisms that could be employed by PCGs at other levels to solve such problems appear to be lacking. The issue of clinical governance and the move to greater collective responsibility for resources (Malcolm and Mays 1999) is probably the most significant challenge inherent in the creation of PCGs, yet its implications for clinical and corporate accountability have yet to be resolved.

# 12

# EVALUATING COMPLEX POLICIES: WHAT HAVE WE LEARNED FROM TOTAL PURCHASING?

## David Evans, Nicholas Mays and Sally Wyke

This chapter explores questions that are related to, but distinct from, the next and final chapter, which summarizes the policy lessons learned from the total purchasing experiment for the future of primary care organizations. It will ask, what can be learned from the experience of designing and undertaking the evaluation itself? What can other evaluators learn from the experience of the TP-NET? What would the members of this team themselves do again, and what would they avoid?

These questions are particularly pertinent since the evaluation of total purchasing became the first of a series of similar commissions for the evaluation of complex policy innovations in the UK, some of which have parallels in other developed countries. Following total purchasing, both Conservative and Labour governments in the UK commissioned evaluations of general practitioner commissioning groups (in 1997), primary medical services pilots (in 1997), the *Health of the Nation* strategy (Department of Health 1998a), Health Action Zones (in 1998) and PCGs (in 1999). Underlying these commissions was a cross-governmental approach to policy implementation which emphasized the need for evaluated pilots and experiments, not just in the health field (for example, pilot employment action zones and 'beacon' councils in local government; Miller 1998).

As Chapter 2 indicated, the total purchasing initiative was a challenge to policy evaluation. It showed all the features that are typical of important developments in public policy, but which make evaluation demanding. They are summarized (following the issues outlined in Chapter 2) in Box 12.1.

Despite these constraints, because of its novelty and high profile, the evaluation tender was very attractive to researchers, and the bidding process was competitive. The successful consortium bid, led by the King's Fund, involved a number of the leading organizations in UK health policy analysis and related research. Ultimately, the total purchasing evaluation took over four years to complete and involved over 30 researchers working in 11 academic departments and research units. It was an ambitious, complex and a relatively expensive project in terms of UK health programme evaluation. Did the evaluation team get it right? This chapter reflects on five issues drawn from the experience of carrying out the evaluation:

- the disciplinary and theoretical basis of the evaluation;
- developing collaborative approaches to evaluating complex policy innovations;
- improving the evaluation of policy pilots;
- influencing policy;
- the impact on the evaluation of major changes of policy which occurred during the evaluation.

---

**Box 12.1 Features of important developments in public policy, including total purchasing, that make evaluation design challenging**

- The remit, aims and objectives of the total purchasing initiative were not precisely defined.
- The intervention (total purchasing status) was not clearly defined and allowed distinctly different TPP types to emerge.
- There were only limited opportunities for comparisons between the TPPs and other forms of purchasing organizations.
- The programme had a strong political dimension, stemming from the continuing controversy associated with GP fundholding.

## THE DISCIPLINARY AND THEORETICAL BASIS
## OF THE EVALUATION OF TOTAL PURCHASING

The evaluation brief for total purchasing did not explicitly list a set of theoretically grounded hypotheses or research questions, nor did it specify the expected backgrounds of the researchers. However, the scope of the research it outlined made two things clear. First, the evaluation had to be multidisciplinary, and second, the strong emphasis on the assessment of a wide range of costs and benefits implied a need for a firm grounding in evaluative health economics. Members of TP-NET came from a variety of disciplines with different theoretical traditions, with varying methodological skills. However, the limited time available for putting together the evaluation proposal meant that an overarching theoretical stance was not debated, nor were research questions and design transparently related to other bodies of social scientific theory at the outset.

Did the absence of an overarching theoretical position matter? Indeed, was it possible? It was certainly not surprising that it was absent for two main reasons. First, resolving practical issues was a higher priority in writing a proposal and the process of putting together such a complex wide-ranging bid allowed little time for theoretical reflection. Subsequently, team formation and the process of turning the evaluation proposal into practical research activities were pressing, demanding and time-consuming. Although there was a strong effort at central coordination, the eventual design of the total purchasing evaluation was a number of relatively autonomous, but strongly linked, substudies. There was no necessity for the different substudies to be based on a single overarching theoretical position. Second, there are fundamental differences in the assumptions as to what drives human behaviour between different disciplines (such as some branches of economics and sociology). This is always a dilemma in applied, multidisciplinary research. Taking a multidisciplinary approach means that different perspectives can be brought to bear on the programme of interest, and the evaluation team can learn from each other. Taking an interdisciplinary approach, on the other hand, requires a new, shared perspective to be developed. This is much harder to achieve in the context of applied research.

In general, TP-NET observed a careful, pragmatic accommodation between the fundamentally different perspectives on the nature of human behaviour used by different disciplinary traditions. Similarly, pragmatic use was made of different research methods drawn from different disciplines, and the interpretation of the data they produced was also carefully handled. Instead of attempting interdisciplinary theory at a 'high' or philosophical level, the proposal made reference to 'middle-level' theory drawn from economics and organizational sociology. It reviewed the impact of the quasi-market in the NHS, and this review informed the construction of detailed research questions and the design of subsequent data collection instruments.

However, this is not to say that there were no vigorous discussions between the evaluation team members about research design, about the most important questions that the research should tackle, or about how these should be approached empirically. Disciplinary differences of emphasis and opinion in relation to the overall design of the evaluation were inextricably linked to the fact that the evaluation brief had permitted two quite different sets of questions to be tackled, but without an indication as to which was the more important. The first set of questions asked whether total purchasing was, in some average sense, better than the status quo, while the second set of questions asked which type of TPP was the most successful and should, therefore, be replicated. In the early stages of the research, it is fair to say that the economists, and those researchers with a clinical background, were more interested in the first set of questions than in the second. This led them to quasi-experimental designs to compare the impact of the TPPs (for example, in terms of changes in transactions costs or patterns of hospital use) versus the status quo (that is, health authority purchasing in the absence of the pilots). In contrast, the researchers with more sociological backgrounds were more interested in the second set of questions than in the first. This led them to an observational comparative approach which would allow an understanding of how and why TPPs, in general, operated as they did, as well as permitting comparisons between TPPs in order to identify why some TPPs were more effective purchasers than others. However, the two questions entailed very different hypotheses about the nature of total purchasing, the process of implementation and the approach to evaluation. The evaluation team never wholly resolved the contradiction between the two sets of questions during the life of the evaluation, but collected data to shed light on both.

There was debate within TP-NET as to what constituted success and successful change mechanisms for total purchasers, which also brought out differences between researchers from different disciplinary traditions. Health economists in the team tended to view total purchasing primarily in terms of the incentives generated by the allocation of a budget, which had previously been controlled by the local health authority, to a group of GPs. As a result, their interest was in studying the setting of budgets, budget levels, risk management, contracting for services and the ensuing management of TPP finances. The implicit hypotheses underlying these views were that those pilots which were allocated their own budgets at a relatively early stage and which had the freedom to negotiate their own independent contracts would fare better than the rest and do better than the local health authority in its contracting process. Other members of the evaluation team, while well aware of the importance of budgetary leverage, believed that other sets of incentives were also in operation and that other organizational, contextual and relational factors were likely to be equally, if not more important in whether or not TPPs achieved change. Both sets of concerns were accommodated within the data collection instruments with the result that the first round of face-to-face interviews with TPPs was very long!

Despite disagreements, the multidisciplinary accommodation of views could be productive. For example, there was debate between the economists and the sociologists at one stage about the contribution of formal contracting to TPPs' ability to achieve service change. Fewer of the TPPs than expected by the economists had had budgets allocated to them and had negotiated their own contracts, yet some TPPs, without both, *were* achieving the changes they desired. In a seeming paradox, at interview the lead GPs were generally convinced that budgets and the contracting process were important in bringing about change, even if they did not yet hold budgets. The explanation, which seemed to fit the evidence best, and accommodate the perspectives of the two disciplines, was that the status of being a pilot project with the potential to hold a budget was important in enabling the GPs to initiate discussions with providers about changing services. The success of the discussions depended on the local context and the ability of the TPP to develop good relationships with the providers and its parent health authority. Whether or not contracts were signed was of little relevance in itself. It was therefore possible to conclude that having access to a budget was necessary, but far from sufficient to achieve service change. Economic incentive structures were relevant, but so too were other aspects of the local context and the leadership and vision of key players in the TPP.

The recognition that the evaluation process was pursuing two quite different sets of research questions, and that debate between disciplines had not been tackled in a fundamental, interdisciplinary way, increasingly troubled some members of the team. However, midway through the evaluation, a new book was published – *Realistic Evaluation* by Ray Pawson and Nick Tilley (1997) – which set out a distinctive theoretical approach to the evaluation of complex social programmes. The authors offered an alternative both to the conventional quasi-experimental and the naturalistic or 'fourth-generation' approaches to evaluation (Guba and Lincoln 1989; Patton 1990; Ovretveit 1998). These approaches were not considered by TP-NET because they did not usually aspire to identify causality or to rigorously assess the outcomes of policy. Pawson and Tilley's approach seemed to offer a solution to a number of the theoretical and design concerns thrown up by the evaluation of total purchasing.

Pawson and Tilley criticize the traditional experimental approach to social programme evaluation because it seeks to control for, or cancel out, the varying social contexts within which a programme is implemented and which shape its effects. In their view, the context is essential for understanding the success of a programme. The simple 'A versus B' structure of many experimental evaluations cannot accommodate this dimension. However, criticizing most naturalistic evaluators, Pawson and Tilley strongly argue that social phenomena (in this case, the effects of social programmes) are 'real' in the sense of embodying cause and effect relations. As a result, an understanding of causality is fundamental to evaluation. They argue for a theory of 'generative causation' that gives contextual factors their proper place in investigation (see Figure 12.1).

In this conceptualization, innovative social programmes work by introducing new ideas or resources (i.e. mechanisms) into existing social relations (i.e. context). The crucial task of evaluation is to investigate, via hypothesis making and testing, the extent to which the context (which precedes the intervention) enables or disables the intended mechanism for change. Outcomes of programmes are explained by the action of particular mechanisms operating in particular contexts. In Pawson and Tilley's elegant equation, Context + Mechanism = Outcome.

For a programme like total purchasing, the crucial question therefore concerned the causal relationships between the different contexts ($C_1$, $C_2$, $C_3$ ...) in which TPPs operated, the mechanisms ($M_1$, $M_2$, $M_3$ ...) used by the TPPs and the resultant outcomes ($O_1$,

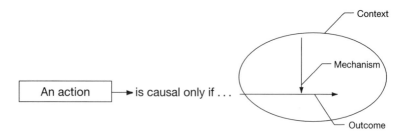

... its outcome is triggered by a mechanism acting in context

**Figure 12.1**   Generative causation
*Source*: Pawson and Tilley (1997). Reprinted by kind permission of Sage Publications Ltd., copyright 1997.

$O_2$, $O_3$ ...). Pawson and Tilley call these causal relationships 'Context–Mechanism–Outcome configurations'. They conclude: 'The task of a realist evaluation is to find ways of identifying, articulating, testing and refining conjectured Context–Mechanism–Outcome configurations' (Pawson and Tilley 1997: 77). The ultimate goal is to identify regularities in the relationships between context, mechanism and outcome within social programmes.

In retrospect, the total purchasing evaluation would have greatly benefited from the explicit application of Pawson and Tilley's Context–Mechanism–Outcome framework from the outset. It would have obviated the need for a great deal of confused discussion within the team and would have provided common ground for the different disciplines to share. The team was aware of previous case study work on the importance of context in policy evaluation (Pettigrew *et al.* 1992) and had used it to generate hypotheses about the likely causes of variations between pilots (Mays *et al.* 1998a). However, before the publication of Pawson and Tilley's book, the team did not have a conceptual system explicitly linking context with hypotheses about processes (mechanisms) and outcomes which could accommodate both quantitative and qualitative data and which was explicitly comparative.

One of the attractions of the Context–Mechanism–Outcome framework was that it could be applied using the diversity of quantitative and qualitative methods within the total purchasing evaluation. The *a priori* identification of Context–Mechanism–Outcome configurations would have enabled the team to use middle-level theory on the impact of quasi-markets to generate an explicit set of hypotheses about how total purchasing might work in practice, despite the lack of clear aims for the initiative at the outset. As a detailed understanding emerged of the heterogeneity of the 53 first-wave TPPs during the first live year, the emerging analysis of important contextual factors (e.g. degree of health authority support) and mechanisms for change (e.g. budget holding and independent contracting) could have been used to hypothesize predicted outcomes for different TPPs. Therefore, these predicted Context–Mechanism–Outcome configurations could have been compared with observed outcomes in the second live year of total purchasing. The comparison of predicted and observed outcomes would have added a coherent and systematic analysis of causality to the assessment of total purchasing presented in preceding chapters.

As the Context–Mechanism–Outcome framework is not limited to any particular method of data collection and analysis, it is potentially applicable to a wide range of future evaluations of complex policy. Its utility should at least be considered in planning such evaluations. Members of TP-NET have used the Context–Mechanism–Outcome framework explicitly in designing subsequent evaluations, for example an evaluation of the role of primary care pharmacists in new primary care organizations responsible for managing prescribing budgets, and in an evaluation of the novel provision of emergency contraceptives for women to keep at home.

However, Pawson and Tilley's approach and the notion of Context–Mechanism–Outcome configurations was in time to influence the data collection, analysis and presentation of results in the final year of the evaluation. The sampling and analysis of data from the TPPs which were selected for more intensive study in 1997/98 were strongly influenced by Context–Mechanism–Outcome thinking, even if it was not possible to construct hypotheses and empirical tests of all the possible Context–Mechanism–Outcome configurations to be found across the TPPs.

## WORKING IN A LARGE, MULTIDISCIPLINARY, GEOGRAPHICALLY SPREAD EVALUATION TEAM

One of the many ambitious elements of the total purchasing evaluation was the attempt to incorporate a range of substudies using qualitative and quantitative methods into the overall evaluation design. The mainly qualitative process part of the evaluation collected data on, and analysed in detail, the developmental processes, internal organization and contexts of the individual TPPs. It also included two sweeps of self-report data from a range of local stakeholders on the achievements of the TPPs against their previously stated objectives. However, it also included quantitative process data, for example on the different contractual forms used by TPPs. The more quantitative part of the evaluation focused mainly on identifying activity changes and the transaction costs generated by total purchasing. In addition, the evaluation included four service-specific substudies in which there was a mixture of qualitative and quantitative data (for example, the study on maternity services purchasing discussed in Chapter 6).

The complexity of this mixed-method design was both a strength and a weakness of the evaluation. It was a strength in that it allowed a sharing of contrasting data and analysis between different substudies, with the potential for improved data completeness, reassurance when several analyses seemed to be tending to the same conclusions, or prompts to further analysis of apparent contradictions. In particular, detailed data from the process evaluation were often useful in informing the analysis of quantitative studies. This was particularly so in the case of the analysis of hospital activity changes brought about by TPPs (see Chapter 7). It was also possible to collect and analyse the qualitative descriptive data far more quickly than, say, data on changes in hospital activity rates. This early intelligence on the progress of the TPPs was found to be particularly valuable to policy makers at central government level, and has been adopted in a number of subsequent Department of Health-commissioned policy evaluations (e.g. the evaluation of PCGs and PCTs).

The weakness of combining methods and substudies in essentially a programme of evaluation rather than a single study was more an issue of practical coordination than of principle. Due to the heterogeneity of the sites and the Department of Health's requirement that all TPPs be included in the evaluation, the qualitative process evaluation generated more data than could easily be processed for rapid reporting. At the same time, data collection and analysis for most of the quantitative studies took longer than anticipated. Consequently there were major logistical difficulties in processing and analysing the data from the different substudies in time to allow useful sharing and discussion to inform the emerging analyses. Pulling together and making sense of all the contributions to the programme of evaluation took far longer than was predicted at the outset. Despite a series of rapid briefings for policy customers in the Department of Health and NHS Executive during the life of the study, all the components necessary for inclusion in the final report to the Department of Health could not be assembled until May 1999, just over a year after the pilots had officially come to an end.

These logistical difficulties were compounded by sensitivities within TP-NET over how to ensure that each participant in the large team was given appropriate recognition when analyses were prepared for publication. Publication has long been a major criterion against which academic performance is judged. The competitive nature of publication has been exacerbated over the last decade by the demands of the UK universities' Research Assessment Exercise. Despite the attempt by the senior managers of the project to plan publications and allocate fair authorship, there were times when some team members felt either that their work had not been adequately recognized in publications, or that others had published without sufficient consultation or without involving them as authors. This was particularly likely to occur in the case of those part-time research assistants working in parallel on other studies, whose main contribution was simply to carry out fieldwork. Their input was essential to covering all the TPPs, but their data made no sense without data collected by other centres and, as a result, they had very limited, if any, chance to contribute intellectually to the project. Finally, various individuals and institutions within TP-NET also found themselves competing for research contracts to carry out other evaluations relevant to total purchasing, which inevitably coloured relationships within the team.

These tensions within the evaluation team were largely managed through the mechanism of discussion at regular team meetings. Depending on the number of team members who chose to attend, these meetings were more or less useful fora for sharing information and resolving differences of view. They were often fun and usually stimulating, given the wealth of experience and insight in the full team. On a few occasions, there were more in-depth 'retreats' in order to attempt to develop a shared interpretation of emerging findings and to give some attention to internal team processes. The cross-institutional membership of the team, the autonomy and seniority of many team members, and other contextual factors, such as the Research Assessment Exercise and competitive funding environment, necessarily meant that the the evaluation team could be managed only in a non-hierarchical, *laissez faire* manner. This was despite the fact that the King's Fund was the principal contractor to the Department of Health, with most of the other institutions subcontracted to the Fund. Senior staff in other institutions could not be line managed or forced to agree with one another, only encouraged to value their participation within the evaluation sufficiently to honour their commitments. More explicit processes of team development might have facilitated greater shared ownership of the evaluation and might have prevented some tensions from arising, but would have added still further to the already high transaction costs of running a multi-institutional collaboration.

With the benefit of hindsight, several members of the evaluation team felt that it had been simply too large and the project too complex to allow the establishment of the degree of closeness in working relationships which they would have preferred. In addition, the agenda at team meetings was often so crowded with operational-level questions of data collection, data processing, analysis and reporting that there was little time to address internal development issues. So an important lesson for future evaluations of complex policy is the need to consider the external contextual pressures on multidisciplinary and multi-institutional evaluation teams, and the appropriate size, structure and internal process arrangements for the teams undertaking such evaluations. In particular, teams will need to consider the balance of benefits and costs between large teams with wide-ranging expertise and small teams, which are likely to be more cohesive and easier to manage, but which cannot claim expertise in all necessary areas. The Department of Health evaluation brief required an exceptional breadth of knowledge and skills. The King's Fund chose to recruit subject area experts in all relevant areas. The result was an exceptionally large team, which was a management challenge in itself, regardless of liaising with almost 100 TPPs. The evaluation team also reflected the emphasis of the period on large, complex health services research collaborations such as the Department of Health's own National Primary Care Research and Development Centre, involving three universities, and the Medical Research Council's Health Services Research Collaboration, involving even more.

## IMPROVING THE EVALUATION OF POLICY PILOTS

There are at least three questions worth reflecting on, which relate to the evaluation of complex pilots such as the TPPs. First, what are the design and methodological implications for the evaluation of such pilots? Second, can evaluators help policy makers plan pilots in more effective ways? Finally, how should evaluators respond to emerging evidence of more and less successful models among the pilots? That is, to what extent does the evaluator have a responsibility to share learning and promote good practice among the pilots, even if, as in the case of total purchasing, there was no commission to do so?

The answer to the first question has already been suggested in the discussion of theory above. The solution is to identify the context and mechanisms operating in the different pilots, and hypothesize predicted outcomes using Pawson and Tilley's equation, Context + Mechanism = Outcome. By establishing Context–Mechanism–Outcome configurations for a range of pilot types, theoretically coherent and empirically tested regularities can be established. To some extent this happened implicitly within the total purchasing evaluation. Consequently, important contextual factors (e.g. the level of health authority support) and mechanisms (such as budget holding and having independent contracts) were linked to self-reported outcomes (e.g. a higher level of achievement in service areas new to GP-led purchasing). Where such findings are consistent across a number of pilots, a regularity is suggested. If a regularity is not identified, then the hypothesis needs to be refined and retested.

The second question relating to how evaluators might help policy makers frame and develop pilots in more effective ways is problematic. Even asking the question presupposes that policy makers want, and should want, clarity in any pilot initiative, but this is not necessarily so, and for good reasons. In the case of total purchasing, the lack of precise definition of the scope of the initiative most probably reflected a desire, within limits, to see what happened when GPs were given incentives, freedoms and opportunities which they had previously not had. The vagueness may also have been a deliberate way of wooing GPs into the scheme and not intimidating them with rules and regulations. Therefore, although TP-NET was free to inform the Department of Health that total purchasing had not been adequately defined, this was unlikely to have had great policy influence in the short term. Indeed, perhaps deliberately naively, such feedback was given in the first total purchasing reports, but did little to influence the Department of Health, either regarding the total purchasing initiative or subsequent pilot initiatives. As a result the Personal Medical Services pilots launched in

1997 exhibited the same unclear aims and lack of definition as TPPs (NHS Executive 1997b). It can be argued that evaluators have an ethical responsibility to point out to their funders the lack of clarity and incoherence in policies. In practice, however, the most evaluators could reasonably expect is to point out at a later stage which subtypes within a pilot initiative appear to be more effective than others. It is possible that TP-NET's strictures about the need for a clearer definition of total purchasing and/or clearer aims and objectives for the pilots would have been better received had it been targeted at individual TPPs rather than national policy makers.

This leads to our third issue: the responsibility of the evaluators to share learning and promote good practice among the inevitably heterogeneous pilots. Despite their very different local contexts, TPPs did share a number of objectives and intended mechanisms for change rooted in their experience of using budgets as fundholders. As the preceding chapters have made clear, some TPPs were much more successful than others in implementing their plans and achieving their objectives. For example, some TPPs succeeded in changing contract currency from finished consultant episodes to reflect length of stay, thereby freeing resources to invest in other services, while others did not (see Chapter 7). Systematic sharing of learning derived from the more successful TPPs might well have assisted less successful ones in developing effective local strategies. However, this was not part of the Department of Health research brief. This decision was most likely to have been taken on the grounds that researchers should concentrate on their main task to make sense of their data; that the main purpose of the research was to inform national policy development, not the course of individual pilots; that researchers were not necessarily seen as skilled in helping local pilots; and that involvement in more hands-on, local dissemination of good practice might confuse roles and relationships, jeopardizing the research. Indeed, at the beginning of the evaluation, TP-NET had to work hard to reassure participants at TPPs, particularly those from within the NHS bureaucracy, that the researchers were not a covert arm of the NHS Executive Regional Offices' performance management function. As researchers, it was easier to get interviewees to talk openly and honestly about their pilots! The Department was also acutely aware of the scale and cost of commissioning dedicated help to individual TPPs given that there were almost 100 of them in the two waves.

Despite the fact that interactive working with the TPPs was not within the remit of the evaluation team, members of the team did give extensive general and informal feedback through regional seminars, conference presentations, interim reports and working papers. On specific topics where the research team had strong practical expertise, such as budget setting and risk management, members of the team gave invited seminars and practical demonstrations (e.g. of a computer simulation model useful for risk management). What was missing, however, was specific developmental feedback targeted at individual failing or less well performing TPPs. To do so, TP-NET would have needed input from colleagues with skills in management consultancy, as well as a large increase in its budget.

**INFLUENCING POLICY**

Over the three years of the study, members of the team were probably involved in over 100 feedback events of various types. The principal grant holder and project leader gave between 40 and 50 seminars, briefings and conference presentations to NHS, general practice and academic audiences in the three-year period, 1995–98. The number of presentations given by members of the evaluation team betrayed the keenness of its members to try to influence policy. A key characteristic of evaluation, which distinguishes it from other forms of academic research, is its concern with policies and programmes that are on the current agenda of policy makers (Berk and Rossi 1990). The evaluator wants to reach assessments that will influence policy makers and the policy they make. Yet, since politicians are central to the policy-making process, evaluation is intrinsically enmeshed in a complex political context. The political nature of evaluation in the NHS in the 1990s was illustrated by the then Conservative government's response to calls for the evaluation of the original quasi-market reforms to the NHS. Speaking soon after the release of his plans for the NHS in 1989, the Secretary of State for Health, Kenneth Clarke, declared that he did not want academics crawling all over his reforms (Robinson 1994). One of his key concerns was that political opponents were calling for evaluation as a mechanism for blocking or delaying change. So no official Department of Health-funded evaluation of the main planks of the 1991 NHS reforms was commissioned, although independent evaluations of parts of the changes were funded by both the King's Fund (Robinson and Le Grand 1994) and the Economic and Social Research Council (Flynn and Williams 1997). However, since the mid-1990s, greater emphasis has been given to the evaluation of major initiatives, partly because the level of ideological heat surrounding the quasi-market fell over time (Department of Health 1993b). Politicians and health policy makers have embraced (at least rhetorically) a commitment to the evaluation of policy innovation. As was noted earlier, total purchasing was the first of a series of major health policy initiatives for which the Department of Health commissioned independent evaluations. What is less clear, however, is the extent to which politicians and policy makers accept the logic (and, indeed, whether they should) that, having commissioned major policy evaluations, they should then base policy decisions on the findings of those evaluations (Ham *et al.* 1998).

The difficulty with this rather naïve position is its deliberate overlooking of the rarity with which individual studies, as against an accumulation of work, ever determine the direction of policy unaided. There is much evidence that supports the contrary view, that evaluation and other forms of research have only a limited direct impact on policy making (Shadish *et al.* 1991; Walt 1994; Ovretveit 1998). Other more political factors are always likely to be more influential. There are also empirical reasons, such as generalizability and changing circumstances, which affect the application of research to policy decisions in a straightforward way. As Mechanic (1993) has observed: 'Research is a form of currency as varying interests negotiate a political resolution, but research is almost never definitive enough to resolve major issues on which strong political interests disagree.' Research is particularly unlikely to be influential where its findings contradict the ideology and policy of politicians (for example, the Thatcher government's rejection of the *Black Report* on poverty and health in the UK; (Townsend and Davidson 1982). In summary, research evidence is only one of the sources of information used when policy decisions are made.

In addition, policy evaluation may have limited impact simply because the findings are viewed as inconclusive due to the methodological difficulties of such complex evaluations. For example, Lord and Littlejohns (1997) argue (perhaps too neatly) that evaluations of clinical audit in the UK have not influenced policy precisely because it has not been possible to apply the rigorous methods of the randomized controlled trial. Where policy evaluation does have an influence, it is likely to be in the longer term and the impact may be diffuse and hard to trace. Walt (1994) draws attention to the fact that the models that best explain how research influences policy are both non-rational and non-linear in form.

In practice, politicians and policy makers may have a range of not wholly consistent motives in commissioning evaluations. We have already noted the portmanteau nature of the total purchasing evaluation brief, which included both the question of whether total purchasing was to be compared with the status quo and whether different forms of total purchasing were to be compared with each other. This ambiguity reflects the fact that policy makers were at one and the same time indicating that total purchasing was the extension of the 'successful' fundholding scheme – and thus a continuation of established policy – but also an experiment that (theoretically at least) might be judged as 'unsuccessful' by the evaluation since it took GP budget holding into service areas that were likely to pose a greater challenge than the elective services in fundholding. In this context, the motives of the policy makers were unclear. They may have genuinely wished an honest answer to the question, 'Is total purchasing more cost-effective than the status quo?' An alternative, and equally plausible, view is that by commissioning the evaluation, they hoped to disarm their political opponents and critics of the existing fundholding scheme. While being free to implement their desired policy, the government could be secure in the knowledge that the evaluation would not report until long after the policy was fully implemented! Although this might be an excessively cynical view, it would have been a rational response from policy makers who had received intense political and academic criticism for their failure to evaluate the original 1991 NHS reforms, including standard fundholding.

The experience of the total purchasing evaluation suggests that, in practice, policy makers make pragmatic political judgements about the sort of evaluative evidence they want and can use. In general, they want to use the findings of evaluations in order to inform policy, but only within the tight limits of policy decisions that they have already taken (i.e. in the case of the TPPs, they tended to have more interest in how to 'optimise' total purchasing rather than in finding out if it were superior or not to the status quo). They also want to use research when it suits their timescales rather than waiting for the findings.

Evaluation findings that contradict recent policy decisions are particularly unwelcome. The response of the incoming Labour government in 1997 to the interim findings of the total purchasing evaluation is a perfect example of this phenomenon. In opposition, the Labour Party was committed to the abolition of the NHS internal market, and fundholding in particular (Labour Party 1995). On entering office, however, Labour had only the outline of a policy with which to replace fundholding and the variety of more informal types of primary care commissioning then in place. The basic idea of all GPs in a locality taking a collectively managed budget had been enunciated in a speech given by the Shadow Health Minister, Chris Smith, in December 1996. However, the more sophisticated concept of PCGs was not developed until the summer and autumn of 1997. At the same time, TP-NET was sharing (and being actively encouraged to share) its emerging findings with the Department of Health. In many ways, the concept of PCGs, as presented in the White Paper *The New NHS* (Secretary of State for Health 1997) in December 1997, demonstrates broad continuity with the total purchasing experiment. Level 2 PCGs, in particular, operate in a very similar manner to TPPs as subcommittees of the health authority with delegated budgets. Although it would overstate the case to suggest that interim results of the TPP evaluation were a determining influence in the formation of policy on PCGs, the evaluation feedback was one of several factors that helped shape the emerging policy. However, what is of as much interest here is the fate of those findings that did not fit with the new political context. For example, a key finding in the interim analysis was that small and single-practice TPPs achieved more in their first live year than larger ones. As small and single-practice forms of primary care commissioning were politically unacceptable to Labour, this finding was ignored. Similarly, the evaluation's warnings about the likely management costs of effective TPPs were unacceptable because of the government's desire to reduce management spending in the NHS. On the other hand, the finding that the TPPs were generally not very adept at purchasing mental health services may have had some influence, as English health authorities retained responsibility for commissioning mental health services under the changes brought in following the *New NHS* White Paper.

More than this, not only were inconvenient findings ignored in policy development, but the Department of Health indicated that it did not want the questions they raised given any priority. During the same period, the TP-NET was concluding negotiations with the Department of Health to define the focus of the final year of the evaluation. In discussion of which pilots to select for detailed case study (all pilots were also monitored straightforwardly in the final year), the Department of Health made it absolutely clear that it did not want the (apparently highly successful) single-practice pilots included since a White Paper had just been published abolishing single-practice budget holding. This generated substantial debate within the team. Some members felt strongly that the single-practice sites should have been included as they represented an important source of evidence about the roots of effective total purchasing, regardless of the fact that they had no future in policy terms. Others took the view that they should be excluded as they were no longer policy relevant. In the end, little or nothing was lost by the decision to exclude the single-practice TPPs, since many of them had already lost motivation and/or local health authority support because of the national policy shift away from standard fundholding. These pilots would not, in practice, continue to the end of the third year of total purchasing. Despite this, the experience of the single-practice pilots had not been in vain – it had emphasized the importance of practice-level incentives in future larger, collective PCGs.

This episode neatly illustrates the limits and the possibilities of evaluation influencing policy. The limits of evaluation are clear. Evaluation is only likely to influence policy directly where it addresses questions on which policy makers have yet to make up their minds, and offers them insights which enable them to develop emerging policy options. And evaluation must also be timely. Quite fortuitously, TP-NET was in a position to share interim findings with the new Labour government at a time in the summer and autumn of 1997 when the policy makers wanted them. In fact, it was a close-run thing. Policy makers wanted the evaluation findings before the TP-NET was quite ready to publish. The main mechanisms for sharing the findings with policy makers were face-to-face presentations and a rapidly produced confidential *Key Findings* paper (Mays 1997). The more detailed and more considered interim report and most of the related working papers were not ready for publication until spring 1998, which would have been far too late to have influenced the central elements of the new policy. The research contract with the Department of Health required annual reports, but policy development rarely fits into neat 12-month periods!

The evaluation team's experience in seeking to influence the formation of policy towards PCGs raises questions about the conventional hands-off evaluation stance assumed in the Department of Health research brief (and the level of funding of the project) and therefore adopted by TP-NET at the beginning of the evaluation. There are inevitable tensions between the relatively short timescales of policy makers, managers and others in the NHS who have to implement policy, and the longer timescales required by evaluators to collect, analyse and interpret data, and to disseminate evaluation findings in a form which is easily assimilated. In order to influence current policy directly, evaluators need to be able to respond with timely feedback of interim findings. It was fortunate that the evaluation team not only had findings which were sufficiently advanced for presentation, but also had a senior member of the team with sufficient time to rapidly produce an unscheduled report.

So although not conceived as an interactive form of evaluation, the total purchasing evaluation increasingly functioned as one. This was also true at a more local level where interim findings were disseminated through workshop and conference presentations throughout the entire study, starting in the very early months and building up over time. In addition, a series of working papers and managerial and professional journal articles appeared between 1996 and 1999. The speed and extent of policy change following the Labour election victory created developmental needs, which the team could not resist responding to. In any case, to have waited for the publication of the final evaluation report and other outputs in the spring and summer of 1999 would have meant missing crucial opportunities to influence policy development and implementation. However, as a result, fine judgements had to be made as to how to interpret and present interim findings, such as the apparent superiority of smaller and single-practice TPPs in the first live year against a background of rapid policy change towards multi-practice purchasing organizations. One solution was to draw attention to the features of single-practice and smaller TPPs which had enabled them to make greater progress, and to point out that larger primary care purchasing organizations would need to give more self-conscious attention to organization building and that this would take more time.

There were, however, drawbacks to this evolving developmental role. At a practical level, the evaluators had not been funded by the Department of Health for this work. The Department had funded some short-term organizational development consultancy (referred to as 'facilitation') in the early months of the preparatory year in 1995, but this had been short-lived, leaving the research team exposed. The evaluation team was not resourced even for basic forms of dissemination of findings and its approach was *ad hoc*. More fundamentally, the pressure to produce feedback at the right time in the policy process risked the researchers over-interpreting what were, after all, only interim findings. In the early winter of 1997, the Department of Health urgently wanted input from the total purchasing evaluation into the formation of PCG policy, yet data had been analysed only from the TPPs' first live year. Such analysis might have been quite misleading.

Given the turbulence of health policy development over the last decade, which seems unlikely to abate in future, evaluators will need to maintain a balance between two stances. Without losing focus on the longer term questions of outcome and cost-effectiveness, evaluators will need to build in a flexible and responsive role (though this does not necessarily include developmental work with individual sites or pilots), if they are to meet the inevitably short-term and changing demands of policy makers. The balance between maintaining a distance and more rapid close-up forms of feedback will always pose a dilemma that can be managed, but is unlikely to be easily resolved. Evaluators will need to be opportunistic in identifying and responding to those key moments when policy makers are particularly open to influence. An open channel of communication between evaluators and policy makers helps this, hence the importance of the research liaison function in the Department of Health.

## MAJOR CHANGES OF POLICY DURING THE EVALUATION

The impact of the 1997 Labour election victory on the TPPs, particularly the smaller projects, has already been emphasized. The change of policy had an equal impact on the evaluation itself. The general election, and the major health policy changes that followed from it, meant that the main evaluative questions changed fundamentally. Rather than, 'Is total purchasing better than the status quo?' and, 'Which is the best model of total purchasing?', the relevant policy questions became, 'Based on the different forms of TPP, which is likely to be the best model for designing PCGs?' and, 'What can we learn from total purchasing about making PCGs work well?' As importantly, the change of policy meant that the third year of the evaluation was significantly altered. Once the new Labour government's policy began to emerge during the second live year of total purchasing (1997/98), a number of stakeholders in TPPs recognized the implications and began to alter their behaviour in response. Some health authorities withdrew their support for pilots. Many GPs and managers leading TPPs shifted their focus from their TPPs' objectives to PCG formation – to take place in April 1999 – and to attempting to place the former TPP in an influential position within the emerging PCG. Providers recognized that they could avoid or ignore TPP pressures as the initiative was coming to an end. Single-practice and 'non-locality' TPPs were particularly vulnerable to the disruptive impact of the new policies; but even multi-practice locality TPPs which continued to receive health authority support as precursors to PCGs often shifted their focus from achieving service change through their purchasing towards PCG organizational development. Therefore, the evaluation team's ability to collect useful data on the achievements of many TPPs in their second live year was limited by this radical shift in the national context and in what TPPs were seeking to achieve locally.

The response of TP-NET to this major contextual change was three-fold. First, the team continued to collect and analyse data relevant to the original evaluation questions, while recognizing the impact of the change on the validity and relevance of these analyses. At the same time, where possible, new data were collected relevant to the new policy questions about PCGs. This was particularly possible in the in-depth TPP case studies carried out in 1997/98, where PCG development became as important a focus of data collection as exploring progress regarding TPPs' achievements. Finally, reflection on the importance of the national contextual change stimulated thinking as to how to address the local context more explicitly in the analysis, thereby contributing to the incorporation of Pawson and Tilley's Context–Mechanism–Outcome framework into the team's analysis (see above).

Future evaluators of national policy initiatives would be wise to prepare for major changes in policy that may have a similar profound impact. They should be ready to identify how policy change may affect the validity of their data collection and analysis, and to identify how the relevant policy questions may change. If possible, they should be prepared to be responsive and collect new data to answer new questions thrown up by changing contexts. Crucially, evaluators need to able to reflect on the impact of such policy change in their analysis, possibly using Pawson and Tilley's Context–Mechanism–Outcome framework. Of course, it is easy to say that evaluators should be ready for contextual change, but harder to build such flexibility into the detail of the design of commissioned studies. In the case of the total purchasing evaluation, the design was helped by the fact that John Major's government had looked vulnerable for a considerable time before the May 1997 general election!

## CONCLUSIONS

The evaluation of total purchasing was a major learning opportunity in its own right for the researchers and for the Department of Health in managing such a large study. It was the first time a major NHS quasi-market budgetary and organizational initiative had been subjected to an official external evaluation. The total purchasing evaluation sought to assess the value of a complex and very broadly defined policy within a changing policy context. As the preceding chapters have acknowledged, there were a number of limitations to the knowledge generated through the evaluation. However, the value of the total purchasing evaluation was that, despite its limitations, extensive policy-relevant data and analysis were produced to inform the development of PCGs in England and primary care organizations more widely.

In its methods and diverse approaches, the total purchasing evaluation offers a case study of the strengths and weaknesses of a collaborative, multidisciplinary approach to policy evaluation. The evaluation demonstrated the importance of early attention to theory (i.e. clear explanatory frameworks), even in applied policy research. More particularly, the experience highlighted the importance of addressing the influence of context in the processes of hypotheses generation, testing and analysis. A useful theoretical framework was identified in the *realistic evaluation* advocated by Pawson and Tilley (1997) and their concepts of generative causation and Context–Mechanism–Outcome configurations. The impact of Labour's election victory in May 1997 and the development of a new NHS policy convinced the evaluation team of the need to address context by incorporating this major policy change into analysis, and into data collection, where possible.

Equally, the evaluation team recognized the need to be reflexive and responsive to the needs of policy makers for a more interactive approach to the evaluation, which included early and continuous feedback. The experience of the total purchasing evaluation has appeared to influence the commissioning style of the Department of Health. Subsequent evaluation briefs have encouraged prospective researchers to include more explicit plans for dissemination and feedback of findings throughout the study. Some evaluations have been resourced to include more interactive activities such as workshops with staff and managers from the health system. On the other hand, the fundamental stance of most Departmental evaluations is to maintain a clear separation between the participants in the policy implementation process and the researchers. This tends to draw the line at approaches such as 'action research' and more developmental styles of evaluation. The researchers are still clearly separate from the initiatives they are evaluating, despite being encouraged to communicate their findings and insights more vigorously and frequently.

The total purchasing evaluation reminded health services researchers (if they ever needed to be reminded) that policy evaluation is inevitably a more complex and messy process than more clinically orientated types of health services research such as health technology assessment. The frequent lack of clear policy objectives, the ill-defined nature and fluidity of policy interventions and the impact of political factors on policy change all present methodological challenges to the evaluator. Therefore it is unlikely that there will ever be a single model for policy evaluation as dominant as the randomized controlled trial in clinically orientated health services research. Nevertheless, the experience of the TPP evaluation suggests that policy researchers can usefully reflect on their range of theoretical and methodological approaches, and learn from the evaluation process as well as directly from the policy under scrutiny.

# 13

# THE TOTAL PURCHASING EXPERIMENT: INTERPRETING THE EVIDENCE
## Nicholas Mays and Sally Wyke

This chapter attempts to draw together the wide range of empirical material and analysis presented throughout the rest of this book and tries to explain why the pilots developed as they did, with particular attention to the context in which they operated and the incentives facing their participants. An understanding of the constraints faced by the TPPs is necessary for any interpretation of the scale and nature of their achievements and of the potential contribution of primary care-based commissioning to the development of health systems more generally. In the final chapter we assess the significance of the total purchasing experiment for current primary care organizations in the NHS and for future policy in other health systems.

## BALANCING THE EVIDENCE

There is little doubt that standard fundholding was the most innovative part of the NHS internal market changes of the early 1990s. For example, there was clear evidence that fundholders had improved waiting times for elective surgery significantly more than their local health authorities (Dowling 1997). On the other hand, the NHS incurred additional costs to support standard fundholding practices and by no means all of them made good use of their budgets (Goodwin 1998). Only a small proportion of fundholders was able to transform the services available to their patients (Audit Commission 1996). The successes of fundholding may be attributed to the fact that standard fundholding practices, unlike health authority purchasers, faced clear incentives to improve the quality and efficiency of their prescribing and the elective services which they purchased in order both to make 'savings' and to attract more patients. 'Savings' could be used to buy more services for their patients, but also to invest in equipment and facilities, which were subsequently owned by the GPs, thereby adding value to their practices as small businesses. On the other hand, there is evidence, from the same period, of some non-fundholding practices achieving comparable and even superior efficiency improvements, suggesting that budgetary incentives alone are inadequate to explain practice-level innovation (Petchey 1995). The abilities of individual practitioners, and the context in which they work, play their parts.

The total purchasing initiative began life as a direct extension of the standard fundholding scheme to allow volunteer practices, either individually or in groups, to purchase services beyond the scope of the elective services contained within standard fundholding. Like standard fundholding, the total purchasing initiative was originally conceived as giving general practitioners greater influence over hospital and community health services through the contracting process. The total purchasing GPs were expected to change provider behaviour principally by contracting, rather than by building organizational links between primary, community and secondary care. Unlike standard fundholding, the professional and financial incentives for GPs to take part in total purchasing, and for them to bring about change in health services, were less obviously apparent since the total purchasing budgets remained technically the responsibility of the health authority.

So, on balance, was the total purchasing experiment a good thing? Was it a sensible idea to extend general practitioners' involvement in purchasing hospital and community health services beyond the scope of standard fundholding? Were the TPP general practitioners motivated to, and capable of, purchasing services not directly influenced by their day-to-day clinical practice (e.g. unplanned use of acute hospitals)?

As is frequently the case with complex social and economic interventions, evolving in a changing policy environment, it is extremely difficult to come to simple and incontestable answers to these questions. The preceding pages have revealed a shifting balance of costs and benefits, of achievements and limitations, of opportunities and problems. Producing a single, simple summary of the case for and against the TPPs is complicated at the outset by the lack of specific, measurable goals set out by the Department of Health for the pilot scheme. This, in turn, led to a wide range of interpretations of the concept of total purchasing in terms of the aims of the scheme, the nature of the objectives pursued and the organization of pilots.

Furthermore, in conventional evaluation, an innovation is often judged in comparison, either with what came before, or with some contemporaneous setting unaffected by the innovation. As stated above, TPPs were originally set up as health services' purchasing organizations. Yet, the appropriate purchaser for comparison was never entirely clear and changed over time (see Chapters 2 and 12). For example, should the appropriate comparison have been with the previously established standard fundholding regime, which existed at each practice in each TPP alongside total purchasing? In large part, this was the stance adopted in the original Department of Health research brief, but such a comparison (although under-standable at the time), became increasingly irrelevant as time passed and the likelihood grew that standard fundholding (i.e. with budgets held by individual practices) would be abolished.

Alternatively, should the comparison have been with the purchasing achievements of the local health authority of each TPP? The difficulty with this approach was the fact that the TPPs were subcommittees of their local health authorities and frequently relied on substantial input from health authority staff. The distinction between health authority purchasing and GP-led purchasing via the TPP was thus fuzzy. In some cases, for example, the health authority envisaged using the TPP to pilot new ways of securing services which the authority could then build on.

Thus the TPPs were a new hybrid of general practitioner budget holding and health authority purchasing with budgets which remained the ultimate responsibility of the health authority. So should the comparison have been with the other, non-budget hold-ing models of local GP commissioning which existed in most of the health authorities where TPPs also operated? The problem with this sort of comparison was the great variety of forms and levels of locality or GP commissioning operating in different places at the time (Mays and Dixon 1996). Some groups were no more than modest advisory forums used by the health authority as it saw fit, while others were very close to the TPPs in their aims and degree of budgetary delegation from the health authority.

It also became apparent as the evaluation progressed that the TPPs were acting not only, or even mainly (in some cases), as pur-chasers, but also as providers, developing services in and around their constituent general practices. In retrospect, perhaps total purchasing should have been viewed from the outset as a form of primary care development initiative as much as a purchasing innovation. It is not surprising that the TPPs blurred the purchaser–provider separation since to general practitioners, who also provided services directly themselves, the distinction between the two functions was not as clear-cut as it was for health authority purchasers and NHS trusts. Indeed, part of the rationale for standard fundholding had been that it enabled general practitioners to build purchasing into their roles as providers of general medical services and as referral agents for their patients. Many of the service innovations brought about by TPPs were as much to do with extending their primary care role as purchasing services from others (see below for more on this). In some cases, they were able to pay their constituent practices to provide new services outside their contractual general medical services commitments, thereby, in a small way, bringing about 'vertical integration' of services. In other cases, their activities in trying to reduce their patients' dependence on acute hospitals by attempting to reinvest resources elsewhere contributed to a form of 'virtual integration' in which the pilot contracted with other providers of intermediate and community care (Dixon *et al.* 1998b).

Seen in this light as developers of primary care, the TPPs could have been compared with other innovative ways of developing primary care and vertical integration, including the NHS Executive's own Primary Medical Services pilots, although these began later than the TPPs (NHS Executive 1997b). Although not conceived as such, in the end both the TPPs and the Personal Medical Services pilots were concerned with broadening the range of services provided outside hospital on a flexible locally determined basis. The former scheme attempted to do this by giving general practitioners control over the hospital and community health services budget for their patients; the latter approached this goal by encouraging GPs to step outside their national contract for general medical services, and by allowing health authorities to commission primary care and related services from any local provider within the 'NHS family'. For example, contracts were negotiated for nurse-led provision of primary care services for patients with specific chronic conditions or employment of salaried GPs in deprived areas where the national GP contract had failed to attract sufficient practitioners. The convergence between the TPPs and the Personal Medical Services pilots was recognized in the specification for Primary Care Groups in the *New NHS* White Paper (Secretary of

State for Health 1997) since Primary Care Groups will gradually assume responsibility for both the general medical services and hospital and community health services budget. In particular, level four Primary Care Groups, known as Primary Care Trusts, are fully integrated 'purchaser-providers' responsible for securing a full range of health services for their patients including both general medical services and hospital and community health services. They differ from Scottish Primary Care Trusts which are responsible only for the provision of primary care and community health services.

As the evaluation developed, and as the total purchasing initiative unfolded, it became increasingly apparent that a straightforward comparative design would provide relatively limited insight relevant to future policy development, for all the reasons discussed above (see Chapter 12 for more on this and related study design issues). In circumstances in which health policy was constantly evolving, there was considerable variation in the intervention under study, the context of the intervention was influencing its impact and appropriate comparators were difficult to identify, other approaches were called for. While it is useful to attempt some contemporaneous comparisons (for example, the current study included useful comparisons of TPP and non-TPP populations' use of hospital emergency services), equally, if not more, valuable knowledge for future policy development can be gleaned from asking and attempting to answer a different set of questions. For example, policy makers are likely to be as interested in the characteristics of, and circumstances surrounding, the most successful forms of TPP as in whether, in some invariant (or average) sense, total purchasing is 'better' than another form of innovative purchasing. Policy makers are likely to derive insight from learning which forms of TPP activity work best for which services and which patients, and in which contexts (see Chapter 12 for more on the relation between the evolving theoretical insights supporting the evaluation, its design and the identification of appropriate policy-relevant research questions). This is particularly so in a period when there is widespread support for some form of primary care-based purchasing within the NHS.

Thus the summary verdict on total purchasing and the assessment of the potential of primary care-based budgetary delegation which follows has been constructed with these considerations of policy relevance in mind in order to help inform the discussion of future policy and practice development in Chapter 14.

## OVERVIEW OF THE EVIDENCE FROM THE TOTAL PURCHASING EXPERIMENT

### Organizational development

The TPPs began the process of breaking down the boundaries which exist between general practices in the UK and building new forms of GP leadership and interpractice organization which sit somewhere between the conventional professional partnership and a hierarchical bureaucracy (see Chapter 3). TPPs also enabled practices to develop new relationships with other health and social services agencies including the health authority and NHS trusts (Wyke *et al.* 1999; Goodwin *et al.* 2000). This process had begun under standard fundholding as hospital and community health services' providers were obliged to develop some sort of relationship with GPs, often for the first time, because of their new control over hospital and community health services' resources. However, the process of organization building took more time and effort in the larger, multi-practice pilots. After three years, some pilots were still at a relatively early stage in becoming effective service purchasing or commissioning organizations (Mays *et al.* 1998a; Killoran *et al.* 1999b). For example, the research team was able to identify five different types of TPP at the end of the first 'live' year (1996/97): 'commissioning' (purchasing directly with a devolved budget and some independent contracts); 'co-purchasing' (contracting jointly with the health authority rather than in their own right); 'primary care developer' (focusing on developing primary care either as 'commissioners' or 'co-purchasers' rather than changing secondary care via contracting); 'developmental' (preparing to bring about change in service areas outside standard fundholding); and 'stalled' (showing little sign of being able to make changes in services beyond standard fundholding).

In some cases, the existence of a TPP stimulated organizational learning on the part of the health authority as it sought to find ways of developing relationships with a range of GP-led organizations in order to increase the degree of devolution of its service commissioning role. This process was seen most clearly in a unique 'whole district' TPP in which the health authority devolved its entire commissioning budget to five total purchasing localities based on groups of general practices. This approach attracted national attention and may be seen as the precursor of the establishment of primary care groups in England (Killoran *et al.* 1999b).

**Accountability**

The TPPs were subcommittees of the local health authority. Within this basic constraint, occasioned by their informal status, the pilots were given considerable freedom from regulation. The 'upward' accountability regime for TPPs was relatively loose and informal (see Chapter 11). The only systematic quantitative monitoring of performance related to the financial position of the projects, which were expected to stay within budget. Seeing themselves as agents for their patients, the GPs gave relatively little attention to developing 'downward' forms of accountability. As a result, they did not, on the whole, involve their patients in their total purchasing decisions.

**Management support and transaction costs**

The level of spending on management support varied widely between pilots, reflecting the lack of a 'blueprint' as to how to implement total purchasing (see Chapter 8). Pilot projects struggled to establish themselves without competent, full-time management support to 'weld' the individual practices and their GPs together into a single organization. Greater investment in management and the management infrastructure was clearly associated with more effective purchasing.

The existence of the TPPs increased the total level of transaction costs in the local health system. However, 85 per cent of the additional transaction costs attributable to total purchasing were associated with activities at practice level within the TPPs, such as communication, coordination and decision making, rather than with commissioning services and negotiating contracts with other agencies.

**Budgets and information**

Three basic methods were used to set TPPs' budgets: historical spending levels; some form of capitation; and a mix of historical and capitation funding. In the first 'live' year, of those pilots which received a budget, 43 per cent were historically set, 14 per cent were set by capitation and 43 per cent had a mix of the two (see Chapter 9). There was a shift towards capitation by the second 'live' year when 65 per cent of pilots were using capitation formulae. There was a general desire to shift towards a fair, needs-based allocation system for pilots.

The vast majority of the lead general practitioners in the TPPs reported that they found the process of budget setting difficult. This is reflected in the fact that only a quarter of first-wave TPPs had known their allocation before the start of the 1996/97 financial year. TPP respondents regarded these delays as a serious impediment to achieving desired changes. A delegated budget was particularly important for pilots which were aiming to change their patients' use of hospital services.

All the TPPs experienced similar difficulties in obtaining adequate routine information on their patients' use of services and service quality to inform the contracting process. Pilots undertook relatively little systematic work to assess the health care needs of their populations.

### Leadership and collective responsibility

Despite the fact that each practice in the TPP tended to be represented on the project board, most TPPs were dependent on the leadership exercised by a small number of GPs and found it difficult to engage all the GPs in, for example, the operational management of a shared budget (see Chapter 10). Most TPPs were led by one or two enthusiasts with a remainder of acquiescent GPs. By contrast, the most effective forms of project management combined small, active executive groups, which determined the direction of the project and ran it day-to-day, with wider involvement of all participants both in ratifying strategic decisions in order to ensure project sustainability and legitimacy and in implementing TPP policy day-to-day (see Chapter 3). Those projects which were able to distinguish and link the strategic and the operational tended to be more effective in implementing their goals and staying within budget (Baxter *et al.* 1998). However, in most TPPs, only the lead GPs were actively involved in taking financial decisions relating to managing the budget. This was particularly the case in multi-practice versus single-practice pilots. In a multi-practice environment, there was a greater risk of GPs 'free-riding' (i.e. accepting the benefits of total purchasing such as additional services, but not the restraints on their clinical freedom to commit resources) than under single-practice standard fundholding. Multi-practice TPPs found it more difficult to adapt their expenditure in-year (see below).

TPPs tended to avoid becoming involved in direct efforts to influence the clinical practice, prescribing or referral habits of individual GPs since it was assumed that these were outside the scope of the total purchasing budget. The implications for managing a collective total purchasing budget of differences in patterns of behaviour between practices and GPs were rarely explored. The TPPs were not viewed by their participants as a basis for peer review and audit (unlike the Primary Care Groups which have followed them, which have a wider remit *vis-à-vis* their general practices). The presence of a TPP did little in itself to shift the professional culture of general practice towards peer review, with a small number of exceptions. This was probably because the TPPs came into being principally to purchase secondary care services. Although they ended up developing primary care-based services they did not see their role as managers of GPs' own clinical activity. They remained aggregations of still distinct, independent practices.

## Managing budgets and managing risk

Over 80 per cent of TPPs shared information on activity and spending between the practices as their main way of managing their budgets in 1996/97 (Chapter 10). Many fewer had any protocols for changing activity or spending patterns as a result of this information. It appeared that many TPPs were hoping that information alone would be sufficient to lead to the necessary changes in behaviour. Single-practice TPPs were more often able to keep their spending in line with their budgets than multi-practice pilots. This is the opposite of what might have been expected on actuarial grounds, but was probably a result of the fact that it took the larger projects longer to develop as coherent organizations and for their general practitioners to work together.

Few pilots had undertaken a thorough assessment of their financial risk, perhaps because three in four shared risk with their parent health authorities. Despite inadequate provision for risks (e.g. generated by rare, costly cases) and worries that overspends might occur, surprisingly few pilots reported problems due to overspending. In part, this was because they lacked good up-to-date information on their spending and partly because they knew that the health authority was most unlikely to be able to impose any penalty for overspending.

## Selective purchasers and non-purchasers

The title 'total purchasers' was misleading. All the TPPs were *selective* purchasers, choosing which service areas they wished to devote their energies to changing. Their initial choices reflected their local experience of problems encountered in their work as general practitioners rather than a careful analysis of local needs and service responses (Chapter 4). Furthermore, although the concept of total purchasing emerged as the extension of standard fundholding, 22 per cent of 'first-wave' TPPs were either not formally offered a budget or failed to agree their allocation in 1996/97 (see Chapter 9). Thus there was considerable variety between the TPPs in the scope of their budgets and their ability to use budgets and contracts to bring about change.

### Impact on service equity

There was little hint that TPPs engaged systematically in either cost shifting to other organizations (e.g. the health authority) or 'cream skimming' (getting rid of high-risk (cost) patients to other practices), both of which might have been expected on theoretical grounds and both of which would have threatened equity of funding and of access between TPP and non-TPP populations. However, the reliance on historical or a mix of historical and capitation funding of TPPs, together with the lack of competition between pilots for patients may have blunted incentives to behave in these ways. In addition, the pilots were aware that the health authority would have to subsidize them if they got into financial difficulties.

Although there was little sign that TPPs' actions were motivated directly by self-interest, some of the changes in services which they brought about could have indirectly increased inequity of access to services in their locality. In particular, there were examples where TPPs had been able to reduce their costs, for example by negotiating a length of stay-sensitive contract for an acute in-patient service, which had led the provider to recoup the lost revenue by increasing its prices to other purchasers of the same service. As a result, the other purchasers were able to purchase fewer services for their populations than the TPP. This is similar to the 'two-tier' situation under standard fundholding, in which benefits secured by fundholders were not available to non-fundholding practice populations.

Conversely, there were also examples of TPPs acting to push up standards across an entire district. Some TPPs were able to persuade their health authority to revise its contracts so that service improvements could be generalized.

## Achievements and their determinants

In the main, the goals of the TPPs were to bring about small-scale, incremental and locally focused service developments. Based on their self-reports, the TPPs displayed a wide range of achievement both in 1996/97 and 1997/98. Simply conferring the status of 'TPP' on a practice or group of practices was insufficient to enable the project to attain its goals in the medium term (see Chapter 4).

Overall, the proportion of purchasing objectives which TPPs reported that they had successfully implemented, rose from 54 per cent in 1996/97 to 70 per cent in 1997/98. In the second period, fewer objectives were set in the service areas which had presented the most difficulties in the first period (namely, mental health services and managing emergency services), suggesting that the pilots were becoming more realistic. Over the two years, TPPs were more successful in making developments in primary and community care than in any other service areas. The practices could set up and manage services in these areas without the need to negotiate with secondary care providers.

Indeed, some TPPs were either not able to start or uninterested in trying to influence secondary care providers or negotiate contracts to bring about service change. Instead, they simply worked to extend the range of primary care services available at the practices (e.g. using the total purchasing budget to pay for advice on general practitioner prescribing from a local pharmacist). Other more ambitious TPPs (typically, those with a relatively high degree of budgetary autonomy and their own contracts) tried to bring about service change in more challenging service areas beyond the conventional scope of primary care (e.g. reducing their patients' use of hospital emergency care or improving mental health services), but they also tended to do so using primary and community-based developments with which they were more familiar (e.g. nursing home beds and intensive home support). For example, rather than negotiating a contract with protocols specifying that hospitals would review in-patients of the TPP after so many days of stay, they tended to invest in alternatives to hospitalization to prevent the initial admissions. Rather than acting as a managed care organization might to compel hospital staff to abide by treatment protocols designed to reduce resource use, they developed primary care and intermediate care facilities of their own in the hope of lowering their patients' admission rates. In sum, the vast majority of the TPPs focused on primary care-based and intermediate care developments. A small minority of these TPPs did so, not simply to extend primary care, but with a more systemic set of goals in mind to substitute non-hospital care for the use of more expensive secondary care in order to release resources for investment elsewhere.

There are a number of possible reasons why TPPs preferred not to use contracting with acute hospitals as a means of implementing reductions in lengths of stay and admissions: relative unfamiliarity with more specialized hospital services; deference to the knowledge of hospital consultants; specialists' resistance to general practitioners' interference in their work; and unwillingness of trust managers to release resources from previous contracts as patient activity was redirected away from the hospital. It is likely that all these factors played some part in the strategies employed by TPP general practitioners.

TPPs did bring about some service change through contracting and in some cases this was in the acute sector. However, contract-led service change was most common in relation to community health services NHS trusts rather than acute hospital NHS trusts. For example, TPPs used the contracting process to alter the delivery of community nursing services so that they were organized around individual general practices rather than geographic areas.

The influences shaping the level of self-reported achievement of the pilots were complex, but could be reduced to the interaction between the receptivity of the context, the content of the TPP's objectives, the mechanisms used to achieve the objectives and the organizational capacity of the TPP (see Chapters 5 and 6). In 1997/98, TPPs with more experienced fundholders, a more supportive health authority, their own independent contracts (at least for some services) and higher management costs were more likely to have realized their objectives than those without. The stage of organizational development clearly influenced the pattern of achievement. Whereas, in 1996/97, *smaller* TPPs were more likely to be higher achievers, by the second 'live' year, 1997/98, *larger* TPPs were more likely to be higher achievers. This was because the larger pilots had taken longer to grow to organizational maturity and because the new Labour government had made it plain during 1997/98 that single-practice budget holding of all types was shortly to be abolished. Having a budget was necessary, but not sufficient on its own for making progress. Neither the size of the budget per capita, nor whether the TPP had 'gained' or 'lost' in relation to past levels of spending appeared to be associated with the level of achievement.

As indicated above, only a small minority of TPPs' achievements were brought about directly by altering contracts with other, specialist providers, despite the fact that the presence of one or more independent contracts was associated with a higher level of self-reported achievement by TPPs. Over three times as many achievements were the result of using the TPP's budget directly to bring about a straightforward expansion or improved coordination of workers in the primary health care team (Wyke *et al.* 1999b). However, it was apparent that having a budget and, therefore, the *potential* to negotiate contracts for a wider range of services than standard fundholding had encouraged TPP practices to look at the balance and location of the care offered to their patients. It had also encouraged health authority staff and providers to engage with TPPs in negotiating options for service change (Malbon *et al.* 1999). It may be that having a few contracts, similarly, was a marker of the *potential* of the particular TPP to shift resources from NHS trusts and, therefore, encouraged trusts to cooperate with the TPP. The vast majority of project managers were convinced that independent contracting was important in both 'live' years of total purchasing in achieving service change, despite the fact that approximately a quarter of the pilots had no contracts of their own in either 1996/97 or 1997/98 (Robison *et al.* 1998).

**Managing emergency use of secondary care**

From a strategic, health system-wide perspective, one of the toughest, but most important, tests of GP-led purchasing as a contributor to overall health system efficiency is whether the purchaser is able to alter the pattern of unplanned (i.e. 'emergency') use of acute in-patient services (see Chapter 7 and McLeod and Raftery 2000). Of the 16 first-wave TPPs which pursued objectives either to reduce emergency admissions to acute hospital or lengths of stay over the two 'live' years of the initiative, nine were multi-practice pilots and seven were single-practice TPPs. Seven of the nine multi-practice TPPs and four of the seven single-practice TPPs experienced a reduction in the bed days consumed by their patients in the targeted specialties compared with local practices. These findings suggest that the pilots' use of a range of alternative services to prevent mainly older medical patients from requiring admission to local acute hospitals was particularly successful for the multi-practice pilots. Despite the fact that these TPPs were able to demonstrate that primary care-based purchasers can influence their patients' use of emergency as well as elective services, only one of the 'successful' multi-practice pilots reported being able to release sufficient resources through the introduction of activity-sensitive contract pricing at its main acute hospital to fund its alternative services. This was partly because health authorities failed to agree budgets in a timely manner (see Chapter 9), thereby handicapping the pilots. More fundamentally, however, hospitals were resistant to having resources shifted out of their contracts and generally refused to move away from activity-based contracts based on payments for each finished consultant episode to length of stay-sensitive pricing. Ideally, TPPs would have wished to extract resources from acute hospitals at average cost, but hospitals argued that marginal cost reductions were the most that they could contemplate, at least in the short term. Most health authorities did not intervene to support their pilots to remove resources from acute hospital contracts in line with planned or actual reductions in hospital use. As a result, the alternatives to hospital services put in place by the TPPs were generally funded from growth monies or 'winter pressures' budgets.

**Integration of care**

Delegating a larger share of the health authority budget to an organization based on general practices encouraged the development in many TPPs of initiatives which led to greater integration between primary and secondary services, between primary and community care, or between primary, community and social care services (i.e. both vertical and horizontal integration). These developments resulted both from a relatively straightforward intention to develop better primary care and more ambitious and complex attempts to reduce dependence on the local acute hospital system (Killoran *et al.* 1999b).

Many of the integrative developments embodied elements of case or care management familiar in 'managed care' settings in other systems (see Chapter 5). In the NHS, where the relationship between health services in the community and social services controlled by local government is a vexed one, TPPs showed some signs of getting to grips with the problems of collaboration at the operational, practice level (Goodwin *et al.* 2000). They were also developing more ambitious ideas for integrated provision for people with complex and enduring needs when the pilots came to an end (see Chapter 6 and Wyke *et al.* 1999c). Although it would be difficult to argue that the developments made by the TPPs were, in any fundamental sense, unique or could not have been developed by other means, the delegation of a budget to the practices in the TPPs increased the likelihood that collaborative initiatives were implemented rather than simply discussed. On the other hand, it was very rare to see budget pooling between the TPPs and local social services being used to develop new patterns of service; rather, the focus was on developing a shared vision of service developments, sometimes accompanied by a shift in the boundary of responsibility between the NHS and local government social services.

### Impact of total purchasing on users

It was easy to criticize the design of the national evaluation of total purchasing by pointing out that it did not consider the impact of changes in responsibility for purchasing on users. This criticism was not considered justifiable for most of the services purchased by total purchasers, as changes in service organization or delivery could not be expected to change people's health status at least in measurable ways over the life of the study. However, in the area of maternity care comparison of women's experiences of information, choice, control and resource use between GP-based purchasing and non-GP-based purchasing practices was judged to be both feasible and important.

Following the national policy recommendations in *Changing Childbirth* (Department of Health 1993a), GP-based purchasers might have been expected to be more effective in shifting services towards a model which delivered quality of care defined from women's perspectives. As budget holders, they might also have been expected to reconsider resource use, and to encourage services that provided more effective use of resources. However, as Chapter 6 described, although GP-based purchasers seemed to be more likely to be associated with more integrated, less traditional models of maternity care, these did not appear to produce a measurable effect sufficient to improve women's experience of care, or alter their use of resources.

## CONCLUSIONS FROM THE EVALUATION EVIDENCE

Like many social policy initiatives, TPPs were far from uniformly 'successful' or 'unsuccessful'. The circumstances in which an innovation is implemented play a crucial role in its effectiveness (Pawson and Tilley 1997). Whether a particular TPP was able to achieve its objectives and/or bring about change in local health services depended on interactions between the context in which the TPP was operating, the content of its objectives and the mechanisms which it developed to achieve those objectives (see Chapter 5). Specifically, the most successful TPPs had strong leadership, general practitioners experienced in purchasing and fundholding, support from the local health authority and the ability to develop collaborative relationships with local providers. Those pilots which invested time and effort in developing these organizational competencies (with their associated management costs) were more likely to make progress. As a result, some developments worked well in some places, some of the time. The primary care groups which have replaced fundholding and total purchasing in the NHS in England are likely to repeat this experience of differential progress, at least in their first few years.

While recognizing the variation between individual TPPs, and the fact that the TPP practices were a voluntary and selected group from the half of NHS practices already involved in standard fundholding in 1995, it is still possible to draw conclusions from the initiative as a whole. Starting on the debit side, the TPPs undoubtedly increased the cost and complexity of local health services, and were far from consistently successful in achieving their objectives (especially in shifting resources out of hospitals to reflect service changes and to fund developments such as alternatives to hospital care). The TPPs varied widely in their abilities and levels of reported achievements and there were no demonstrable benefits to users of maternity services in the life of the pilots. However, on the credit side, granting general practitioners control over a wider range of hospital and community health services resources enabled new relationships with providers to develop and new services to be built up. Particularly in multi-practice pilots, total purchasing stimulated investment in corporate capacity building and schemes which, in time, led to the extension of primary care and inter-mediate care services, together with improvements in the ability to commission services from others. In the toughest of areas for general practitioner-based purchasers – altering the use of hospital emergency care by their patients – those TPPs which made this a priority showed the potential contribution to the entire NHS of GP-led organizations in managing a reduction in dependence on acute hospital services. This, in turn, has the potential to improve overall efficiency in the use of hospital and community health services resources. By putting purchasing decisions in the hands of clinicians with direct experience of local services and the incentive to take responsibility for their patients' total NHS resource use, including their emergency use of acute hospitals, TPPs were able to develop more integrated approaches to service delivery. TPP status gave the GPs the opportunity and the total purchasing budget gave them the leverage, in principle, to manage their patients' use of acute services more actively than previously.

The pilots focused particularly on developing primary and community care and intermediate care services, in order to increase both vertical and horizontal integration of local services. Many aimed to do so using the contracting process to shift resources and influence providers' behaviour. Indeed, many did develop independent contracts and these were the more successful at bringing about service change. However, very few TPPs were able to use contractual relationships with NHS trusts to shift resources out of trust contracts to reflect actual or planned shifts of activity and, thereby, to fund their new integrated care schemes.

## EXPLAINING THE FINDINGS

How can the relatively modest impact of the total purchasing initiative, both for good and ill, despite its substantial *potential* for the future, be explained? In large part, the explanation lies in the way in which total purchasing was introduced and the changing circumstances within which the pilots had to operate.

### Pilot status

The first part of the explanation focuses on the pilot status of the TPPs. Total purchasing was unusual in the internal market era in being implemented on a 'pilot' basis. Standard fundholding, for example, had not been introduced in this way. The reasons for this decision were not fully apparent, but probably related to some scepticism on the part of ministers and officials in the Department of Health as to whether or not GPs could become knowledgeable and motivated purchasers of services in areas where they had little direct experience and only modest leverage. Given that the NHS had become accustomed in the recent past to policy change driven by strong political convictions, brooking no dissent, the 'pilot' status of the TPPs was interpreted by some in the Service as an expression of uncertainty rather than as a desire to learn by experimenting.

'Pilot' status meant that the projects began life with an explicit time limit. It also meant that the government chose not to legislate the TPPs into existence, allowing them to be defined as subcommittees of their local health authority. These two features had profound implications. The subcommittee aspect meant that the budgets delegated to the TPPs remained ultimately the responsibility of the health authority, not the TPP. TPPs also had to negotiate with the health authority to obtain a management budget, unlike under standard fundholding where they had received a generous management allowance by right and 'owned' the fundholding budget. Both features set external limits on the autonomy of the pilots. The fact that the TPPs' budgets were still legally the responsibility of the health authority also prevented the practices from managing their standard fundholding and total purchasing budgets as one. Pilots were precluded from shifting money between standard fundholding and total purchasing. In addition, the General Medical Services payments to the individual GPs remained outside the scope of total purchasing. Some TPPs complained that these artificial restrictions had handicapped their purchasing and service development goals.

The 'hybrid' nature of the TPPs – part formal health authority bureaucracy, part general practice collective – was unusual for the NHS. TPPs did not fit neatly into the NHS organizational chart. They also presented problems for the health authority accountability regime. The NHS Executive wished to give the pilots considerable autonomy and freedom to innovate, yet organizationally they were part of the local health authority and subject to its accountability regime.

'Pilot' status may have influenced the responses of providers, especially acute hospital trusts, to the TPPs. Some NHS trusts voiced concerns that the actions of TPPs would threaten the viability of their services, thereby harming the remainder of the local population. Others were worried that the GPs would act unilaterally and bring about major changes without warning and consultation. The hospitals and health authorities were anxious to avoid the problems, which they perceived standard fundholding had created. They could see that the TPPs would, in principle, control far bigger budgets than fundholders had done. In practice, the pilot status of the TPPs meant that they were dependent on the local health authority for their resources. Delay in finalizing TPPs' budgets was one tactic for restricting the TPPs and reducing the risk that they might destabilize local providers by shifting resources around the system.

Involvement in total purchasing gave the practices visibility and higher status as part of an NHS Executive-supported initiative. In some cases, pilots could influence significant purchasing power (see Chapter 9). However, pilot status also encouraged a perception among trusts that the TPPs were not necessarily going to be an enduring part of the NHS landscape. There was always the hope that they would disappear after three years and their demands could, therefore, be resisted. Indeed, the more ineffectual the providers could make the TPPs appear, the more likely this outcome would become!

### Shifts in national policy

The second set of related explanations for the degree of impact of the TPPs relates to the wider national policy context. Provider resistance to the TPPs increased over time, as the Conservative government's hold on power appeared to weaken with the approaching 1997 general election. The May 1997 Labour electoral victory took place one month into the second 'live' year for the first-wave pilots. The new government promised to abolish standard general practitioner fundholding. As a result, TPPs found it even more difficult to engage the attention of providers. Labour had made it plain that if any form of general practitioner budget holding were to replace standard fundholding, it would not be based on self-selected practices, but all practices in a defined area working together. This contributed further to the difficulty faced by TPPs in negotiating length of stay-sensitive contracts. Single-practice TPPs were particularly badly hit by this national political change in their second 'live' year (1997/98). Seen in this light, the TPPs' achievements appear more rather than less impressive.

The primary care groups and local health groups which have replaced standard fundholding and total purchasing in England and Wales at least have the advantage of being permanent (some would argue pivotal) features of the NHS structure in the two countries. Indeed, in the *New NHS* developed by Labour after April 1999, the relationships between the players in the local health system are governed by a statutory duty of 'partnership'. As a result, primary care groups and local health groups are accepted as having a central role in the development and delivery of local health services. They may have greater leverage over other providers than the TPPs enjoyed.

National policy appears to have been crucial both for facilitating and inhibiting the actions of the TPPs in other ways. Maternity care provides a vivid example. Health authority and provider support for TPPs which wished to implement the recommendations contained in the *Changing Childbirth* strategy (Department of Health 1993a) and related maternity care initiatives was present as long as *Changing Childbirth* remained a high priority at national level (Chapter 6). As it was displaced by other initiatives, so the TPPs found it more difficult to obtain the cooperation of the health authorities and trusts.

One of the paradoxical consequences of the internal market changes to the NHS after 1991 was the way in which, far from becoming *less* responsive to central directives, the system was reshaped to become *more* responsive to 'bureaucratic incentives' generated at the centre rather than market signals generated at the periphery (Hughes *et al.* 1997). As a result, once enthusiasm for GP fundholding began to wane at the centre, this mood was transmitted rapidly to the periphery. Since TPPs were dependent on the goodwill of their local health authority for their existence, this had a decisive, negative influence on a number of TPPs. Standard fundholding and total purchasing were increasingly seen as divisive and contrary to emerging trends towards involving all GPs in commissioning services and towards a more collaborative Health Service rather than one based on quasi-market transactions between purchasers and providers.

## The political economy of the quasi-market

The third set of related explanations for the performance of the TPPs focuses on politicians' perceptions of risk and the fact that, at national level, ministers were responsible for both the purchase and most of the provision of publicly funded health care. This had profound implications for the kind of quasi-market which was tolerated. The interests of the two sides of the internal market could conflict and ministers and their officials had to negotiate a route between the two. Throughout the Conservatives' internal market (1991–98), ministers were torn between following the logic of their market rhetoric and allowing lower quality or higher cost providers to lose business (and even go bankrupt), and intervening to ensure stability, particularly in the acute hospital sector, in order to avoid adverse political repercussions. The high profile of hospitals in the public's mind meant that provider interests tended to prevail, thereby weakening the legitimacy and influence of purchasers.

TPPs were affected by this since the larger pilots were large enough for their purchasing decisions to affect the financial position of large acute hospitals (unlike individual standard fundholding practices). In short, TPPs were part of a wider internal market in which, it can be argued, 'the incentives were too weak and the constraints were too strong' (Le Grand *et al.* 1998; Mays *et al.* 2000) for major change. Ministers wanted innovation driven from primary care, but not at the price of destabilization of providers. Yet destabilization of at least some participants is essential to the dynamics of markets. Following this line of interpretation, it can justifiably be argued that

> the British quasi-market in health care neither succeeded nor failed, simply because it was never tried. Moreover, perhaps the quasi-market never could have been tried . . . it may be that health is too sensitive an issue in Britain for central government ever to let the relevant agents have enough freedom.'
> (Le Grand 1999: 37)

Particularly in their attempts to shift resources from secondary to primary care (see Chapters 4, 5 and 7), the TPPs faced many of the same obstacles encountered by other primary care initiatives developed in the 1990s in the NHS. While successive Conservative and Labour governments had promoted national policies to transfer decision making, funds and services to primary and community care settings and away from traditional providers, especially acute hospitals, local progress was more modest. O'Cathain *et al.* (1999) identified stakeholders' perceptions of the barriers to shifting services from secondary to primary care in the context of two failed initiatives, one of which was a pilot extension of general practitioner fundholding similar to total purchasing. They concluded that the issue of disinvestment from existing providers was the main barrier to success in schemes aiming to shift services to primary care. As they pointed out, whether in a competitive or a more collaborative service environment, disinvestment will be seen by potential losers as a threat to their survival, especially where there are substantial fixed costs, as in acute hospitals. Providers were only willing to see marginal costs withdrawn from their budgets in order to preserve their ability to provide their remaining services. Unfortunately, marginal costs were insufficient to establish new alternative services. TPPs were in a similar bind (see Chapters 7 and 9). When local providers and the health authority told the TPPs that they could only make savings from changes in use of services at marginal cost, this greatly reduced their incentive to try, since it narrowed the scope of alternative services which they could establish.

It remains to be seen whether the new primary care groups in England will find the process of negotiating shifts of resources as well as services out of acute hospitals any easier than their TPP predecessors despite the duty of partnership between primary care groups and NHS trusts.

### Incentives facing GPs

The fourth set of explanations for the behaviour and achievements of the TPPs relates to the incentives facing individual practitioners in the pilots. The GPs in TPPs faced fewer direct, personal incentives to manage resources efficiently than they had encountered under standard fundholding. It is not difficult to argue that, as a hybrid of health authority purchasing and standard fundholding, total purchasing was a 'diluted' form of GP practice-based budget holding. Practices were not financially at risk for their TPP budgets. In addition, standard fundholding was based on practice level budgets, whereas multi-practice TPPs' budgets were held in common between practices. In principle, the prospect of exerting influence and achieving service improvements through the use of larger, pooled budgets created incentives for GPs to work for the collective good of the combined patient population of the TPP practices. However, 'savings' which, under standard fundholding, had remained unequivocally the property of the individual practice, to be used, within limits, as the practice saw fit (e.g. to invest in building and equipment which added to the value of the practice), had to be shared and negotiated with the local health authority and the other practices in the project. Thus, although risk was shared with the health authority and, in theory, with other practices in the TPP (though there were no sanctions for overspending save removal from the scheme), so too were the benefits of any potential 'savings' made by individual GPs.

It was also more difficult than under standard fundholding

(though not absolutely impossible) to use total purchasing 'savings' in ways which could benefit the individual practices and practitioners. TPPs were expected to purchase additional services with any surplus. On the other hand, TPP GPs were able to pay themselves (within locally agreed limits) to provide services outside their general medical services national contracts. Thus some TPP GPs provided a range of specialist outpatient services themselves rather than using hospital specialists, and they were paid accordingly. Furthermore, the introduction via total purchasing of new services at practice level stood some prospect of reducing the GPs' workloads or, at least, of improving the skill mix available to practices. These incentives had to be weighed against the fact that involvement in total purchasing frequently imposed significant time and locum costs on the lead general practitioners which were not always compensated by the health authority through the management budget for the pilot. Thus, in some ways, there were major *disincentives* for all but the most enthusiastic GPs to take part.

The relatively weak financial incentives acting on the TPP GPs because of the 'hybrid' nature of the scheme also had some advantages. The combination of the fact that the GPs were not personally at risk financially for TPP overspends; that the TPPs' budgets frequently included substantial historical funding levels; that the budget belonged ultimately to the health authority; and that the pilots were not in competition with other purchasers for patients, but part of the health authority, probably explains why 'cost shifting' and 'cream skimming' did not appear to have been problems under total purchasing. The health authority staff involved in supporting the pilots had no incentive to encourage either form of behaviour since both would increase the demands on the remainder of health authorities' budgets.

## Clout and capacity

The final set of explanations for the impact of the TPPs relates to the scale of the initiative and related organizational capacity. Although the total purchasing venture comprised 53 projects in the first wave and another 35 in the second, on average each TPP only comprised three general practices; that is, the pilots were mostly small players in their local health 'market'. While a typical health authority might have a population of 300,000–400,000 people, TPPs were normally a tenth of the size. They rarely employed more than one or two staff, although they made extensive use of health authority expertise. For example, a third of TPPs did not even have a full-time project manager. Some of the health authorities with TPPs were reluctant to invest in management support for the pilots since they themselves were under pressure from the NHS Executive to reduce their headquarters management expenditure as part of the Labour government's 'war' on the bureaucracy generated by the Conservatives' internal market. Despite the significantly increased budgetary and commissioning responsibility over standard fundholding, there was little appreciation of the need to invest systematically in building organizational competencies. Perhaps, again, this was a consequence of pilot status. From such a base, TPPs were expected to develop their own approach to health services' purchasing across a range of new services outside the scope of standard fundholding. Compared with successful purchasing agencies in the United States of America, TPPs were at a considerable disadvantage, prompting one North American commentator on the United Kingdom scene to ask whether the NHS was indeed serious about developing the purchasing side of the Service (Light, 1998). Efficient not-for-profit health maintenance organizations in the United States of America frequently have management costs equivalent to £1300 per capita per year (quoted in Chapter 10). The costliest TPP was spending less than a thirtieth of this sum. Seen from this perspective, TPPs were too small, had too little expertise and lacked managerial firepower. In addition, they lacked most of the essential information needed for purchasing and were handicapped by the reluctance of health authorities and the NHS Executive to allow them to make significant changes, particularly if this involved reducing the operating budgets of acute hospitals where most of the resources were locked up. Light's view was that efficiency and quality gains in service delivery could only be realized in the NHS by investing more heavily in the development of the purchasing function than successive governments had been willing to do since the early 1990s. On the other hand, the bigger the commissioning organization, in a politically sensitive, highly managed system such as the NHS, the greater the risk that the purchaser represents too large a proportion of local providers' incomes for the purchaser to be able to move its business elsewhere without destroying the providers (Le Grand 1999). This is sometimes referred to as the 'nuclear deterrent' problem in purchasing.

## CONCLUSIONS

The impact of the TPPs was variable. Their achievements tended to be small-scale, local and incremental. The pilots increased the costs of running the local health system. Yet some were able to alter their patients' emergency use of hospital services by providing a range of early intervention and alternative forms of care in ways which demonstrate the potential of primary care-based commissioning organizations for improving the use of resources.

Their modest achievements start to look more substantial when the constraints under which they operated and the wider policy environment of the period are taken into account. Time-limited 'pilots' which relied on health authority goodwill to have control over their own budgets and which were mostly about a tenth the population size of the health authority had limited bargaining power and managerial capacity in relation to providers. Their position was not assisted by the shift in national policy away from standard fundholding on which they had been based.

Despite their limitations, TPPs did enough to continue the momentum begun with standard fundholding to shift the balance of influence in the NHS from the hospital towards other parts of the wider health system. TPPs and GP commissioning pilots have been replaced by primary care groups and primary care trusts in England which have much in common with the TPPs. GPs and primary care professionals also play an enhanced role in the local NHS in the other parts of the United Kingdom. The final chapter draws out the implications for these developments which can be derived from the total purchasing initiative. It also attempts to derive wider lessons for health policy which transcend the boundaries of the NHS.

# 14

# THE TOTAL PURCHASING EXPERIMENT: A GUIDE TO FUTURE POLICY DEVELOPMENT?

## Nicholas Mays, Gill Malbon, Sally Wyke, Amanda Killoran and Nick Goodwin

Now that the total purchasing initiative is over and all GPs in England and Wales are required to take part in large collectives which betray marked similarities to the former TPPs, charged with both commissioning a large proportion of NHS hospital and community health services and delivering primary care services, how should the episode be viewed? Where does it fit in the recent history of the NHS? Was total purchasing the last gasp of the expiring Conservatives' ill-fated internal market experiment? Was the centrality it gave to GPs as purchasing agents for their patients a blind alley in policy development? Or was the 'hybrid' nature of total purchasing a necessary bridge between the supposedly 'competitive', or at least 'contestable', internal market of 1991–97 and Labour's more explicitly 'collaborative' NHS after 1998? Is there any sign of policy learning from the experience of the TPPs? Does primary care-based service commissioning have a continuing role in publicly financed health systems? In this final chapter we put the total purchasing initiative into the policy context which both preceded and followed it, before drawing out its implications for primary care organizations in Britain and elsewhere.

## THE TOTAL PURCHASING INITIATIVE IN ITS POLICY CONTEXT

There is little doubt that total purchasing was conceived at the high point of political support for fundholding within central government and ended as the internal market was losing intellectual and practical support ahead of its so called 'abolition' and reinvention by New Labour. The evidence from the national evaluation suggests that small GP-led organizations with little managerial capacity have distinct limitations as purchasers, but that one of the consequences of giving GPs more control over hospital and community health services resources is the development of a wider range of primary and intermediate services outside hospital. On the other hand, it is plain that total purchasing, because it began life as a purchasing initiative, had almost no impact on the way in which the GPs involved provided general medical services under the national general practitioner contract; nor was this a policy goal of the scheme. The TPPs' budgets specifically excluded any element of the general medical services resources received by the participating GPs. TPPs did not see it as part of their role to enquire into, and act on, the quality of general medical services provided by their GPs. This was partly because standard fundholding had already demonstrated that formerly demand-led GP pharmaceutical expenditure could be successfully cash-limited, thereby reducing a major cause of Treasury anxiety about expenditure control in the NHS. It simply remained for government to find a way of introducing all GPs to the joys of managing a prescribing budget (this has now occurred in England, Wales and Scotland with the advent of primary care groups, local health groups in Wales and local health care cooperatives in Scotland. Indeed, the only budget managed by Scottish local health care cooperatives is the prescribing budget). This does mean, however, that total purchasing contributed little to the long-standing concern of policy makers to develop better levers to influence the quality and cost of general medical services. Other policy initiatives were directed at this goal, including successive renegotiations of the national GP contract and the personal medical services pilots in which innovative, local alternatives to the national GP contract were experimented with on a small scale (Coulter and Mays 1997; NHS Executive 1997b).

By contrast, the total purchasing initiative did appear to have acted as a bridge between the practice-level budget holding of standard fundholding and the collective approach of the primary care groups and local health groups. In many ways, the TPPs represented a scaled-down dress rehearsal for the so-called 'level 2' primary care groups. Total purchasing demonstrated that groups of practices could work together without necessarily requiring major change in the constitution of each practice. GPs could collaborate to develop corporate objectives and to implement plans to improve local health services without being placed directly at financial risk. The total purchasing initiative produced a cadre of GPs, practices and health authorities with some experience of a more devolved system of service commissioning. It also put in place some of the organizational building blocks for this. However, the costs of coordinating independent practices were considerable and exceeded the costs of negotiating contracts with other providers. There did not seem to be obvious economies of scale in managing the larger TPPs because of their basis in the aggregation of individual practices (Posnett *et al.* 1998 and Chapter 8). Total purchasing also showed how difficult it was to engage all practices and all practitioners in the effective management of a shared budget when there was no clear link between the financial health of the TPP and that of the individual practices and practitioners. In addition, total purchasers did not undertake population-based needs assessment; nor did they systematically engage with patients when they were seeking solutions to local health problems. These issues remain as challenges for the primary care groups and local health groups in the NHS.

## IMPLICATIONS OF TOTAL PURCHASING FOR NEW PRIMARY CARE ORGANIZATIONS IN THE NHS

### Similarities and differences between TPPs and new organizations

The implications of the research findings for the development of the new primary care organizations need to be considered in the light of differences between them and TPPs. The differences and similarities are set out in Table 1.1. Although these relatively recent primary care-led commissioning organizations in England and Wales have a great deal in common with the former TPPs (for example, they have budgets, are allowed to retain surpluses and are able to switch providers as a last resort), they are considerably larger. The relationship between the financial incentives facing the organisation as a whole and its constituent practices is even more indirect. Primary care groups rest on the assumption that all GPs in an area working together compulsorily as part of a larger organization will deliver greater benefits than the same general practitioners working either as individual budget holding practices or smaller self-selected groups like TPPs (Street and Place 1998). The risk with primary care groups is that service improvements, for example, may accrue to the primary care group as a whole rather than to the specific practices, which have been active in bringing them about. Conversely, individual practitioners may choose to ignore the collective budgetary constraint (since their contractual relationship with the NHS to deliver general medical services will remain largely separate from the operation of the primary care group, at least in the early stages of development), thereby putting pressure on the rest of the primary care group to alter behaviour to manage a potential overspend. The evidence from the evaluation of the TPPs indicates that these sorts of 'free-rider' problems could be a significant difficulty, since the larger pilots, particularly in the first 'live' year, found it more difficult to develop interpractice links in order to engage with all their GPs (Mays *et al.* 1998b) and to take steps actively to manage their spending to stay within budget (Baxter *et al.* 1998 and Chapter 10). Whereas the GPs in TPPs were, at least nominally, all volunteers, the main incentive for GPs initially to cooperate with the objectives of the wider primary care group appears to be access to practice development funds which are allocated by the primary care group to practices on the basis of practice plans. These funds will be used to develop new facilities and services at practice level. It will be important for primary care groups to demonstrate their value to individual general practitioners at a relatively early stage if their support is to be secured.

Most significantly, unlike TPPs, new primary care organizations are a central official component of local health systems. They have a significant and legitimate role in the creation of local health improvement programmes (local health plans) and in their implementation. TPPs had to struggle as minor players, since they were small-scale projects with only pilot status. By contrast, the new primary care organizations are bigger and comprise a mix of practices with varying levels of commissioning experience and different perspectives on the development of local health care. New primary care organizations have a much wider range of responsibilities and functions. Primary care groups/trusts and local health groups in England and Wales are compulsory, while practices can 'opt out' of local health care cooperatives in Scotland.

**The challenge of organizational development**

The experience of total purchasing clearly indicated that the performance of pilots was strongly linked to their development of organizational capability, and that this, in turn, was associated with the level of management costs in a project. This finding predicted that the larger scale of primary care groups, local health groups and local health care cooperatives means that organizational development would present an even greater challenge, particularly given that the new organizations contain a mix of fundholding practices and non-fundholders with varying levels of experience, and practices both ideologically opposed and committed to managing budgets for care. More recent studies of primary care groups/trusts (Audit Commission 2000a; Smith *et al.* 2000a; Wilkin *et al.* 2000) and local health groups (Audit Commission 2000b) have borne this out. The importance of organizational development and board level working was highlighted when primary care group chairs, chief officers and health authority lead managers were asked to identify their most significant achievements to date and barriers to success (Wilkin and Sheaff 2000). Among the most commonly identified achievements were getting the board working together corporately, developing cooperation between the different primary care profession groups at board level and developing the organization of the primary care group. Among the most commonly identified barriers to success were inadequate resources/infrastructure and lack of time/pace of change. Similar findings have been shown in the study by Smith *et al.* (2000a) where almost two-thirds of primary care group board members (in 12 primary care groups studied) highlighted issues relating to organizational development as being key achievements. In particular, these included collaboration and cohesion between primary care group board members and the establishment of the primary care groups' organizational structures and *modus operandi*. Progress in relation to the adoption of corporate governance procedures, the setting up of task specific subgroups, the allocation of roles and responsibilities to primary care group members, and the recruitment of dedicated staff were all singled out as crucial developments to the central objective of establishing the primary care groups' infrastructure. Smith *et al.* argued '. . . it is clear that the PCGs in our study have remained focused largely upon internal issues and process in their first few months' (2000: 33).

Larger TPPs often progressed slowly because not all practices in the project were actively involved, which meant that the behaviour and resource consumption (corporate behaviour) of some of the practices were often uncontrolled. The challenge for primary care organizations will be to develop a management infrastructure that enables 50–100 GPs and other primary care professionals to function corporately, whilst the GPs largely remain independent contractors, with other primary care staff either employed by them, or by the local NHS community trust, or by the primary care trust in Scotland. Complex arrangements are likely to be required that provide different opportunities for, and levels of, engagement in the management of the organization, linked to appropriate incentives and sanctions for different practices and staff groups.

The national evaluation of primary care groups (Smith *et al.* 2000a) has outlined a number of organizational models adopted by Primary Care Groups which vary from a basic structure, relying on health authority links and teams for many functions, comprising fewer than two full-time staff (excluding the chief officer), and operating on a management budget of £2.75 per head, to the extended primary care group structure which has, on average, five to ten full-time staff working as part of a dedicated support team. Posts in these structures typically include the chief officer, a business support manager, finance manager(s), health improvement/needs analysis staff, primary care development managers, prescribing advisers, and secretarial and administrative support. The management spending for this type of primary care group averages £4.25 per head. The evidence from the TPPs suggests that the higher management spending primary care groups will be able to achieve more. However, just like the TPPs, primary care groups face difficulty in obtaining sufficient management resources, encouraging mergers and sharing of functions.

As yet, there is no evidence to show which, if any, organizational model is better placed to manage expenditure on services in the primary care groups' first year (1999/2000). Early hints suggest that most primary care groups were unable to stay within their expenditure envelope in the first year. This casts some doubt on the assumption underlying primary care groups that large groups of GPs are able to function collectively and collaboratively, particularly when the incentives to do so are not overtly apparent.

However, having a primary care group-wide budget may encourage greater consistency of clinical practice and gradually encourage greater involvement of practitioners across the primary care group.

For example, if one practice considerably overspends on its pre-scribing budget, this would have a knock-on effect for all the other practices within the primary care group since the responsibility to stay within the cash-limited prescribing budget is the corporate responsibility of the primary care group. In a situation such as this, the primary care group may well be expected to produce savings and claw back overspends, *as a whole*, rather than looking to the individual practice to offer up savings elsewhere. This introduces a new dynamic which may produce a stronger incentive to operate collectively.

### Changing roles of health authorities and primary care organizations and their management cost implications

The evidence from total purchasing demonstrated that the success of the new primary care organizations will depend on investment in an effective management infrastructure. When primary care groups were first proposed, the government announced that it would set a cap on their total management costs at £3.00 per head of popu-lation. The total management costs of TPPs (including their stan-dard fundholding functions) were between £6.00 and £8.00 per head. The assumption is that by making primary care groups the size of small districts (with approximately 100,000 population) management costs per capita can be reduced through economies of scale and the elimination of duplication of functions throughout the local health system. The evidence from the TPPs indicated that the reality is likely to be more complex, since there was no reduction in per capita management costs in the larger projects. This was because, while there were some management functions where straightforward economies of scale could be realized, there were other organizational costs which increased in step with size. These costs were typically associated with communication and coordi-nation between practices and with paying GPs for their time spent on TPP work. Moreover, since TPPs comprised 'leading edge', volunteer practices operating as fixed-term pilots, the scheme was able to count on a high proportion of uncosted additional time given by key participants, particularly on the part of the lead gen-eral practitioners who were enthusiastic for GP commissioning and budget management. The implication is that the costs of coordinat-ing GPs across more, and non-volunteer, practices under primary care groups are unlikely to be less than they were for the TPPs. Early signs suggest that this is not far from the case. Evidence from the Audit Commission's study noted wide differences in the per capita management budgets available to primary care groups (Audit Commission 2000a). Primary care group budgets ranged from £119,000 to £1.28 million, or between £1.54 and £5.57 per resident, the average being £2.96. The 'average' primary care group spends over a third (£99,000) of this management budget on the chair, board and other clinicians' remuneration and allowances, and rather less than one-half (average £120,000) on staff salaries, including that of the chief executive. Staff budgets reported by primary care groups ranged from £39,000 to £836,000. Salaries offered by different primary care groups for similar posts seem to vary considerably. Small primary care groups in particular have very limited funds for staff once board costs are met.

In the long term, the effective deployment of management costs, and any reduction of costs, will depend on agreeing the respective roles and functions of health authorities (and health boards in Scotland), local authorities and primary care organizations, and eliminating the overlap of functions that characterized the TPP case. In particular, new ways of fulfilling the tasks associated with operational commissioning will need to be tested to secure the most effective and efficient distribution of management costs.

In the short term, the pressure on management costs is likely to be particularly intense; since health authorities will have to continue to operate as important commissioners locally, while at the same time investment is needed to develop the functions of primary care organizations in the same areas. But if these organizations are to succeed, health authorities/boards will increasingly need to 'let go' – by devolving and sharing functions, and management costs, with the new organizations. According to the national tracker survey (Leese and Wilkin 2000), most health authorities have made the first steps towards 'letting go' and all have put in place the basic mechanisms for holding primary care groups accountable for their actions. However, the future role of health authorities in providing strategic leadership for their local 'health economies' is not sufficiently well defined or understood to know how far management spending can be reduced.

### GP-led organization versus a partnership model

A key principle of the *New NHS* (Secretary of State for Health 1997) is the duty placed on health organizations to work in partnership with each other and with local authorities and other agencies.

In contrast, total purchasing was explicitly a GP-led model of commissioning and based on the experience and views of GPs. Priority setting was seen largely as a GP-dominated process. By contrast, most primary care groups appear to be explicitly committed to involving and representing the interests of their local stakeholders (Smith *et al.* 2000b). However, although primary care groups are working hard to develop an inclusive approach to the operation of the board, there continue to be concerns about the extent to which general practitioners dominate the board and the limited involvement of nurses in priority setting and decision making. In addition, most primary care groups have made little progress in developing mechanisms for involving lay people in the work of the group beyond the contribution of lay board members and consultation with Community Health Councils. The TPP experience predicted that this would be so as small local organizations had very limited capacity for sophisticated stakeholder management activities. As Anderson and Florin (2000) recognize, 'within an overwhelming operational and development agenda, public involvement has rarely been a high priority for primary care group boards'. For many primary care groups in England, the first major test of their ability to engage and respond to the views of stakeholders will be in relation to decisions about applications for primary care trust status and/or mergers between neighbouring primary care groups. The capacity of primary care groups/trusts to deliver policy goals will depend significantly on their ability to develop new ways to debate and set priorities that engage other interest groups, particularly community nurses, local authorities – including housing, urban regeneration and education services as well as their social services – and local people.

Allied to this duty of partnership working is the duty to improve the local population's health. The evidence from total purchasing shows that the assessment of population needs was highly underdeveloped. Given that new primary care organizations are to have responsibilities for the wider public health of their communities, they will need to give far more attention to this area than TPPs. Greater support from public health specialists – including health promotion staff – will be essential, although this may be problematic given the limited expertise available in some health authorities. Alternatively, the public health role of community nurses could be developed (e.g. in data collection relevant to needs assessment). As recent research on primary care groups has shown (Abbott and Gillam 2000), the skills to support health needs assessment are in limited supply. Timescales and the pressure of other tasks for primary care groups have precluded them contributing much to the first health authority health improvement programmes; national public health priorities (e.g. the *Health of the Nation* targets) have not previously attracted strong commitment from within primary care; and, health improvement is not a concept with an agreed definition giving clear direction to primary care groups. However, there are examples of some primary care groups becoming key players in a range of health promotion activities (Audit Commission 2000a). Those activities most commonly reported centred around implementing national priorities for coronary heart disease and stroke, including involvement in healthy living centres; appointment of a healthy lifestyles officer and healthy schools initiative; a healthy village project centred on a 'beacon' practice; and partnership working to develop healthy living programmes and networks. Other examples were 'exercise on prescription', 'start to exercise' or 'exercise for nursing home patients' initiatives.

### Prospects for integrated care

Integration of services around the needs of patients across conventional boundaries can be pursued through structural reorganization, explicit planning, budgetary incentives, or by a combination of these strategies. Total purchasing was designed to use budgetary delegation to give general practitioners an interest for the first time in potentially all the hospital and community health services used by their patients, thereby encouraging more vertical integration of services. For example, the TPPs had an incentive to avoid inappropriate hospital admissions and to facilitate earlier discharge from the acute hospital sector. Horizontal integration had to occur more informally because TPPs were not in a position to take on local authority budgets for the social care of their patients – instead, they engaged in more informal collaboration and budget alignment activities with their local social services counterparts.

The introduction of primary care groups/trusts and more recently the English *NHS Plan* (Secretary of State for Health 2000) of July 2000 has been associated with more fundamental changes in the National Health Service budgetary framework – although it has built on the general principle heralded in the total purchasing experiment that primary care professionals will take responsibility for most of the resources. The resource allocation formulae used previously to distribute hospital and community health service expenditure have been extended to cover all types of health care expenditure, except non-cash limited general medical services. Budgets have begun to be devolved from health authorities to primary care groups. In turn primary care groups are being encouraged to develop notional budgets for their constituent practices. Thus primary care group budgets are now unified, so that the funds generated by the separate sub-formulae for hospital and community health services, GP prescribing and cash limited general medical services may be spent on any service, though with a one-way valve operating to ensure that expenditure on cash limited General Medical Services does not fall below the formula-generated target. The *NHS Plan* (Secretary of State for Health 2000) goes even further and outlines future potential arrangements for a single organization (namely a care trust, a new type of 'level 5' PCT) to commission and deliver primary and community health services *and social care*. Thus a single organization may, in future, provide health and social services through a single care network. However, the vast majority of primary care groups in England are a long way from being able to take advantage of this new opportunity for horizontal integration, with the majority concentrating on the delivery and development of primary and community health services.

In Scotland, the approach to vertical integration laid out in *Designed to Care* (Secretary of State for Scotland 1997) was to be different. Rather than relying on the incentives for vertical and horizontal integration generated by devolving an ever-widening scope of budget to groups of GPs, there was to be a Joint Investment Fund in each district designed to be spent exclusively on initiatives that involve both hospital and community (including primary care) providers, thereby fostering vertical integration. Joint plans or bids would be drawn up to justify the use of the Joint Investment Fund within the framework of the local health improvement programme. In the event, the potential of a Joint Investment Fund has not been achieved. Other approaches to vertical integration, including the development of *'managed clinical networks'* and *'service redesign'* are being used, using planning and regulation rather than market forces to drive change. GPs and other members of the primary care team will concentrate on horizontal integration by developing primary and community care services within a single financial envelope for general medical, prescribing and community health services in the local health care cooperatives and primary care trusts, but they will not be required to commission/purchase any secondary care. It remains to be seen how the Scottish system will make GPs conscious of the resource implications of their referral behaviour to secondary care under this arrangement.

The total purchasing initiative provided several examples of how better integration could be achieved. These have been discussed in more detail in earlier chapters of this book. Research from the national tracker survey of primary care groups and trusts (Malbon 2000) shows that primary care groups are adopting similar approaches for improving the coordination of services through integrating primary and secondary care. These include developing care pathways and shared protocols between primary and secondary care clinicians in the treatment of patients with diabetes and the frail elderly, and paying for specialists to be on call to prevent patients entering hospitals.

**Primary care development versus commissioning services**

As noted elsewhere in the book, the evidence shows that although the focus of total purchasing was ostensibly on purchasing of hospital and community health services, particularly secondary care, in practice the initiative proved to be an important vehicle for developing and elaborating services in a primary care setting. The development of community health services and intermediate care schemes, together with initatives to increase the number of specialists working in the community by primary care groups, has continued to shift the boundary with secondary care. Early findings from two major evaluations of primary care groups in their first year, 1999/2000, show that primary care groups have also tended to focus their attention on organizational development, primary care investment plans, clinical governance and improving GP prescribing (Malbon and Smith 2000).

In principle, primary care groups and their counterparts are strategic players in the development and implementation of health authority-wide health improvement programmes. In practice, only a minority of primary care groups have felt involved in the design stage of their local health improvement programme, which sets the scene for development locally over a five-year period. It is anticipated that this will improve and primary care groups will play a more active role. In the same way, in principle, primary care groups and local health groups in Wales are able to commission almost all the health care for their local populations. The first year of primary care groups suggests, however, that they are more concerned with taking stock of their basic practice infrastructure, including the workforce, premises and equipment, than taking up the opportunities of a greater commissioning role. Commissioning was not generally regarded by primary care groups as their main priority in the first year. Many had inherited service agreements already negotiated by their health authority. However, joint commissioning with neighbouring primary care groups was common.

On the other hand, primary care groups/trusts as service commissioners have the advantage of size over TPPs – it was often apparent to TPPs that changes to the local acute hospital could only be sensibly implemented on a wider scale than a single TPP, since the average population of a TPP was just 30,000. The involvement of primary care organizations in the development and monitoring of health improvement programmes is likely to prove a crucial mechanism to achieve strategic change in the pattern of service delivery, particularly if any significant shift of resources from acute hospital and mental health trusts is to be achieved – this perhaps explains why there was little movement in the commissioning field amongst primary care groups in the first year. Like TPPs, they wished to make strategic change but recognized that this needed to be managed at a higher level in the system.

**Resource allocation and budgets**

The experience of total purchasing supports the principle of devolving budgets to groups of practices, with the potential for them to contract independently for services. TPPs that received their own budgets and had their own contract made the most progress. This insight has been applied by those primary care groups, which devolve budgets to practice level, in order to develop incentive schemes to influence GPs' behaviour (Smith 1999). However, as the TPP evaluation discovered, holding a budget is not sufficient to bring about immediate change – progress also depends on organizational development and relationships with clinicians and others. The key to using resources effectively, and particularly if primary care groups/trusts are to develop their role as effective gatekeepers to secondary care and efficient prescribers, is for all the GPs to become involved in the collective management of resources but within a framework which depicts good quality of service. Engendering good interpractice relations and supporting less motivated practitioners will be essential in primary care organizations if they are to function effectively as commissioners and providers of primary care. The roles of the clinical governance lead GP and the prescribing lead GP have been found to be the key in bringing about GP involvement in quality improvement within a budget by taking a facilitative and educational approach. Extending clinical governance to primary care as one way of ending the clinical isolation of some general practices is a key priority for improving quality of patient care and encouraging GPs to develop the most effective and efficient way of delivering care. There will, inevitably be tensions between quality and efficiency on occasions and these will need to be carefully worked out within individual primary care groups.

Sharing practice information on patterns of activity and expenditure is also likely to be an essential tool underpinning this process. Lack of appropriate, accurate and timely information was a recurring complaint from primary care groups in their first year (Jones and Wilkin 2000), whether it was information to support primary care development, to monitor service provision, to develop clinical governance or to support commissioning. Again the frustrations of the primary care groups were prefigured by the TPPs. Early signs suggest that this is not far from the case. National information targets and milestones tend to focus on technology (e.g. connectivity or electronic patient records). These are often seen as unhelpful because they do not address immediate needs and they do not provide the resources to implement change. To deliver their core functions successfully, primary care groups will need to have access to accurate, reliable and timely information about the health needs of their population, the services provided and the outcomes of treatment. Achieving this will require both additional resources and a stronger focus on information needs as well as improvements in the technology available.

## DRAWING THE WIDER LESSONS FROM TOTAL PURCHASING FOR FUTURE POLICY

Moving beyond the recent history of the NHS and the early stages of the development of primary care groups/trusts, what are the wider policy implications of the NHS experiment with TPPs? Perhaps the main lesson is that there is still considerable potential for better cost control, demand management, efficiency improvement and service innovation in publicly funded health systems through bringing clinical decision making and resource management closer together in the system in the hands of primary care professionals. Some of the tools of United States 'managed care' organizations such as utilization review (discharge planning) and widening the scope of generalist care outside the hospital can be applied powerfully by primary care-based budget holders in quite different systems than the USA. Giving responsibility for service purchasing to primary care organizations is also a way of encouraging the integration of previously separate budgetary streams, thereby allowing more flexible use of resources. In many health care systems, primary care and hospital care have been traditionally separately funded, leading to perverse incentives and cost shifting on both sides. Initiatives such as total purchasing have the potential to mitigate greatly these risks by moving towards the emergence of organizations at local level with the resources and mandate to secure *all* health services for a defined population.

The total purchasing initiative also showed that primary care professionals, in this case volunteer GPs, could be encouraged to take greater responsibility for relatively larger budgets and could begin to think more broadly about their integrated use in the local health system. Finally, the TPPs were valuable in continuing the NHS cultural revolution, begun through standard fundholding, in which general practitioners, and primary care professionals more widely, gradually ceased to be subordinate and marginal figures in the health system and gained in centrality and influence. After total purchasing, it became impossible to doubt that the management of the acute hospitals and the rising demand for their services could only be made sustainable with the direct involvement of the staff and organizations providing non-hospital care. The TPPs showed great promise in all these ways, albeit in difficult circumstances.

The fact that the TPPs faced significant constraints was a product of the particular circumstances of the NHS in the mid-1990s rather than the result of intrinsic limitations in the underlying concept. Pilot status, shifts in national policy, the politics of managing the quasi-market and the lack of clear incentives acting on individual general practitioners and TPPs limited the clout and capacity of the pilots (see Chapter 13). Both an opportunity and incentives to use that opportunity are needed for health professionals to engage in the planning, rationing and purchasing of health services. However, potentially beneficial service changes can be brought about without necessarily placing the professionals involved at full financial risk for their decisions. Risk sharing with, for example, public authorities or government is possible and can change behaviour desirably. Likewise, although there is no doubt that some financial incentives are needed to encourage clinicians to participate in resource management, financial self-interest is not the only effective form of incentive. This finding is corroborated by experience in other health systems similar to the UK's. For example, the budget-holding 'savings' in expenditure on laboratory tests and general practitioner pharmaceuticals brought about by independent practitioner associations in New Zealand took place in the absence of individual GP liability for overspends or opportunity to profit personally from 'savings' (Kerr *et al.* 1996; Malcolm *et al.* 1999). Opportunities to pursue professional concerns (e.g. to improve services to patients and/or to increase the influence of GPs over the health system) can be equally potent. This is particularly the case in solidaristic health systems such as the NHS.

Seen in this light, both standard fundholding and total purchasing appealed to a subtle mix of what Le Grand calls 'knavish' (self-interested) motives and 'knightly' (altruistic) incentives (Le Grand 1997). Thus, standard fundholding practices could generate and retain 'savings', but they were restricted from putting the money straight into the pockets of their general practitioners. 'Savings' had to be used to buy more services for patients or facilities such as equipment and buildings. Being able to offer more services to their patients appealed both to the GPs' professional concern to do the best for the patients on their lists and to their more self-interested desire to ensure that their practices were more attractive to patients than those of other local GPs. 'Savings' could be spent on buildings and equipment, thereby increasing the value of the GPs' own property. Similarly, practices volunteered to become involved in TPPs both to use their distinctive clinical perspective to improve local health services ('knightly' motives) and in order to be able to increase the range and depth of services available to their patients and which they directly controlled or provided ('knavish' motives). Although the latter motive was not directly concerned with financial gain, it is likely that practices which are able to boast a wider range of services will be able to attract and retain more patients, thereby potentially increasing their GPs' incomes. Both standard fundholding and total purchasing also appealed to certain GPs' competitive desire to be seen to be at the forefront of developments both in the profession and in the wider NHS.

The challenge for the future in health care systems which are based on principles of equity and public service is to develop incentive structures which appeal to both the 'knight' and the 'knave' in order to be able to assure taxpayers that services are being delivered efficiently (Le Grand 1999). Perhaps this is what the Blair Labour government in the UK meant when it trumpeted its so-called 'third way' in health care reform (Ham 1999). In terms of primary care groups in England, this may involve developing a range of different incentives which operate at both the corporate (primary care group) and individual practice level. Some primary care groups are already tentatively going in this direction, as was seen above (Smith 1999).

The second broad lesson from the total purchasing experience is that GPs as purchasers have great potential, but considerable limitations. While they may have distinctive insights into the needs of their patients and the capacity to act in ways in which larger, more remote public bureaucracies cannot, they tend to see the same set of solutions to a wide range of perceived problems in the local health system. Thus the TPPs tended to use their budgets to extend the scope of primary care and to increase intermediate care. Very few of their initiatives as purchasers involved attempts to influence the behaviour of secondary care providers directly; for example, by altering the quality standards in contracts or by insisting on new protocols of care. Rather, their focus was on developing services of a type with which they were familiar in their work as GPs. In addition, certain service areas appeared to present particular difficulties for the TPPs. One such area was mental health services, despite its salience for the day-to-day work of GPs. The TPPs also did little systematically to assess the health care requirements of their patients, preferring to rely on the GPs' personal experiences, and mostly failed to involve or even consult their patients about their decisions as total purchasers. The TPPs were set up and run as GP-led organizations. Other primary care professionals were rarely involved in contributing to their decisions and few TPPs fully exploited the potential of more multi-professional and multi-agency options for service development, for example by involving social care agencies. In addition, in the only area in which it was possible to examine user experience of care – maternity care – GP-based purchasers did not have a measurable impact on women's experience and assessment of care.

The implication of the foregoing is that any straightforward expectation that GP-based purchasing organizations will rapidly improve quality of patient experience of care or alter their use of resources should be treated with caution. GP-based purchasing organizations are likely to be more appropriate in circumstances where the main purchasing task is to alter the balance and location of care between hospital and extramural settings. Other, more expert, forms of purchasing may be more appropriate when the principal challenge facing the system is to improve the allocative efficiency of specialist services by, for example, altering the mix of patients treated or substituting more for less cost-effective procedures (e.g. in response to new research evidence). In the recent past, the NHS has required both sorts of service change to be pursued. In future, primary care-based purchasers in the NHS in England will have the additional support of evidence-based National Service Frameworks, which will be promulgated by the National Institute for Clinical Excellence. The National Service Frameworks will set national standards and define service models for specific services or client groups (Secretary of State for Health 1997). It may be that the National Service Frameworks will enable primary care groups successfully to extend the scope of their service commissioning by providing them with the expertise they may lack. However, the existence of detailed National Service Frameworks raises more fundamental questions as to the precise role of the local purchaser in the NHS in the future.

The final lesson for policy from the total purchasing initiative concerns the importance of context for understanding the likely effectiveness of organizational and budgetary innovations. Setting aside the skills of the GPs and managers concerned, the precise effects of this form of budgetary delegation depended on the extent to which the pilot was operating in an environment conducive to GP-led service change (Goodwin *et al.*, 2000 and Chapter 5). For example, in the first 'live' year of the scheme, the progress of the pilots was frequently influenced by their ability to bridge the professional cultures of general practice and the host health authority, the help of whose staff was important for the development of the pilots. In the second 'live' year, 1997/98, changes in the wider NHS policy environment overrode all other contextual influences. Early in 1997, Labour's critique of the 'two-tierism' of standard fundholding and its desire to abolish the scheme grew in salience, as the party led at the opinion polls. This weakened all forms of GP purchasing or commissioning, including total purchasing, before the pilots could complete their second 'live' year. At the end of the year, the new Labour government published its plans for the future of the NHS, which included a determination to end standard fundholding and total purchasing by April 1999. In their place, all practices in England in each defined area of between 50,000 and 150,000 people would be required to join primary care groups (Secretary of State for Health 1997). There was to be no place for the far smaller, volunteer groups of self-selected practices which were often not organized on an area basis. In this sense, the balance between central control and uniformity and local autonomy and diversity was given a marked push in the direction of the former.

As a result of this national change of direction, health authorities began to work towards configuring the new primary care groups before the TPPs had completed their work. Larger and more locality-based TPPs were at an advantage since they most nearly resembled the primary care groups which were to replace them. As a result, some larger TPPs experienced relatively smooth progressions into primary care groups. By contrast, many non-locality TPPs faced being divided between primary care groups. Having been higher achieving projects in the first 'live' year, the smaller pilots found it much more difficult in the second year, 1997/98, to achieve their objectives. In all TPPs, the uncertainty created by yet another NHS reorganization affected managerial staff concerned for their future employment and the GPs' willingness to initiate developments which might be lost as soon as the TPP was disbanded.

Budgetary incentives are not 'magic bullets' which have similar effects on behaviour wherever they are introduced. Considering the fact that all the TPPs were operating within the NHS, widely regarded as one of the most uniform and planned health care systems in the world, their progress in organizational maturity and purchasing achievements varied widely. These disparities persisted over the three-year life of the scheme. Holding budgets and having independent contracts, while important prerequisites for being taken seriously in the internal market, were not sufficient for effective total purchasing. The pilots also needed determined leadership, a robust management infrastructure, good information systems, structures to enable wide GP involvement in decision making and budget management, a supportive health authority and well-developed relationships with other provider organizations to make headway.

As well as having implications for the design and conduct of policy evaluations (see Chapter 12), this insight into the significance of context suggests that policy makers should be trying to work out not which approach to purchasing (and any other feature of health system design) is 'best', but which approach is best for whom and in which circumstances. The experience of the total purchasing experiment would suggest that when GPs purchase health care, they can make a difference only for some services in some contexts.

# REFERENCES

Abbot, S. and Gillam, S. (2000). Health Improvement. In D. Wilkin, S. Gillam and B. Leese (eds) *The National Tracker Survey of Primary Care Groups and Trusts: Progress and Challenges, 1999/2000*. Manchester University of Manchester.

Anderson, W. and Florin, D. (2000). *Involving the Public – One of Many Priorities: A Survey of Public Involvement in London's Primary Care Groups*. London: King's Fund.

Appleby, J. (1996). *A Measure of Effectiveness? A Critical Review of the NHS Efficiency Index*. Birmingham: National Association of Health Authorities and Trusts.

Armitage, P. and Berry, G. (1987). *Statistical Methods in Medical Research*. Oxford: Blackwell Scientific Publications.

Ashton, T. (1998). Contracting for health services in New Zealand: A transaction cost analysis. *Social Science and Medicine*, 46(3), 357–67.

Audit Commission (1992). *Lying in Wait: The Use of Medical Beds in Acute Hospitals*. London: HMSO.

Audit Commission (1996). *What the Doctor Ordered: A Study of GP Fund-holders in England and Wales*. London: HMSO.

Audit Commission (2000a). *Local Health Groups in Wales*. London: Audit Commission.

Audit Commission (2000b). *The PCG Agenda: Early Progress of Primary Care Groups in 'the New NHS'*. London: Audit Commission.

Bachmann, M. and Bevan, G. (1996). Determining the size of a total purchasing site to manage financial risks of rare costly referrals: computer simulation model. *British Medical Journal*, 313, 1054–7.

Balogh, R. (1996). Exploring the role of localities in health commissioning: A review of the literature. *Social Policy and Administration*, 30, 99–113.

Barbour, R. (1999). Combining qualitative and quantitative approaches in health services research. *Journal of Health Services Research and Policy*, 4, 39–43.

Baxter, K., Bachmann, M. and Bevan, G. (1998). *Survey of Budgetary and Risk Management of Total Purchasing Pilot Projects, 1996–97*. National Evaluation of Total Purchasing Pilot Projects Working Paper. London: King's Fund.

Berk, R. and Rossi, P. (1990). *Thinking About Program Evaluation*. Newbury Park: Sage.

Bevan, G. (1997). *Resource Allocation within Health Authorities: Lessons from Total Purchasing Pilots*. National Evaluation of Total Purchasing Pilot Projects Working Paper. London: King's Fund.

Bevan, G. (1998) Taking equity seriously: A dilemma for government from allocating resources to Primary Care Groups. *British Medical Journal*, 316, 39–43.

Bevan, G., Copeman, H., Perrin, J. and Rosser, R. (1980). *Health Care Priorities and Management*. London: Croom Helm.

Black, D., Birchall, A. and Trimble, I. (1994) Non-fundholding in Nottingham: A vision of the future. *British Medical Journal*, 309, 930–2.

Butler, P. (1998). Primary Care Trusts go live in 18 months. *Health Service Journal*, 12 November, 2–3.

Butler, T. and Roland, M. (1998). How will Primary Care Groups work? *British Medical Journal*, 316, 214.

Coulter, A. and Mays, N. (1997). De-regulating primary care. *British Medical Journal*, 314, 510–13.

Crombie, D. and Fleming, D. (1988). General practitioner referrals to hospital: The financial implications of variability. *Health Trends*, 20, 53–6.

Cumming, J. (2000) *Management of Key Purchaser Risks in Devolved Purchase Arrangements in Health Care*. London: Treasury Working Paper; Wellington: The Treasury.

Cumming, J. and Scott, C. (1998). The role of outputs and outcomes in purchaser accountability: Reflecting on New Zealand experiences. *Health Policy*, 46, 53–68.

Dawson, D. and Goddard, M. (1998). *Longer-term Agreements for Health Care Services: What Will They Achieve?* Discussion paper 157. York: Centre for Health Economics, University of York.

Dawson, D. and Street, A. (1998) *Reference Costs and the Pursuit of Efficiency in the 'New' NHS*. Discussion Paper 161. York: Centre for Health Economics, University of York.

Day, P. and Klein, R. (1988). *Accountabilities in Five Public Services*. London: Tavistock Publications.

Department of Health (1991a). *Local Voices*. London: HMSO.

Department of Health (1991b). *The Patient's Charter*. London: HMSO.

Department of Health (1992). *A Health Strategy for England*. London: HMSO.

Department of Health (1993a). *Changing Childbirth*. Report of the Expert Maternity Group. London: HMSO.

Department of Health (1993b). *Research for Health*. London: HMSO.

Department of Health (1996a). *More than 50 per cent of Patients Are Now Served by GP Fundholders*. London: Department of Health.

Department of Health (1996b). *The National Health Service: A Service with Ambitions*. London: The Stationery Office.

Department of Health (1996c). *Promoting Patient Partnership: Building a Collaborative Strategy*. Leeds: NHS Executive.

Department of Health (1998a). *The Health of the Nation: A Policy Assessed*. London: The Stationery Office.

Department of Health (1998b). *Information for Health: An Information Strategy for the Modern NHS 1998–2005. A National Strategy for Implementation*. London: HMSO.

Department of Health (1998c). *The New NHS. Guidance on Out of Area Treatment Consultation Document*. London: Department of Health.

Department of Health (1998d). *Partnership in Action (New Opportunities for Joint Working between Health and Social Services)*. London: HMSO.

Department of Health (1999). *Health Act 1999*. London: HMSO.

Department of Health Research and Development Division (1995). *National Evaluation of Total Purchasing Pilot Schemes: Research Brief*. London: Department of Health.

Department of Health and Social Security (1976). *Sharing Resources for Health in England*. Report to the Resources Allocation Working Party (RAWP Report). London: HMSO.

Department of Health and Social Security (1988). *Review of the Resource Allocation Working Party Formula (Final Report by the NHS Management Board)*. London: DHSS.

Dixon, J. (1994). Can there be fair funding for fundholding practices? *British Medical Journal*, 308, 772–5.

Dixon, J., Dinwoodies, M., Hodson, D. *et al.* (1994). Distribution of NHS funds between fundholding and non-fundholding practices. *British Medical Journal*, 309, 30–4.

Dixon, J., Goodwin, N. and Mays, N. (1998a). *Accountability of Total Purchasing Pilot Projects*. National Evaluation of Total Purchasing Pilot Projects Working Paper. London: King's Fund.

Dixon, J., Holland, P. and Mays, N. (1998b). Developing primary care: Gatekeeping, commissioning and managed care. *British Medical Journal*, 317, 125–8.

Dowling, B. (1997). Effect of fundholding on waiting times: Database study. *British Medical Journal*, 315, 290–2.

Earwicker, S. (1998). *Commissioning Groups – The Nottingham Experience*. London: Office of Health Economics.

Enthoven, A. (1995). *Reflections on the Management of the NHS*. London: Nuffield Provincial Hospitals Trust.

Evans, R. (1987). Public health insurance: The collective purchase of individual care. *Health Policy*, 7, 115–34.

Flynn, R. and Williams, G. (1997). *Contracting for Health: Quasi-markets and the National Health Service*. Oxford: Oxford University Press.

Gask, L., Lee, J., Donnan, S. and Roland, M. (1998). *Total Purchasing and Extended Fundholding of Mental Health Services.* National Evaluation of Total Purchasing Pilot Projects Working Paper. London: King's Fund.

Glennerster, H., Cohen, A. and Bovell, V. (1998). Alternatives to fundholding. *International Journal of Health Services*, 28, 47–66.

Glennerster, H., Matsaganis, M. and Owens, P. (1994). *Implementing GP Fundholding: Wild Card or Winning Hand?* Buckingham: Open University Press.

Goodwin, N. (1998). GP Fundholding. In J. Le Grand, N. Mays and J.-A. Mulligan (eds) *Learning from the NHS Internal Market: A Review of the Evidence.* London: King's Fund.

Goodwin, N., Abbott, S., Baxter, K. *et al.* (2000). *The Dynamics of Primary Care Commissioning: A Close-up of Total Purchasing Pilots. Analysis and Implications of Eleven Case Studies.* National Evaluation of Total Purchasing Pilot Projects Working Paper. London: King's Fund.

Graffy, J. and Williams, J. (1994). Purchasing for all: An alternative to fundholding. *British Medical Journal*, 308, 391–4.

Griffiths, J. (1996). *Defining the Essentials: The Functions, Roles and Costs of Health Authorities and GP Purchasers.* Milton Keynes and London: NHS Executive Anglia and Oxford, North Thames and South Thames.

Guba, Y. and Lincoln, E. (1989). *Fourth Generation Evaluation.* London: Sage.

Ham, C. (1999). The third way in health care reform: Does the emperor have any clothes? *Journal of Health Services Research and Policy*, 4, 168–73.

Ham, C., Hunter, D. and Robinson, R. (1998). Evidence based policy making. *British Medical Journal*, 310, 71–2.

Hughes, D., Griffiths, L. and McHale, J. (1997). Do quasi-markets evolve? Institutional analysis and the NHS. *Cambridge Journal of Economics*, 21, 259–76.

Jones, D. and Wilkin, D. (2000). Information management and technology. In D. Wilkin, S. Gillam and B. Leese (eds) *The National Tracker Survey of Primary Care Groups and Trusts: Progress and Challenges, 1999/2000.* Manchester: University of Manchester.

Kerr, D., Malcolm, L., Schousboe, J. and Pimm, F. (1996). Successful implementation of laboratory budget holding by Pegasus' Medical Group. *New Zealand Medical Journal*, 109, 354–7.

Killoran, A., Abbott, S., Malbon, G., Mays, N. and Wyke, S. (1999a). *The Transition from TPPs to PCGs: Lessons for PCG Development.* National Evaluation of Total Purchasing Pilot Projects Working Paper. London: King's Fund.

Killoran, A., Mays, N., Wyke, S. and Malbon, G. (1999b). *Total Purchasing: a Step Towards New Primary Care Organisations.* National Evaluation of Total Purchasing Pilot Projects Working Paper. London: King's Fund.

Klein, R. (1995a). *The New Politics of the National Health Service*, 3rd ed. London: Longman.

Klein, R. (1995b). Self-Inventing Institutions: institutionalised design and the UK welfare state. In R. Goodin (ed.) *The Theory of Institutionalised Design*. Cambridge: Cambridge University Press.

Labour Party. (1995). *Renewing the NHS: Labour's Agenda for a Healthier Britain*. London: Labour Party.

Leese, B. and Mahon, A. (1999a). The information requirements for total purchasing projects: Implications for primary care groups. *Journal of Management in Medicine*, 13, 13–22.

Leese, B. and Mahon, A. (1999b). Management and relationships in total purchasing pilots. Relevance for primary care groups. *Journal of Management in Medicine*, 13, 154–63.

Leese B. and Wilkin, D. (2000). The role of health authorities. In D. Wilkin, S. Gillam and B. Leese (eds) *The National Tracker Survey of Primary Care Groups and Trusts: Progress and Challenges, 1999/2000*. Manchester: University of Manchester.

Le Grand, J. (1997). Knights, knaves or pawns? Human behaviour and social policy. *Journal of Social Policy*, 26, 149–69.

Le Grand, J. (1999). Competition, Cupertino, or control? Tales from the British National Health Service. *Health Affairs*, 18, 27–39.

Le Grand, J., Mays, N. and Dixon, J. (1998). The reforms: Success or failure or neither? In J. Le Grand, N. Mays and J.-A. Mulligan (eds) *Learning from the NHS Internal Market: A Review of the Evidence*. London: King's Fund.

Le Grand, J., Mays, N., Mulligan J.-A. *et al.* (1997). *Models of Purchasing and Commissioning: A Review of the Research Evidence*. London: London School of Economics and the King's Fund.

Light, D. (1998). *Effective Commissioning: Lessons from Purchasing in American Managed Care*. London: Office of Health Economics.

Lord, J. and Littlejohns, P. (1997). Evaluating healthcare policies: the case of clinical audit. *British Medical Journal*, 315, 668–71.

McCay, C., Smith, J., Goodwin, N. and Donnelly, M. (2000). *Northern Ireland Primary Care Commissioning Pilots: First Annual Report*. Belfast: HSCRU, Queen's University of Belfast.

McLeod, H. and Raftery, J. (2000). *Total Purchasing and the Management of Emergency Hospital Activity*. National Evaluation of Total Purchasing Pilot Projects Working Paper. London: King's Fund.

Mahon, A., Leese, B., Baxter, K., Goodwin, N. and Scott, J. (1998). *Developing Success Criteria for Total Purchasing Pilot Projects*. National Evaluation of Total Purchasing Pilot Projects Working Paper. London: King's Fund.

Majeed, A. and Malcolm, L. (1999). Unified budgets for primary care groups. *British Medical Journal*, 318, 772–6.

Malbon, G., Mays, N., Killoran, A., Wyke, S. and Goodwin, N. (1999). *What Were the Achievements of TPPs in their Second Year and How Can They Be Explained?* National Evaluation of Total Purchasing Pilot Projects Working Paper. London: King's Fund.

Malbon, G. and Smith, J. (2000). Commissioning. In D. Wilkin, S. Gillam and B. Leese (eds) *The National Tracker Survey of Primary Care Groups and Trusts: Progress and Challenges, 1999/2000*. Manchester: University of Manchester.

Malcolm, L. and Mays, N. (1999). New Zealand's independent practitioner associations: A working model of clinical governance in primary care? *British Medical Journal*, 319(7221), 1340–2.

Malcolm, L. and Powell, M. (1996). The development of independent practice association in New Zealand. *New Zealand Medical Journal*, 109, 184–7.

Malcolm, L., Wright, L. and Barnett, P. (1999). *The Development of Primary Care Organisations in New Zealand*. Wellington: Ministry of Health.

Malcolm, L., Wright, L., Seers, M. and Guthrie, J. (1999). An evaluation of pharmaceutical management and budget holding in Pegasus Medical Group. *New Zealand Medical Journal*, 112, 162–4.

Martin, S., Rice, N. and Smith, P. (1997). *Risk and the GP Budget Holder*. Discussion Paper 153. York: University of York, Centre for Health Economics.

Mays, N. (1997). *Key Findings to Date from the National Evaluation of First Wave Total Purchasing Pilot Projects in England and Scotland*. Prepared as Briefing for the Department of Health/NHSE (unpublished).

Mays, N. and Bevan, G. (1987). *Resource Allocation in the Health Service*. London: Bedford Square Press.

Mays, N. and Dixon, J. (1996). *Purchaser Plurality in UK Health Care: Is a Consenus Emerging and Is It the right One?* London: King's Fund.

Mays, N. and Goodwin, N. (1998). Implementing the White Paper: Pitfalls and opportunities. In R. Klein (ed.) *Primary Care Groups*. London: King's Fund.

Mays, N., Goodwin, N., Bevan, G. and Wyke, S. (1997a). *Total Purchasing: A Profile of National Pilot Projects*. National Evaluation of Total Purchasing Pilot Projects Working Paper. London: King's Fund.

Mays, N., Goodwin, N., Bevan, G. and Wyke, S. (1997b). What is total purchasing? *British Medical Journal*, 315, 652–5.

Mays, N., Goodwin, N., Killoran, A. and Malbon, G. (1998a). *Total Purchasing: A Step towards Primary Care Groups*. National Evaluation of Total Purchasing Pilot Projects Working Paper. London: King's Fund.

Mays, N., Goodwin, N., Malbon, G. *et al.* (1998b). *What Were the Achievements of Total Purchasing Pilots in their First Year and How Can They Be Explained?* National Evaluation of Total Purchasing Pilot Projects Working Paper. London: King's Fund.

Mays, N., Mulligan, J.-A. and Goodwin, N. (2000). The British quasi-market in health care: A balance sheet of the evidence. *Journal of Health Services Research and Policy*, 5 (January).

Mechanic, D. (1993). Social research in health and the American socio-political context: The changing fortunes of medical sociology. *Social Science and Medicine*, 36, 95–102.

Millar, B. (1997). Nine to five. *Health Service Journal*, 107(5535), 12–13.

Miller, C. (1998). *Joint Action on Health Inequalities: The Policy Drivers for the Health Service and for Local Authorities.* London: Health Education Authority.

Mulligan, J.-A. (1998). Locality and general practitioner commissioning. In J. Le Grand, N. Mays and J.-A. Mulligan (eds) *Learning from the NHS Internal Market: A Review of the Evidence.* London: King's Fund.

Myles, S., Wyke, S., Popay, J. *et al.* (1999). *Total Purchasing and Community and Continuing Care: Lessons for Future Policy Developments in the NHS.* National Evaluation of Total Purchasing Pilot Projects Working Paper. London: King's Fund.

National Audit Office (1995). *General Practitioner Fundholding in England.* London: HMSO.

New, B. (1993). Accountability and control in the NHS. In A. Harrison and S. Bruscini (eds) *Health Care UK 1992/93.* London: King's Fund.

NHS Confederation (1997). *Tackling Emergency NHS Admissions: Policy into Practice*, Best Practice Paper 1. Birmingham: NHS Confederation.

NHS Executive (1994a). *Developing NHS Purchasing and GP Fundholding: Towards a Primary Care-led NHS.* EL(94)79. Leeds: NHS Executive.

NHS Executive (1994b). *An Accountability Framework for GP Fundholding: Towards a Primary Care-led NHS.* EL(94)92. Leeds: NHS Executive.

NHS Executive (1995). *NHS Responsibilities for Meeting Continuing Health Care Needs.* HSC(95)8. Leeds: NHS Executive.

NHS Executive (1996a). *General Practitioner Fundholder Budget-setting: The National Framework.* EL(96)55. Leeds: NHS Executive.

NHS Executive (1996b). *1997–98 Health Authority Revenue Cash Limits Exposition Book.* Leeds: NHS Executive.

NHS Executive (1996c). *NHSE Guidance Notes for Total Purchasing Sites.* HSC(96)57. Leeds: NHS Executive.

NHS Executive (1996d). *NHS Priorities and Planning Guidance 1996/97.* Leeds: NHS Executive.

NHS Executive (1997a). *Involving Patients: Examples of Good Practice.* Leeds: NHS Executive.

NHS Executive (1997b). *Personal Medical Services under the NHS (Primary Care) Act 1997. The Contractual Framework for PMS Provider Pilots.* Leeds: NHS Executive.

NHS Executive (1998a). *Commissioning in the New NHS: Commissioning Services 1999–2000.* HSG 1998/198. London: NHS Executive.

NHS Executive (1998b). *The New NHS: Modern and Dependable. Developing Primary Care Groups.* HSC 1998/139. Leeds: NHS Executive.

NHS Executive (1998c). *The New NHS: Modern and Dependable. Primary Care Groups: Delivering the Agenda.* HSC 1998/228. Leeds: NHS Executive.

NHS Executive (1998d). *The New NHS: Modern and Dependable. Government Arrangements for Primary Care Groups.* HSG 1998/230: LAC(98)31. Leeds: NHS Executive.

O'Caithan A., Musson, G. and Munro, J. (1999). An evaluation of pharmaceutical management and budget holding in Pegasus Medical Group. *Journal of Health Services Research and Policy*, 4.

Office of Health Economics (1995). *Compendium of Health Statistics*. London: Office of Health Economics.

Ovretveit J. (1998). *Evaluating Health Interventions*. Buckingham: Open University Press.

Patton, M. (1990). *Qualitative Evaluation and Research Methods*. Newbury Park: Sage.

Pawson R. and Tilley, N. (1997). *Realistic Evaluation*. London: Sage.

Petchey, R. (1995). General practitioner fundholding: Weighing the evidence. *Lancet*, 346, 1139–42.

Pettigrew, A., Ferlie, E. and McKee, L. (1992). *Shaping Strategic Change*. London: Sage.

Place, M., Posnett, J. and Street, A. (1998). *An Analysis of the Transactions Costs of Total Purchasing Pilots*. National Evaluation of Total Purchasing Pilot Projects Working Paper. London: King's Fund.

Posnett, J., Goodwin, N., Griffiths, G. *et al.* (1998). *The Transactions Costs of Total Purchasing*. National Evaluation of Total Purchasing Pilot Projects Working Paper. London: King's Fund.

Raftery, J. and McLeod, H. (1999). *Hospital Activity Changes and Total Purchasing in 1996/97*. National Evaluation of Total Purchasing Pilot Projects Working Paper. London: King's Fund.

Raftery, J., Robinson, R., Mulligan, J.-A. and Forrest, S. (1996). Contracting in the NHS quasi-market. *Health Economics*, 5, 353–62.

Regen, E., Smith, J. and Shapiro, J. (1999). *First off the Starting Block: Lessons from GP Commissioning Pilots for Primary Care Groups*. University of Birmingham: Health Service Management Centre.

Reinhardt, U. (1997). A social contract for 21st century health care: Three-tier health care with bounty hunters. *Health Economics*, 5, 479–99.

Robinson, R. (1994). Introduction. In R. Robinson and J. Le Grand (eds) *Evaluating the NHS Reforms*. London: King's Fund.

Robinson, R. and Le Grand, J. (1994). *Evaluating the NHS Reforms*. London: King's Fund.

Robinson, R., Robison, J., Raftery, J. (1998). *Contracting by Total Purchasing Pilot Projects 1996–97*. National Evaluation of Total Purchasing Pilot Projects Working Paper. London: King's Fund.

Robinson, R. and Steiner, A. (1998). *Managed Health Care: US Evidence and Lessons for the National Health Service*. Buckingham: Open University Press.

Robison, J., Robinson, R., Raftery, J. and McLeod, H. (1999). *Contracting by Total Purchasing Pilot Projects 1997–1998*. National Evaluation of Total Purchasing Pilot Projects Working Paper. London: King's Fund.

Round, A. (1997). Emergency medical admissions to hospital – the influence of supply factors. *Public Health*, 111(4), 221–4.

Saltman, R., Figueras, J. and Sakellarides, C. (1998). *Critical Challenges for Health Care Reform in Europe*. Buckingham: Open University Press.

Scheffler, R. (1989). Adverse selection: The Achilles heel of the NHS reforms. *Lancet*, i, 950–2.

Scottish Office (1998). *Modernising Community Care: An Action Plan*. Edinburgh: The Stationery Office.

Secretaries of State for Health (W, NI and S) (1989). *Working for Patients*. Cm 555. London: HMSO.

Secretary of State for Health (1996). *Choice and Opportunity*. Cm 3390. London: The Stationery Office.

Secretary of State for Health (1997). *The New NHS: Modern, Dependable*. Cm 3807. London: The Stationery Office.

Secretary of State for Scotland (1997). *Designed to Care*. Edinburgh: The Stationery Office.

Secretary of State for Wales (1998). *Putting Patients First*. Cardiff: The Stationery Office.

Secretary of State for Health (2000). *The NHS Plan: A Plan for Investment. A Plan for Reform*. Cm 4818-I. London: The Stationery Office.

Shadish, W., Cook, T. and Leviton, L. (1991). *Foundations of Programme Evaluation: Theories of Practice*. London: Sage.

Sheldon, T., Smith, G. and Bevan, G. (1993). Weighting in the dark: Resource allocation in the new NHS. *British Medical Journal*, 306, 835–9.

Smith, J., Knight, T. and Wilson, F. (1999). Supra troupers. *Health Service Journal*, 14 January, 26–8.

Smith, J., Regen, E, Goodwin, N., McLeod, H. and Shapiro, J. (2000a). *Getting in to their Stride: Interim Report of a National Evaluation of Primary Care Groups*. University of Birmingham: Health Service Management Centre.

Smith, K., Leese, B., Pickard, S. and Chapple, A. (2000b). Involving stakeholders. In D. Wilkin, S. Gillam and B. Leese (eds) *The National Tracker Survey of Primary Care Groups and Trusts: Progress and Challenges, 1999/2000*. Manchester: University of Manchester.

Smith, P. (1999). Setting budgets for general practice in the new NHS. *British Medical Journal*, 318, 776–9.

Starr, P. (1982). *The Social Transformation of American Medicine*. New York: Basic Books.

Strawderman, T., Mays, N. and Goodwin, N. (1996). *Survey of NHSE Regional total Purchasing Lead Officers*. Unpublished report. London: King's Fund.

Street, A. and Place, M. (1998). *The Management Challenge for Primary Care Groups*. National Evaluation of Total Purchasing Pilot Projects Working Paper. London: King's Fund.

Townsend, P. and Davidson, N. (1982). *The Black Report*. Harmondsworth: Penguin.

Walt, G. (1994). *Health Policy: An Introduction to Process and Power*. London: Zed Books.

Webster, C. (1998). *The Health Services since the War, Volume 1: Problems of Health Care. The Health Service before 1957.* London: HMSO.

Weiner, J. and Ferris, D. (1990). *GP Budget Holding in the UK: Lessons from America.* London: King's Fund.

Wilkin, D. and Sheaff, R. (2000). Organisational development and governance. In D. Wilkin, S. Gillam and B. Leese (eds) *The National Tracker Survey of Primary Care Groups and Trusts: Progress and Challenges, 1999/2000.* University of Manchester: NPCRDC Publications.

Wilkin, D., Gillam, S. and Leese, B. (2000). *The National Tracker Survey of Primary Care Groups and Trusts: Progress and Challenges, 1999/2000.* University of Manchester: NPCRDC Publications.

Wyke, S., Hewison, J., Piercy, J. *et al.* (1999a). *National Evaluation of General Practice-based Purchasing of Maternity Care: Preliminary Findings.* National Evaluation of Total Purchasing Pilot Projects Working Paper. London: King's Fund.

Wyke, S., Mays, N., Abbott, S. *et al.* (1999b) *Developing Primary Care in the New NHS: Lessons from Total Purchasing.* National Evaluation of Total Purchasing Pilot Projects Working Paper. London: King's Fund.

Wyke, S., Myles, S., Popay, J. *et al.* (1999c). Total purchasing and community and continuing care: Lessons for future policy developments in the NHS. *Health and Social Care in the Community*, 7(6), 394–407.

Yuen, P. (1999). *Compendium of Health Statistics*, 11th ed. London: Office of Health Economics.

# INDEX

# CONTEMPORARY PRIMARY CARE
## The challenges of change

**Philip Tovey (ed.)**

Primary care is currently going through a period of substantial change. The high profile alteration of structures is occurring at a time when many issues of practice are presenting new or renewed challenges. These are issues grounded in the complexities and dissatisfactions of contemporary society as well as in the changing policy context.

This book has been produced in order to bring together critical and thought-provoking pieces on these wide-ranging challenges, by authors from an equally wide range of disciplines, including anthropology, clinical psychology, disability studies, public health, sociology, as well as general practice.

Beginning with a think piece on the nature of primary care and what an emerging vision for it might look like, the book continues with contributions on the changing form, organization and delivery of primary health care, before going on to examine specific areas of provision and some significant research issues. The book will be of interest to all those involved in the study or development of primary health care services.

## Contents

*Introduction – Part 1: Challenges of context and organization – Vision and change in primary care: past, present and future – The changing character of service provision – The changing nature of primary health care teams and interprofessional relationships – Part 2: Challenges of practice – Commissioning services for older people: make haste slowly? – Disability: from medical needs to social rights – The new genetics and general practice: revolution or continuity? – Socio-economic inequality: beyond the inverse care law – Part 3: Challenges of research – Locality planning and research evidence: using primary care data – Counselling: researching and evidence base for practice – Complementary medicine and primary care: towards a grassroots focus – Postscript – Index.*

c. 192 pp     0 335 20009 5 (Paperback)     0 335 20452 X (Hardback)

## MANAGING PUBLIC INVOLVEMENT IN HEALTHCARE PURCHASING

**Carol Lupton, Stephen Peckham and Pat Taylor**

Public involvement is a key theme within the post-reform NHS, with a growing emphasis on involving people in healthcare decision making, improving accountability to the public and developing a stronger focus on the consumer or user of services. This challenging book establishes a framework for public involvement in healthcare. With a focus on purchasing, the authors draw on recent research understanding to describe the central factors 'driving' involvement and the organizational structures and processes by which it is under pinned. Current progress in respect of public involvement is assessed and recommendations made for the developement of effective strategies. The discussion of current issues and debates is set within a wider theoretical and historical examination of the concepts of 'citizenship' and 'accountability', detailing the changing role of the 'consumer' in the context of the major developments in the organization and delivery of public services that have taken place in Britain in the last two decades.

### Contents
*Health and citizenship – Restructuring public services – Politics, markets and accountability – Understanding public involvement – The history of public involvement in health – Healthcare purchasing: a new framework for public involvement – Public involvement: health authority responses – Involvement: the response from the public – The future of public involvement – Bibliography – Index.*

176 pp    0 335 19632 2 (Paperback)    0 335 19633 0 (Hardback)

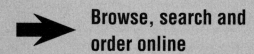